WHO KILLED CREATIVITY?

...And How Can We Get It Back?

Seven Essential Strategies to Make Yourself, Your Team and Your Organisation More Innovative

ANDREW GRANT | GAIA GRANT

with Dr JASON GALLATE

D0840038

JOSSEY-BASS
A Wiley Imprint
www.wiley.com

First published in 2012 by Jossey-Bass
A Wiley imprint
www.josseybass.com

John Wiley & Sons Australia, Ltd
42 McDougall St, Milton Qld 4064
Office also in Melbourne

Typeset in Bembo Regular 11.5/12 pt

© Andrew and Gaia Grant 2012

The moral rights of the authors have been asserted

National Library of Australia Cataloguing-in-Publication data:

Author:	Grant, Andrew.
Title:	Who killed creativity? ... and how can we get it back?: seven essential strategies to make yourself, your team and your organisation more innovative / Andrew Grant, Gaia Grant and Jason Gallate.
ISBN:	9781118232521 (pbk.)
Notes:	Includes index.
Subjects:	Creative ability in business.
	Creative ability.
Other Authors/	Grant, Gaia.
Contributors:	Gallate, Jason.
Dewey Number:	658.4063

Cover design by Adrian Morgan
Cover images: Tape © iStockphoto.com/Ivan Bliznetsov; Bullet holes © Thinkstock/iStockphoto.com

Printed in China by Printplus Limited

10 9 8 7 6 5 4 3 2 1

To Zoe and Kallen, our wonderfully creative children who have inspired us to continue to innovate and teach about the importance of creative thinking for the next generation.

Contents at a glance

Table of contents

About the authors

A dynamic husband-and-wife team, Andrew and Gaia Grant are the founders and directors of the consultancy Tirian International. Focusing on organisational innovation, they design and deliver highly creative educational experiences for leaders and teams. Over more than 25 years and in more than 30 countries they have worked at all levels — from the classroom to the boardroom, from tribal education to corporate coaching. Tirian's seminars and experiential learning programs are now presented under licence in a number of countries around the world. Andrew is a highly sought after and engaging keynote speaker for senior executives from Fortune 500 companies, and Gaia is the author of a number of books and other resources, including *A Patch of Paradise* and *The Rhythm of Life*. They have also co-authored educational resources directed at all levels, including the 'Schools Total Health Program', which has helped improve the lives of more than 25 million children in developing countries worldwide. When not travelling, Andrew and Gaia live with their two children between Sydney and Bali.

Dr Jason Gallate, a special guest contributor to this book, is an award-winning scientist and a registered psychologist with a doctorate in neuroscience. Jason's experiments in creativity have established the importance of non-conscious processing for innovation. His research has been published in several international peer-reviewed scientific journals.

Visit <www.whokilledcreativity.com> for more information and resources, including: seminars, workshops, keynotes, articles, blogs, surveys, videos and the 'Who Killed Creativity?' whodunit-style board game. Visit <www.tirian.com> for the full range of programs Tirian offers. Readers can email <book@whokilledcreativity.com> for a complimentary download pack.

Acknowledgements

In preparing this book we worked closely with our team at Tirian, who contributed to case studies and stories and assisted in revising the ideas and information. Tirian executives Lloyd Irwin and Carol Fusek helped design and rework the seminar material, and contributed to relevant sections of the text, so we are extremely thankful for their input. Many thanks also to the creatively talented Bruce Haddon, who was there when we started on this journey and helped to shape our initial ideas. We also appreciate the valued feedback we received from other members of our team, including our creative comedy mastermind Darren McCubbin along with Dr Peter Downey, Cindy Malifa and Rowena Wynfeld.

Introduction

Murder and mayhem in paradise

On 1 October 2005 at 6.50 pm two unassuming men dressed in t-shirts, jeans and sport shoes and carrying small backpacks walked into two beach cafes in Bali, Indonesia, and blew themselves up. By that simple act they instantly killed 20 people and wounded up to a hundred others. The remnants of the backpacks and their severely mutilated legs and heads were found later, but no torsos were recovered—an indication that they were suicide bombers. Although not the biggest suicide bombing to hit Bali (200 people had died in a coordinated car bomb attack just two years earlier almost to the day) this event had a particular impact on us. You see, the restaurants they attacked were located only 50 metres from the front doorstep of our quiet home.

The Indonesian island we had chosen as our home was a peaceful tropical retreat when we had first moved there 13 years earlier. Bali has a fabulously rich cultural heritage that has been preserved over time, and its people have a unique creative energy that comes from living in a lush, fertile land. The small corner where we had chosen to live out our escapist dreams, Jimbaran Bay, had been the epitome of exotic tropical perfection. But as international events such as 9/11 changed the shape of the world, local tensions grew and our own quiet haven was no longer immune.

For us the bombing was not just a one-off, random incident. It was the culmination of a long series of increasingly alarming events, as though there had been a scheme to destroy this unsuspecting patch of paradise. We share this story with you because we think in many ways it mirrors the dramatic chain of events that we believe may be leading to the death of creativity...

First, a bit more on the background. Ten years before that fateful day our sleepy fishing village at the southern tip of the island was relatively unspoiled and pristine. Although barely 10 kilometres from the hustle and bustle of the overcrowded tourist centre of Kuta, it was so quiet and unaffected it could have been on another planet. The women made beautiful colourful daily offerings and decorations for the gods; the men carved incredibly delicate images from wood and stone. Then the tourists came, and hot on their heels, the entrepreneurs, keen to get a piece of the tourist action. And that is when the focus changed dramatically.

The first changes seemed innocent enough. Then, six months after a few locals had opened four small barbecue seafood cafes on the beach, we woke one morning, not to the usual gentle sound of waves lapping on a sandy shore, but to the grinding crunch of a cantankerous chainsaw. The trees out the front were being ruthlessly cut down to make way for a string of identical seafood cafes. Soon the trees were pretty much gone, the cows had been moved to greener pastures, and the field was radically transformed into a huge paved car park ready to take large numbers of tourist buses. The locals no longer had time for their religious devotions and cultural arts, and there was friction over who owned the cafes, who got the jobs and who made the money. As the trucks carrying building materials rolled in, the green field edging the sand in front of our house was transformed. It became the site for an amazing 110 tightly packed, smoke-filled cafes, each an almost exact replica of the one next to it. No originality or creativity, just rows and rows of sameness driven by the promise of financial reward.

Now thousands of tourists packed into the area, and soon the garbage piled up, the tourist buses clogged the tiny streets, soupy polluted water started lapping up on the once pristine sands. Suffocating smoke from the barbecues clogged the air, leaving your eyes streaming as you walked through, and no doubt poisoning the local people daily.

Yes, tourism had arrived big time in our patch of paradise, and it was going to leave an indelible mark. Over time, our local area had been trampled by a mass influx of people, smothered in smoke, hit by commercial greed and finally invaded by terrorists.

This was no longer the place we had fallen in love with—it had become something else entirely. And the once-innocent village was heading towards almost certain self-destruction. The degeneration of this pretty beach community was not due to one thing in particular but to a combination of factors, an apparently irreversible chain of events. No-one deliberately set out to destroy the beach or the village community. No-one would have admitted even to contributing to the slow and painful murder. And yet the impact was clear.

In the same way, we believe creative innocence is being gradually trampled, suffocated and more directly attacked in all areas of life and all around the world. In our individual lives, in our communities and in our organisations, we are confronted by the realities of radical change so rapid that we are finding it difficult to cope. One of the first victims of this process is usually creativity, which cannot easily withstand such external pressures. Like the destruction of Jimbaran Bay, the suffocation of creativity is not necessarily deliberate. No criminal or institution (we hope!) has a master plan to turn us into unimaginative zombies. The creative naivety that defined and characterised us as children simply seems to be lost in the pursuit of personal or institutional goals. It's as though we lose sight of the principles and passions that give us purpose, and in the process lose our creative drive and ability. While everyone in Bali was busy making money from the tourists, the pristine beach was dying and the core values of the creative Balinese community were being destroyed. Many organisations today are falling into the same trap—chasing short-term profit at the expense of long-term values. This is a clear example of innocence lost.

The latest research shows that while average IQ has been rising with each generation, CQ (the Creativity Quotient) has stagnated and since 1990 has actually fallen. Many of us lose the creativity we had as kids over time. We enter school enthusiastic, open and with fresh ideas, but we leave 12 years later having learned, in most cases, the importance of being 'correct' rather than 'creative'. This suppression of creativity can be seen in many organisations as well. Although entrepreneurs start with fresh, innovative ideas, those who ultimately run the organisations learn to create systems and structures that ensure stability, and that process can often be at odds with the need for creative thinking.

So what exactly is creativity, and why do we feel it is so important to save it from destruction? Although everyone seems comfortable to use the term in daily conversation, readily asserting that someone has 'more' or 'less' of it, the experts struggle to come up with a simple definition. It is generally accepted that it involves the process of using the imagination to develop new, original ideas. For pragmatic creative thinking, the practical application of creativity, it is agreed that two key qualities are involved: *originality* and *usefulness*. This wide net captures a lot of things (see if it fits with the way you define creativity), but it also misses what is most special about the quality. We believe that creativity is far more important and broad than this—we believe it is an essential response to life.

After all, life is a series of choices or forks in the road. At each fork you can choose to do things the way you have always done them or to do something different, something new and original. You can accept the established wisdom or methods, or you can find a better way, making adjustments and improvements as you go. Each approach to life has pros and cons, and a successful life probably involves a combination of both. However, we will argue throughout this book that many people and organisations have become far too comfortable with, or addicted to, doing 'what already works' or what is risk free. Sometimes this apparently safe choice can unintentionally lead to degeneration and destruction. Sometimes, also, more sinister forces are at work that will directly attack your freedom of choice and limit your ability to think creatively.

Rather than simply passing on a set of principles and strategies for rescuing creative thinking, we are first going to examine how and why we believe creativity has died through a comprehensive murder investigation, asking and investigating the question: *Who killed creativity?* The inquiry into why we often choose the more destructive path, and who or what is responsible for this, will inform the initial stages of our investigation. We will then examine the alternate path—the more original and perhaps idealistic path that rescues creativity and leads to a richer quality of life.

Is it important to spend time considering the impact the death of creativity may have? We think so. Although the cost of simply doing what works or what is safe is not always immediately obvious, the problem is that it will work only until someone else does it better, and it may not work for everyone or in the best possible way to benefit all. This pragmatic argument for the necessity of innovation — for example, developing new products, processes, markets and business models — although strong, is by no means the only reason why creativity is important. It has a myriad other more and less tangible benefits. But the jewel in the crown, the boon that we hope this book amply illustrates, is that creativity makes life much richer and more interesting, and when applied well can also make life more meaningful and satisfying. What a truly amazing gift this is! Any boring or negative or unsatisfying process, place or thing can be brought to life by bringing creativity into the picture. We hope this book will give you some practical ideas as well as the passion to rescue this process in your life, in your community and in your work.

We will need you to enter into the spirit of our chosen approach, though. Instead of simply offering straight principles, we personify these into characters with whom you can readily identify. We then conduct a crime scene investigation to uncover any evidence that may exist for the murder of creativity through these characters. Consider how glamourised crime scene television has become big business: the hugely popular *CSI* TV franchise has had an estimated worldwide audience of over 73.8 million viewers.[1] These shows, in which the usually mundane and tedious job of analysing evidence is represented as incredibly slick and sexy, are believed to have changed the way many real trials are run today, with prosecutors now pressured to deliver more forensic evidence in court. Much of what is presented is pure Hollywood fabrication, but the shows do help to reveal a meticulous process, and that is the process we would like to utilise here.

One of the ways we will approach our investigation is through a 'pre-mortem', since prevention is always going to be preferred to conducting a post-mortem after the fact. This will mean that ideas, systems and processes can be improved before disaster occurs. Through imagining that an event has already occurred (applying what is known as prospective hindsight), people have actually been found to be able to correctly better identify reasons for future outcomes by as much as 30 per cent,[2] so this will no doubt be an invaluable tool.

In Part I we investigate the crime scene and explore why we believe creativity is on the decline (chapter 1) before using psychological profiling to identify the potential murder suspects and analyse their motives (chapter 2). We will also look at possible locations for the murders (chapter 3) and discuss in more detail why it is important to save creativity (chapter 4). In Part II we delve into the latest exciting brain research to explore how the skill of creative thinking can be acquired (chapter 5). We provide psychological profiles of the potential rescuers and explore some simple strategies that can be used to save creativity (chapter 6), as well as the locations creativity can be saved (chapter 7). At the end of Part II we will leave you with a challenging twist to the tale—as with a real crime scene, reality is usually not uncomplicated. We therefore hope to challenge you to engage more deeply in the rescue process (chapter 8), and to provide you with a practical case study as an example and template for change (chapter 9). But rather than presenting all this in a dry, scientific way, we plan to involve and entertain you by combining convincing evidence and fascinating facts with insightful case studies and stories. While many books offer creative thinking 'tools', we hope that in this book we will help to fill a gap—and perhaps fittingly to make the synaptic leap—in the information revolution by connecting all the great information and ideas out there with *your own* personal experience.

If you played any kind of whodunit-style game as a child you will already have a sense of the simple murder investigation approach we are using. In true whodunit style, we will be attempting to find out together:

\ *Who* or *what* kills creativity?

\ *How* is it killed—with what weapon?

\ *Where* is it killed?

During the investigation we will show how creativity has been killed, not by a single agent, but by a combination of contributing factors. And we will together discover that many of these factors are actually within our control. The good news is that, unlike physical death, creativity can never be fully extinguished. The potential remains ingrained within us. It is possible to go through the whole investigative process in reverse in order to find out:

- *Who* or *what* can rescue creativity?
- *How* can it be rescued—what strategies can be used?
- *Where* can it be rescued?

That will be the second stage of our investigation—to explore some simple strategies for developing creative thinking and applications at all levels.

Let's now start the process of sifting through the smoke and debris of what may have been destroyed to revive the creativity that has long been left dormant and lifeless. We hope you enjoy playing the detective with us in this complex investigative process.

Part I

Who killed creativity?

Investigating the crime scene

Creative thinking CSI

Crunch.
'Look Dad, a sailing ship!'
Sitting in the back of the car, our five-year-old son Kallen had taken the first bite out of a large, round biscuit—and opened up a world of possibilities.

Crunch.
'Look, it's a moon now!'
Kallen was beside himself with excitement, but he wasn't getting much response from Dad up front. You see, Andrew's mind was engaged in serious work, and he couldn't afford to be distracted by childish play. He had a keynote to prepare for, a presentation on groundbreaking new research into creativity and innovation, but he was having trouble coming up with a creative opening. Feeling under pressure to produce something suitably dazzling for the afternoon session, he knew he needed to maintain his focus on the task at hand.
'Sorry Kallen, I've got work to do.'

Crunch.
'But look Dad, you gotta look! It's become a mountain.'
'Son, not now! I'm trying to be creative.'

Crunch. Crunch.
Undeterred: 'Hey Dad, now it's a bird!'

Mostly out of a guilty sense of parental obligation, and probably also as a way to help stop the interruptions, Andrew turned to look at his son, who held a biscuit wedge a couple of bites short of complete annihilation, and grunted a cursory acknowledgement, before turning his attention back to the serious challenge confronting him.

But then it hit him. In a Eureka moment, Andrew suddenly recognised that while he had been busy trying to conjure up creative solutions, Kallen was expertly demonstrating the creative mind at work. It became apparent that while we approach these sorts of tasks with academic rigor and discipline, creative development is really about being able to imagine and to dream. In that moment Andrew truly appreciated that creativity is more an attitude than an action, and that creative development flies in the face of conventional wisdom. Instead of becoming more 'expert' in the field, instead of accumulating more facts about creative thinking and problem solving, he saw that we need to know how to open ourselves up to new ideas and possibilities, how to better utilise and harness the innate curiosity we are all born with.

This story became the opening of Andrew's presentation later that day. He had bought a packet of biscuits, and for the opening of the keynote Andrew invited six bankers out of the audience of 300 up onto the stage and asked each of them to take a bite out of a biscuit. He then asked the first participant what she could see, and the banker scratched her head, thought deeply, and finally replied with the utmost sincerity and conviction, 'A biscuit with a bite out of it!' Kallen's effortless ability to see seven utterly different objects after seven consecutive bites unexpectedly launched us into the more serious part of our journey in exploring creativity and innovation. (It's interesting to note here a simple creativity assessment exercise in which people are asked to think of a number of different uses for a common object—for example, a brick. While most people struggle to get past five ideas, a creative person can keep going well beyond that.)

This early experience led us to wonder about why, as we age, we seem to move away from that innocent, playful approach to life and appear to lose the ability to think creatively. As the need to think and act creatively has increased with the exponential increase in the demands and pressures of modern life, rediscovering this ability has become more vital than ever.

Is creative thinking *that* important?

A free spirit who would happily skip school or work and spend hours daydreaming in the open fields, creativity is the inner child within all of us dying to break free. When restricted by routine or limited by expectations, creativity struggles to survive. She relies on fresh opportunities to bring new ideas that will oxygenate the mind and soul. Where these are stifled by any number of openly brutal or subtle agents, creativity is murdered.

Creative thinking enables people to approach problems and solutions in more inventive ways. Related to the capacity to put existing ideas together in new combinations, without creative thinking we cannot learn to adapt in order to be able to deal with the future. We will always be stuck in the past, and we will not survive.

The evidence that creativity is now a critically important work and life skill is overwhelming. Many scholars argue that not being able to think creatively is a significant risk factor for any enterprise. In a classic divergent–convergent thinking challenge that measured the ability to think creatively, those who were more successful in problem-finding and problem-solving tasks were found to have better relationships. Creative thinking enabled them to develop more flexibility, which in turn enhanced their ability to handle stress and find solutions rather than seeing problems as setbacks. A study of 1500 US middle-school students found that those with good creative thinking skills tended to have more confidence in the future, believing they would be able to come up with creative solutions to any problems that came their way. It has also been shown that students who have had more exposure to creativity are more engaged at school, achieve better academic results and are more likely to stay at school longer.[1]

Creativity is now widely recognised as a critically important work skill. In a recent IBM[2] survey of more than 1500 CEOs from 33 different industries and 60 different countries, creativity was rated as the most important quality in leadership (60 per cent), more important even than integrity (52 per cent) and global thinking (35 per cent). IBM has identified a number of factors that set apart 'creative leaders' and found that 81 per cent of them rate innovation as a 'crucial capability'. These leaders are able to break with standard approaches and models to come up with new solutions that stand out from the crowd.[3]

Creative thinking enables us not only to deal with existing problems effectively, but also to anticipate potential problems and come up with superior solutions. Yet creativity is undermined unintentionally every day in work environments that were established — for entirely sound reasons — to maximise business imperatives such as coordination, productivity and control. Managers cannot be expected to ignore business imperatives, but in pursuing these imperatives they may be inadvertently designing organisations that systematically crush creativity.[4] As one CEO of a financial institution we have interviewed put it, 'If I tell my team to conquer that mountain they are great, but if I ask them which mountain to conquer they stare blatantly at me'.

According to Dr Geoffrey West, interviewed on the topic of 'Why Cities Keep Growing, Corporations and People Always Die, and Life Gets Faster',[5] innovation is critical for the survival of our civilisation, literally. A physicist and the former president of the Santa Fe Institute, West believes that if you are going to have open cycles of growth (as in our current capitalist system), you must have innovation to support them. The problem is that we need to innovate faster and faster in order to keep up with the pace of growth. West has discovered that the pace of life also increases with size of population. So, he says, 'Everything that's going on in New York today is systematically going faster than it is in San Francisco, than it is in Santa Fe, even the speed of walking. There's a clock that's getting faster and faster. And so you have to innovate faster and faster in order to avoid the collapse. And it all comes out of this exponential growth driven by super linear scaling.' All civilisations and all organisations follow a so-called sigmoidal growth curve, stopping or resetting after a certain period of time, West explains. For large corporations, the growth typically stops at the same value — about half a trillion dollars — or 40 years or three generations. Up to this point, the sigmoidal curve indicates that although sales might have been steadily increasing, the *ratio* of profit to sales has been steadily decreasing. Theoretically, the curve indicates that this ratio eventually goes to zero, but fluctuations in markets end the life of corporations before this point is reached.

It is usually only at the point that an organisation first sees the writing on the wall that they cut back on spending on innovation, for example limiting research and development budgets, and yet this is exactly the time when it is most needed. The lack of foresight organisations usually demonstrate at this critical stage in their life cycle is what ultimately kills them. When companies allow themselves to be dominated by bureaucracy and administration rather than creativity and innovation, as West says is inevitable, they are suffocated by the essentials.

Therefore, creativity is vitally important for individual and organisational survival. Perhaps even more important, creative thinking will help us save the world, because it enables us as a species to dream, to envisage a better future and to implement this vision. When Martin Luther King Jr set out his vision for the future in his famous 'I have a dream…' speech, he epitomised the potential of creative thinking, the ability it has to provide motivation for transformation and to induce a passion for real revolution. Without this creative spark, a spark that needs to live to some extent in all of us, the ember of a meaningful life, and our very existence would have no real substance or purpose. Creative thinking is essential for the evolution of the species and the survival of life beyond just the physical. Looking back, many ideas and ideals that have now become mainstream (such as the environmental movement) started with the creative dream of a few isolated revolutionary individuals who were perceived as radicals at the time but came to have an impact on the future of the whole planet.

Is creative death imminent?
The vital statistics

Research into the decline of creativity has led to some startling conclusions. In a sample of 1500 children aged 3–5, 98 per cent ranked as 'geniuses' in divergent thinking; in children aged 8–10 the figure fell to just 32 per cent; and by age 13–15 it had declined further to a mere 10 per cent. In other words, children become less creative as they grow older. Moreover, in a control test of 2000 adults (aged 25 and over), only 2 per cent ranked as geniuses.[6] When, more than 50 years ago, American psychologist E. Paul Torrance began identifying the key elements in creative thinking and assessing individuals according to these criteria, he had no idea what these assessments would eventually reveal. Torrance and his colleague Garnet Millar, who followed individuals over time, found that the qualities they identified in young children were major predictors for creative professional success. These assessments became the gold standard in the field and have since been used as a reliable predictor of adult accomplishment. By looking at the lifetime data Torrance and his associates collected, and reanalysing it, it was found that the correlation to lifetime creative accomplishments is nearly three times stronger for childhood creativity than it is for childhood IQ.[7]

A shocking new finding from the analysis of Torrance data collected over time is that although IQ levels increase with each generation by about 10 points owing to enriched environments (the Flynn effect), creativity scores are actually *falling* over time. After analysing up to 300 000 Torrance scores from children and adults, it has been discovered that although creativity scores rose along with IQ scores until 1990, creativity scores have since dropped significantly.[8]

Another example of the decline of creativity with age can be seen in an exercise called 'The Marshmallow Challenge'. In this activity, in which participants are asked to build the tallest freestanding structure they can using only marshmallows and spaghetti sticks, children consistently outperform adults. In fact, only half the adults end up with a standing structure, while the children build taller and more interesting structures on every measure of innovation. Adults literally don't measure up.[9]

So why does this happen? Evidently there is some sort of intervention, and unfortunately the evidence points to the very structure that should be encouraging and nurturing creativity — the education system. We found, for example, that when Kallen had not yet started school his enthusiasm for invention and discovery was inspiring. At the same time his older sister Zoe, it seemed, had already become a victim of the system. Zoe was well and truly entrenched in the structure that appeared to be directed towards limiting the child's vision to specific areas of focus and shutting down divergent thinking. In fact, we started to wonder whether, rather than inspiring creative thinking, the education system was actually killing it.

We decided to interview children in the school context to try to understand what happens as children go through the education system.[10] We approached our children's international school in Bali armed with no more than a series of questions and a video camera but were fascinated to get such stark responses from our small sample groups. As we walked into the school, we passed playgrounds with colourful gardens and wonderful play equipment and then moved into a junior classroom adorned with all sorts of creative products made by the children themselves. When we interviewed these young children there was great enthusiasm. Yes, they all felt they were creative, and of course they were proud of it! We felt significant relief and hope that creativity was still well and truly alive in the school. In the senior classrooms, however, the story was different. The wall art had been replaced with maths and science charts, and the children sat in rows, disciplined and subdued. The teachers we interviewed suggested there was 'no need for the additional stimulation in the environment' as students were 'being prepared for high school' and then 'prepared for university'. The students' responses to the questions we asked were also markedly negative. Zoe was horrified to see her parents enter the classroom and ask embarrassing questions about creativity. Our usually chatty and outgoing daughter failed to show any interest in the topic. Like her classmates, she merely shrugged her shoulders and looked away when we asked if she felt she was creative. Her love of learning has continued to diminish rapidly ever since.

We had hypothesised that children might feel they are less creative and as a whole demonstrate less creativity in the school context as they progressed through the system, and our first impressions confirmed our fears. On the premise that children are naturally creative thinkers (for reasons we will discuss throughout this book), we had wanted to see if innocent, non-academic minds could support the academic research on creativity and were fascinated to discover that many of the unscripted answers we received were consistent with the research findings. Children as young as five shared with us startling insights, such as how creative thinking was 'looking for different patterns' and 'coming up with different ideas and putting all the pieces together'. (See 'Hands up' video at <www.whokilledcreativity.com>.)

> *We don't grow into creativity, we grow out of it—or rather we get educated out of it.*
>
> Sir Ken Robinson

Are you creative?

Since our school visit we have surveyed thousands of international seminar participants from companies we have worked with. Asked if they think they were more creative as children than as adults, more than 80 per cent of respondents have agreed. Many have admitted to struggling with being creative in their current work environment, which is probably not surprising when you consider the emphasis in the workplace on reaching pragmatic targets and on the bottom line. And most have reported in our survey that they were more creative when they entered the organisation. It appears that both the education and work systems stifle creativity in some way.

So what can organisations do to help resolve this problem? Smart companies will start taking some responsibility for proactive education, and not simply for training skills. They will start to understand first that training is not always education. Training is about developing a specific skill set, and imparting knowledge and facts in the hope that workers can utilise this information when necessary. Education is about developing skills for ongoing learning and enquiry—ultimately it is all about learning to think creatively. Perhaps we should recognise the shortcomings of many current systems that rely on what educator and theorist Paolo Freire called 'knowledge banking' and start to think about how we might incorporate genuine learning processes into our organisations instead.

It is a mistake simply to assume that the participants in corporate training programs want to learn and want to hear what the facilitator has to say. Adult cynics can provide the greatest resistance to learning. Their poor experiences with the education system can often leave them with little desire for more, and consequently they are not equipped to cope with change. They can have trouble coming up with new ideas and with thinking creatively. When these people end up in management positions, the friction created between their understanding of the way the world is and the way they can see others can have far-reaching effects—and can even grind the company to a halt.

The key to creativity is sustaining that childlike freeform imagination while enriching it with knowledge, rather than replacing it with knowledge!

Bruce Haddon

To help rebuild creativity through *targeted education processes* (rather than simple training), you first need to recognise and deal with the killers to ensure they are no longer having a negative impact on the environment. And that is what we plan to do next.

Who killed creativity, and with what weapons?

Profile of a murderer: the seven deadly creativity killers

'Frighteningly normal' but capable of 'extraordinary cruelty': these were the words used by police surgeon Thomas Bond back in the 1880s to describe the likely profile of history's most infamous serial killer. 'Jack the Ripper' was believed to be responsible for the macabre murders of five London prostitutes, whose throats were cut and bodies mutilated before they were partially disembowelled. The killer's true identity was never discovered—he may have died soon after his killing spree or have been incarcerated for some other crime.

Bond's initial profile was probably remarkably accurate. When he examined the pattern of killings he concluded that the murderer would be 'unassuming in appearance and manner, and daring and calm in the face of unimaginable violence … middle-aged, leading a solitary life and wearing a long coat to cover up any blood from his crimes (since he killed in public spaces)'. The police, however, whose investigative techniques were then still quite crude, did not have enough information to find the killer, and the case was closed after four years. As they were unconvinced by Bond's description, the police failed to recognise that the person they were looking for might not have had a mental illness or appeared unstable, so they were probably searching for the wrong profile type. A recent documentary that re-examined the case using modern methods showed how profiling techniques can help with these types of murder investigations. This documentary revealed how modern psychological profilers have concluded that Jack the Ripper was in fact most likely sane and of normal appearance.[1]

13

The silent serial killers that target creativity can also be 'frighteningly normal' and often escape easy detection. It's time we gathered the evidence and employed the latest profiling tools to help catch and isolate the culprits, disarm them and expose their common haunts. A first step in investigating the murder of creativity is to use 'criminal profiling' to identify the most likely killers suspects. This process will give investigators a general feel for the psychological profiles, and therefore the motivations, of the sorts of characters likely to be involved. Profiling can also assist in analysing the nature of the offence and the manner in which a crime is committed.

After more than 25 years' experience working in both the education system and the corporate sector, our investigations into the killers of creativity have revealed some very clear profiles. We will now introduce you to these qualities and the characters that manifest them, and give you the opportunity to consider whether these killers are lurking undetected in society in general, or are hiding unobserved within your own work environment or your particular realm of experience. The current suspects can be easily identified from these general profile types. They include a range of seedy characters, all of whom personify potentially destructive qualities that can be found in individuals and in systems at all levels of society. It may be interesting for you to consider whether these suspects are loitering in your neighbourhood.

Criminals can be found everywhere—even next door. It can be difficult to recognise the sociopath, who can be adept at fitting in unobtrusively. Every sociopath, like the rest of us, sits somewhere on a continuum that stretches from socially acceptable to psychologically pathological. If you reviewed the characteristics of any personality disorder, you might be shocked to discover how many of them could be applied to you. In fact, it has been found that more than 30 per cent of people globally[2] report meeting some of these criteria at some point in their lives.[3] But while such labels can help with diagnosis and treatment, and in this context can help us to make sense of the world, they are by no means generally indicative or conclusive. The purpose of this book is not to label individuals or to lynch them, but to identify principles and systems that perpetuate negative approaches to creative thinking and to ascertain just how prevalent they are in your daily life or in your organisation.

Psychopaths, or sociopaths as they are also known, make up 4 per cent of the population. This might not sound much, but to put it into context, it is actually a higher percentage than sufferers of high-profile anorexic eating disorders (3.43 per cent) or rates of bowel cancer, which has been targeted as a major health issue. And sociopathic behaviours can have a much greater impact on others. Although sociopaths are generally represented in the media as violent, many more non-violent sociopaths remain below the radar, and their social impact can be incredibly destructive. Rather than fully humanised individuals, they have been described as 'social snipers' who lack 'soul quality' and tend to function as 'efficient machines… with clever social programming'. They can be intellectually brilliant, but often there's a mismatch between their words and actions.[4]

In psychopaths the part of the brain that processes empathy (the amygdala) malfunctions. Psychopaths, by definition, have a personality disorder that is marked by aggressive and antisocial behaviour coupled with a lack of empathy or remorse.[5] This indicates that creativity is also affected, since you need creative thinking to step into someone else's shoes, seeing what they see and feeling what they feel. Psychopaths tend to be very successful precisely because their lack of remorse or guilt means they can become detached 'cold-blooded killers'.

Alarmingly, the higher you go up the ladder of power, the more common psychopaths are. A test called the PCL-R checklist lists 20 personality or behavioural traits typical of psychopaths.[6] They include a grandiose sense of self-worth, lack of remorse or guilt, early behavioural problems and criminal versatility. Have you witnessed any of these traits in your organisation? Have you made the connection between behaviour disorders and the creativity killers? Abnormal, antisocial behaviour that affects others' ability to be creative ultimately kills creativity.

We will now outline the four stages of the murder process and introduce some of the more 'frighteningly normal' psychopathic killers we have identified in individuals and organisations. The stages of destruction of creativity we have identified include:

} Stage 1: oppression
} Stage 2: restriction
} Stage 3: degeneration
} Stage 4: destruction.

As set out in table 2.1, there are seven potential creativity killers and suspected murder weapons we have discovered as contributing to this degenerative process.

**Table 2.1: the Creative Thinking Life Cycle Model™ —
the death of creative thinking**

	THE DEATH OF CREATIVE THINKING: the stages of degeneration		
	Murder process	**Murder weapon**	**Murder suspects**
Stage 1	**Oppression** *The use of CONTROL and FEAR to limit open thinking*		
	Control *(The Control Crew)*	Crushing coercion	*Bureaucracy Bullying leadership Oppression*
	Fear *(The Fear Family)*	Drowning dead	*Fear of Failure Fear of Taking Risks Fear of the Unknown*
Stage 2	**Restriction** *The use of PRESSURE and INSULATION to restrict ideas*		
	Pressure *(The Pressure Pack)*	Strangling stress	*Excess Stress Multitasking Unreasonable expectations*
	Insulation *(The Insulation Clique)*	Bludgeoning bias	*Biased information sources Homogeneity Lack of Diversity*
Stage 3	**Degeneration** *Inhibition of growth driven by APATHY*		
	Apathy *(The Apathy Clan)*	Lacerating lethargy	*Lack of Motivation Lack of Initiative Lack of Drive*
Stage 4	**Destruction** *Destructive NARROW MINDEDNESS and PESSIMISM*		
	Narrow-mindedness *(The Narrow-minded Mob)*	Intractable intolerance	*Blinkered expertise Prejudice Groupthink*
	PESSIMISM *(The Pessimism Posse)*	Noxious negativity	*Negativity Lack of Hope Lack of Trust*

To narrow the field of suspects, we will zero in on the profile groups we have uncovered in our research and experiences. After running creativity workshops involving more than 20 000 people globally — from CEOs and corporate executives to kindergarten kids, from the rich and educated to the impoverished and disadvantaged — we have been able to draw certain general conclusions from our discoveries. For example, most people acknowledge the benefit of creative thinking, but although they support it in principle, they have no idea of how and why creativity is dying in their own experience. At the start of our sessions on reviving creativity we frequently encounter a barrage of protests that 'it won't work for me or in my organisation' and a string of reasons why. But we have found that few people, or books on the topic, have stopped to examine in any detail why this should be so, and indeed how creativity died.

You may be shocked to discover just how close to home many of these killers can strike...

Stage 1: oppression — the use of control and fear to limit open thinking

The first stage of the murder process includes two major killer profiles: the 'Control Crew', who crush independent thought and individual will, and the 'Fear Family', quiet killers who can undermine confidence and overwhelm the individual.

Murder profile 1: the Control Crew

Also known as bully oppressors, the 'control' profile type is usually motivated by the need for power. Individuals and systems with this profile tend to dominate or oppress others. They dictate, and direct towards, specific outcomes rather than empowering and encouraging individual discovery and growth. The targets of the 'control' profile often feel restricted or trapped. The control murderer tends to kill through suppressing the ability to think freely and independently, and the victims usually have their will crushed. These killers can have personality disorders that tend towards the *antisocial* or even *sadistic*. Their preferred weapon is *crushing coercion*.

Institutionalised torture: medieval shackles and meddling systems

In medieval times, convicted prisoners were sometimes confined in an instrument of punishment called the stocks—hinged wooden boards that locked in place over the prisoner's neck and hands. Since an important part of the punishment was public disgrace and ridicule, it took place in a public area, where passers-by were encouraged to throw mud, rotten food or even excrement at the helpless victim. The prisoner might be left in the open for days, exposed to extreme weather conditions, so it was not uncommon for those confined for days at a time to die from hypothermia or heat exhaustion. The idea was to crush the spirit through the exertion of power and humiliation.

You might think that such instruments of torture are a thing of the past, yet there are still 69 known manufacturers of shackles, leg irons and thumb-cuffs today, most of them in the United States and Europe.[7] Through restricting rather than stopping all movement, shackles allow the prisoner limited freedom within the bounds of external control. Amnesty International documents the incredible range of current human rights abuses that use restraint, torture and terror as means of control.[8]

Like stocks or shackles designed to restrict physical movement, many organisational systems are, deliberately or inadvertently, designed to restrict mental and emotional growth and development, crushing the will to create. When systems are set up that restrict freedom of thought, creativity has no room to flourish. This can happen at a national or global level through oppressive dictatorship, at the social or organisational level, and at individual level.

Those who fit the control profile are, in crude terms, thugs. The conduct of characters in this profile is mostly obvious, yet we are often too frightened to confront them, letting them 'get away with murder'. We know where these thugs hang out — they are all around us — but we are afraid to acknowledge their presence. Just as battered wives often stay with their abusive husbands because of emotional attachment to them, we persist in allowing systems that perpetuate control to dominate our lives because they are familiar. And yet as long as these control systems are tolerated, they will continue to crush creativity.

We once worked with an IT management group that struggled with this killer, which had become entrenched in the organisation. By the end of one of our creative thinking workshops, the key leadership team of 30 had generated hundreds of exciting ideas, a number of them developed into specific, workable action plans. By mid afternoon they were excited and motivated, keen to go back to their departments with the fabulous new ideas they had come up with and with the refreshed energy that creative thinking produces. Then the general manager turned up. The session had been organised at the request of this GM, and although in principle he was keen for his team to learn creative thinking, in practice, when he was presented with the specific outcomes, he inadvertently smothered it. After welcoming the group at the beginning of the day, he had headed back to the office to get on with what he called his 'real work', plainly communicating the message that he was not really engaged or even interested in the process. When he was invited to rejoin the session to hear the creative ideas for improvement his teams had come up with, he sat with legs and arms crossed and a serious expression, maintaining a non-responsive, almost negative demeanour throughout. His body language indicated clearly that he was not open to the new ideas or willing to proceed with discussing them.

This GM probably recognised that many of the new ideas were not immediately implementable, and that some could be costly and time consuming. But he missed the point of the process of generating ideas and looking for creative ways of doing things better. Rather than stifling ideas he could have encouraged them and used them as a springboard for further exploration. Later in the session he actively blocked the flow of creative ideas by diverting the follow-up discussion towards his own chosen outcomes rather than allowing for freedom of expression. The long-term result was that nothing changed in the system, there were many dissatisfied employees—a number of them resigned and moved on—while the organisation missed an opportunity to deal with key issues.

The dark story of Lehman Brothers, which has been described as a workplace characterised by extreme coercion, bullying and stand-over bosses, is now well known.[9] As Lehman's Global Head of Strategic Partnerships, David Goldfarb, described it, the end 'came so fast no one was prepared for it. No one at that time had any inkling that we would go down. We just knew we had a lot of work to do'. Bosses had wielded coercion as a formidable weapon, constantly pulling people into line, both formally and informally, and creating such a culture of fear that no-one would dare question the system. As a result, the whole company went down. The bullying culture was so strong that while some may have seen it coming, no-one felt free to question it. A famous banker commented, 'They f----d people. They built a castle to rip people off. Not once in all these years have I come across a person inside a big Wall Street firm who was having a crisis of conscience'.[10]

Through wielding power and authority, and through creating and perpetuating systems that stifle free thinking and new ideas, control effectively kills creativity. There is a saying that there is nothing funnier than a powerful person's jokes. The power and influence that controlling people and controlling systems exert suppress independent thought, and this is incredibly destructive over the long term. The need to be 'in control' can stem from individual insecurities and inadequacies and an attempt to compensate for these, so understanding the motivations underlying this profile can help to diffuse its destructive power.

Key suspects of the Control Crew may include:

- oppressive systems
- systems that stifle (bureaucracy)
- bully bosses.

Murder suspect 1 — oppressive systems

The menacing mafia

Their traditional image — the dark clothing, intimidating manner and strong Sicilian accent, and their reputation for committing violence against anyone in their way and getting away with it — make the Italian mafia easily recognisable today. Not so well known are the origins of this criminal syndicate, which emerged in Sicily in the mid nineteenth century during the period of transition between the end of feudalism and Sicily's annexation by mainland Italy in 1860. The nobility had owned most of the land under

THE CONTROL CREW

Major O. Preshon

MURDER SUSPECT

feudalism, but from 1812 they began to sell off or rent the land to private citizens, and by 1861 there had been a tenfold increase in landowners — from 2000 to 20 000.[11] Without the police resources to monitor the large number of disputes that arose, extra-legal arbitrators and protectors were engaged — protectors who eventually organised themselves into 'companies at arms' or clans. The clans, which became known as the mafia, enlisted former criminals and bandits and relied on violence to enforce their control. They soon became involved in politics. As early as 1889, folklorist Giuseppe Pitre captured the essence of the mafia when he wrote, 'Mafia is the consciousness of one's own worth, the exaggerated concept of individual force as the sole arbiter of every conflict, of every clash of interests or ideas'.

Like the mafia, the Control Crew in organisations exert their power to gain and maintain political control in order to promote their own agenda. This sort of control crushes creativity through a coercion that instils fear.

In order to survive, innovation most often needs to come from the top or at least to be supported at the top. Innovative companies need innovative leaders. Where leaders exert negative, coercive control over their teams through autocratic leadership styles, creative confidence usually suffers. Leaders who express scepticism without exploring the creative potential of new ideas, and who fail to acknowledge and accept creative efforts made by their employees, may not only discourage creativity but actually shut it down. A national campaign to 'defend academic creativity' against the perceived onslaught of red tape and bullying managers was proposed at a conference held in Cardiff in 2007.[12] The speakers at the conference urged participants to 'resist feelings of helplessness in the face of overzealous managers and the requirements of audits, performance indicators and the research assessment exercise. Staff should be prepared to "push back the boundaries" of their working environment and take creative risks. Most importantly creative ideas must be nurtured and "have a home" encouraged and correspondingly bad ideas/ mistakes must be tolerated'.

Murder suspect 2 — bureaucracy

The polite mafia cousin

Bureaucracy can be described as the polite mafia cousin who has grown up in the system and doesn't know any other way. He does not intentionally aim to harm others, but he operates within a controlling world of stifling systems and processes. Like those with obsessive–compulsive personality disorder, he suffers from 'rigid conformity to rules, moral codes and excessive orderliness', including a preoccupation with minute detail and facts. He has a tendency to follow regulations relentlessly, and to make lists and schedules incessantly. Bureaucracy is unaware of the extent of his interpersonal control at the expense of flexibility, openness and efficiency. He is evident everywhere in large, established organisations.

Bureaucracy is like the guy around the office whom no-one likes but everyone knows is there. It's not like he is aggressive or mean, it's just that he is really boring and relentless. And in the end, when you look at his work, he seems to have been involved in everything but to have done absolutely nothing productive. Sometimes bureaucracy kills discreetly — you simply don't notice that the time you had planned to be innovative has been taken up filling out forms; and sometimes it's more obvious — OH&S won't let you have that car-free day because you aren't allowed to store your bike in the office, where it might constitute a trip hazard.

As Dr Jason reveals in his coroner's report, rigid structures cannot accommodate innovation or dimensionality (which, crudely, equates to diversity or multidimensionality). There is simply nowhere for an innovative suggestion to go, and consequently they are not proposed. Fluid structures, on the other hand, allow dimensionality and provide opportunities for cross-pollination and collaboration. At the same time, too much freedom can obviously lead to disorganisation, so it is important to find that ideal but delicately balancing point between flexibility and force.

Bureaucracy has been defined as 'a slow-moving office'. While rigorous systems in the workplace may provide stability, they do not necessarily encourage creativity. Technicalities driven by political will can slow and stifle creative thinking in an organisation.[13] To produce innovative ideas, creative professionals must work in a system that values a bias-to-action and boundary-less collaboration.[14] One hundred years ago bureaucracy meant something positive.[15] It was designed to replace the arbitrary exercise of power by authoritarian regimes. But then, ironically, it became a restrictive system in itself. In his book *Making Bureaucracy Work*, Michael Balle explains that bureaucracy 'is the only known way of coordinating vast numbers of people to treat mass problems', but he also discusses the need to make bureaucracy flexible by knowing where and when to change rules rather than simply being stuck within them. 'What gives bureaucracy such a bad name?' he asks. 'Is it bureaucracy in itself, or the ghosts in the system who, in a million minor drifts, contribute to turning efficiency into red-tape?' Like any tool, Balle believes, it is only as good as the people who use it, and when the users have a set agenda the outcomes will inevitably be biased.[16]

Systems can become oppressive through autocratic leadership, just as they can become inflexible if they are not often updated and refreshed. Unfortunately the profit motive will always place external pressure on an organisation and on individuals, but this imperative must be carefully balanced against the need for freedom of thought in order to innovate.

Murder suspect 3 — bullying leadership
Bullying and the bottom line

A not-too-distant relative of the mafia-style leader who wants to control is the 'bully boss'. It has been found that the bullying boss not only constitutes a distinct leadership profile but also seems to exhibit a distinct set of personality disorders. When British executives and criminal psychiatric patients were set identical personality tests, the results showed that three of the personality disorders were actually more common in executives than in the disturbed criminals.[17][18] The main difference between the executives and the criminals, they concluded, was that the executives were successful psychopaths,[19] while the criminals were unsuccessful psychopaths! The disorders they found were more prevalent in the executives were:

THE CONTROL CREW

Bull E. Boss

MURDER SUSPECT

- ⸙ *histrionic personality disorder*, including superficial charm, insincerity, egocentricity and manipulation
- ⸙ *narcissistic personality disorder*, including grandiosity, self-focused lack of empathy for others, exploitativeness and individualism at the expense of others
- ⸙ *obsessive–compulsive personality disorder*, including perfectionism, excessive devotion to work, rigidity, stubbornness and dictatorial tendencies.

Some other traits they discovered were common among the 'successful psychopath' executives were problems with anger management and a distorted sense of reality.[20] Many bullies experience feelings of inadequacy and difficulties in relating to others, which can come out in inappropriate ways. Narcissistic tendencies were found to be related to bullying motivation and satisfaction with seeing others suffer.[21] Sound familiar? It was concluded that the prevalence of these traits in executive groups might explain why many bullying bosses fail to recognise problems in their leadership and are usually unwilling or unable to change their behaviours when confronted by accusations of abuse. They also tend not to feel remorse or guilt.[22]

As many as one in 25 bosses have been found to be psychopaths,[23] and the incidence of psychopathology among corporate managers (defined as 'madness without delirium'[24]) has been found to be four times higher than in the general population. In bottom-line financial terms, the cost of bullying has been estimated at US$1.2 million for an organisation of 1000 people based on replacement costs of affected individuals, which does not include the cost of potential litigation against the organisation.[25] As it has become more prevalent, bullying has become a mainstream media issue.[26] [27]

While sexual harassment and racial vilification are obvious candidates for the most wanted list, bullying has to date managed to escape attention, perhaps because he's a slippery character who crosses the line when no-one important is looking. He can be like a sniper who picks off his victims when no-one else is around. The bully boss thrives under cover and where people are too afraid to speak out. Although many complain about this killer, few dare to discuss the problems in his presence.

An influential survey on office politics[28] revealed a clear trend towards the 'macho, meddling manager'. As many as one-third of respondents indicated they would like to change jobs because their controlling bosses give them no autonomy at work. Sixty per cent of respondents believed office bullying in general is on the increase, and 79 per cent claimed this escalates to conflict; 9 per cent had experienced actual physical abuse, while 18 per cent had suffered verbal harassment. As many as 64 per cent of survey respondents felt bullied through a culture of enforced long work hours or through being deliberately 'excluded' or 'sidelined'. Other symptoms of this culture included 'basic rudeness', 'unreasonable put-downs', a 'blame culture' and people taking the credit for others' work.

Bully bosses can create environments that are:

- coercive
- reactionary
- judgemental.

These can in turn engender a survival mentality and a culture of:

\ fear
\ anxiety
\ anger
\ self-protection
\ helplessness.

In a hostile work environment, industrial sabotage is common. Employees who feel disempowered, who feel under great pressure but lack support in dealing with this pressure, will often fight back in subtle and subversive ways. There is no room or incentive to think creatively in such a negative environment. 'Producing late, low-quality work, going off sick just when you are most needed or sticking so closely to procedures that you cannot get the job done properly are three increasingly common forms of industrial sabotage,' says occupational psychologist Beverley Stone in an article in the *Guardian*.[29]

Bully bosses also tend to create competitive working environments, which can be destructive. When competition between employees is encouraged so that individual incentives are promoted at the expense of building a cooperative culture, the sort of collaborative creativity that thrives in open and accepting environments can be destroyed. This 'tournament theory' is evident in a large number of organisations today.[30] Indeed, it has been found that in more than three-quarters of poorly performing companies executives set up their successors for failure or deliberately choose weak successors to shore up their own reputation.[31] Managers can also actively destroy creativity by failing to acknowledge creative efforts made by employees. This can be done through not encouraging creative ideas, as well as through actively expressing dislike or scepticism towards ideas without offering a reasonable balance of support and positive feedback.[32]

Finally, if all of this research is true, then a question is screaming out to be addressed: *Why are so many bosses psychopaths?*

All humans cannot be psychopaths, so logic dictates that there are three possible answers:

\ Psychopaths are drawn to positions of power within companies.
\ The organisational system is such that it turns ordinary people into psychopaths, or at least encourages and develops their already existing worst traits.
\ The system is so set up that those who tread on people's heads (metaphorically rather more than literally, we hope!) get promoted.

It is our belief that all three are true, but that the prime culprit is number three: if you are willing to act ruthlessly and deceitfully, and are good at appearing otherwise, you often get ahead in corporate cultures. This is endemically dangerous and incredibly difficult to change.

When a mafia boss dies or retires from his leadership position the reputation of his clan or 'family' often goes with him. The clan will have a better chance of surviving when there are other strong potential leaders within the ranks. But the Control Crew could never have such a strong grip without the close alliance of another not-so-distant set of relatives—the Fear Family—who can easily take over where control leaves off…

Investigator's report

Have you seen this Oppression profile in your neighbourhood or workplace? Profile characteristics can include:

\ organisational systems that stifle ☐
\ a focus on bureaucratic details rather than value-based outcomes ☐
\ autocratic rather than democratic leadership ☐

\ a tendency towards domination ☐
\ restricted freedom ☐

The impact on victims can be:

\ lack of confidence ☐
\ low self-worth ☐
\ resignation—a tendency to give up
  or give in easily ☐

Murder profile 2: the Fear Family

Suspects fitting this profile can appear innocuous, but they are actually silent and deadly killers. Often parented and nurtured by the controllers, and usually closely related to them, the Fear Family are motivated primarily by the need for security. The Fear Family often claim their victims through panic, when they become overwhelmed and sink under the weight of excessive anxiety. The victims usually feel too paralysed to venture out and take the first steps to save themselves. Unable to 'keep their heads above water', they drown easily. Associated personality disorders can include: *obsessive–compulsive, avoidant, self-defeating, generalised anxiety disorder* and *phobic*. The Fear Family's preferred weapon is *drowning dread*.

Franklin Roosevelt and the godfather

So, first of all, let me assert my firm belief that the only thing we have to fear is fear itself—nameless, unreasoning, unjustified terror which paralyses needed efforts to convert retreat into advance.[33]

The man who spoke these words, Franklin Roosevelt, would have understood how crippling fear can be. Struck with polio at the age of 39 and losing the use of his legs, Roosevelt continued to pursue his political ambitions with an iron determination. His wife, Eleanor, recalled, 'I know that he had real fear when he was first taken ill, but he learned to surmount it. After that I never heard him say he was afraid of anything'.

In his time as president, Roosevelt was responsible for leading the US through one of the most challenging phases of its history, a period that included the Great Depression and World War II. In his first inaugural speech in 1933 he called on the nation to face up to its deepest fears. Confronting deep economic woes and further negative forecasts, Roosevelt rallied his nation in an inspirational address that included the memorable passage above, words of defiance that have reverberated down through the generations. As wartime leader in 1941, Roosevelt took a firm tactical approach with a clear foreign policy. In the postwar period he maintained a strong hope that the United Nations would maintain the peace with the cooperation of the former wartime Allies. His achievements remind us that there is indeed 'nothing to fear but fear itself'.

Fear is the godfather of the murdering mob,[34] driving all other murderers before it. Where fear lurks it is impossible to move forward confidently, and without confidence there can be no progress. People who lack confidence tend to stick to the same routines and follow the same patterns, as this brings feelings of safety and security. Rather than taking risks and being prepared to step out of their comfort zones, these people will stay with what's safe and will therefore miss out on opportunities to expand their minds and experiences—to become more creative. Low confidence is also linked to anxiety and the fear of failure, which, like stress, inevitably shuts down creativity. Of course, levels of confidence are affected by many of the factors already listed, including autocratic leadership styles and stifling systems. So dealing with problems of insecurity needs to go hand in hand with dealing with these other issues.

When we live with fear constantly we are in danger of developing a generalised anxiety and insecurity, which in turn cripples creativity. Even perceived (not real) fear can be crippling. It has been shown, for example, that wording a problem differently, even when the situation and facts remain identical, can produce a different impact.[35] Fear kills creativity by continually submersing individuals so they struggle to stay afloat, and the more they struggle, the quicker they will drown. In the water, it takes just three minutes to drown once you start inhaling water instead of air. Similarly, we can give in to fear and be overtaken by its power very quickly. The more we thrash around, sending out feeble or unheard cries for help in a variety of guises, the more quickly we will give up hope and submit to the external pressures that have allowed fear to take control.

Mounting insecurity about the current economic situation is leading to 'a pressure cooker of tension' in many workplaces.[36] So it will be important to address this murder profile openly and directly.

The Fear Family suspects can include:

- fear of failure
- fear of taking risks
- fear of the unknown.

Murder suspect 1 — fear of failure

Making the million-dollar mistake

An overbearing brute who can intimidate the most intrepid, this highly prolific villain thrives on concerns about trialling new ideas and the possibility of failure. Dr Jason argues that creative individuals have to be resilient in the face of rejection, self-sustaining and self-reinforcing. Biographies of great artists and scientists nearly always start with a prolonged period of zero recognition. This is a huge factor that rules out many people from being productively creative. Overcoming insecurity about creativity is for the bold-hearted.

THE FEAR FAMILY

Fear O'Failure

MURDER SUSPECT

Success is a great affirmation but a lousy learning experience. I'd rather climb inside the head of an athlete who failed and came back than one who succeeded.

Edward de Bono[37]

Many inventions have been inspired by accident (3M Scotchguard[38] is a famous example) or come about as a result of people using failure as a learning opportunity—people, that is, who did not fear failure and were willing to get back up and try again and again. Consider these examples of failure and target correction:

- If a ship is blown off course it doesn't simply 'fail'; the pilot recognises that a correction is needed to bring the ship back on track. An organisation's language in relation to 'failure' is crucially important to creativity.

- Egg Bank, based in the UK, risked failure when it tried to be too innovative. Formerly Prudential Banking plc, Egg was established in 1996 as the world's first 100 per cent internet bank. Egg specialises in savings, credit cards and loans but also offers mortgage and insurance products, but an Egg account can be operated only over the internet or via its call centre. In 2007 Prudential sold Egg to Citigroup for a consideration of £575 million.[39]

Failure may actually be encouraged by a company such as 3M. In one, perhaps apocryphal story, when a company employee made a million-dollar mistake, his boss was asked if he was going to fire him, to which he is said to have replied, 'Fire him? We just had a $1 million learning experience!' Not all bosses would or could be so tolerant; organisations that are serious about creativity would, though, if the intentions and approach were positive.

In design it is critical to recognise the importance of 'failing early and often' in order to test and refine the product. Admitting to failure is also an important part of being transparent about the process and seeing and correcting errors as they arise. But we are now being told that only certain types of failure should be tolerated. Of course we need to ensure that, where possible, our failures won't have a deep impact on other people or processes, and we need to be honest about the possible consequences of allowing failure. As designer Jamer Hunt has said, 'Anyone who has experienced staggering failure knows that it is ugly, painful, and psychically destructive. It haunts you when you can't sleep in the wee hours of the night and it can threaten longstanding, valued relationships. Clients may turn away from you, supporters lose confidence in you, and there's a profound and, at times, corrosive level of self-questioning that ensues'.[40]

Creating prototypes is one way failure can be productive. This process allows new approaches to be tested and trialled without the risk and impact of full, unfettered failure. Catching small failures quickly can lead to positive evolution through ensuring a series of incremental improvements. For shareholders, embracing design may require the acceptance of striking failure as a natural corollary of smashing success. Even after major failure, recovery can be superb as a result of taking the initial risk.[41]

To better understand the importance of embracing failure, consider two long-forgotten Apple products and the role they played in innovation history. Apple was able to celebrate the amazing breakthrough success of the Macintosh personal computer only after the crushing failure of the Apple 'Lisa', which was the Macintosh's predecessor. Many of you are probably wondering what the Lisa was. It was a product that faded into oblivion, as it was expensive and slow—a major lesson for Apple. Apple had yet another unmemorable failure in the 'Newton', its first tablet platform, but that failure was followed by the iPad, so was it ultimately worth the cost? Of course it was!

A recent advertising campaign from Apple picked up on the fact that fearlessly creative people are prepared to risk failure. Apple's motto is to 'fail wisely'. The Macintosh was born from the wreckage of the Lisa; the hugely popular iPhone followed on from the failure of Apple's original music phone, produced in conjunction with Motorola. Both times Apple learned from its mistakes and tried again. Its recent computers have been based on technology developed at NeXT, a company Steve Jobs set up in the 1980s that appeared to have failed and was then acquired by Apple. The wider lesson is not to stigmatise failure but rather to learn from it.

According to professional trader and mathematician Nassim Taleb, book publishers often release a number of poor sellers that lose them money before they happen upon the next great breakthrough. Although they must go through the motions and continue to produce books no matter what the outcome, what they are all really banking on is finding the next *Twilight* or *Harry Potter* series. The fact that they might eventually come through with a bestseller can become a focus, so that all the losses involved in the process are forgotten or discounted.[42]

Economist Tim Harford identifies overriding themes based on failsafe failures—what he calls the 'Palchinsky principles': first, seek out new ideas and try new things; second, when trying something new, do it on a scale on which failure is survivable; third, seek out feedback and learn from your mistakes as you go along.[43]

Masked failure can also be dangerous. Although many tend to admire the apparent skill and talent of the big stock market winners, the reality is that at any point in time the richest stock traders in Wall Street are often the most susceptible to failure because of their dangerous 'creative' risk-taking behaviours.[44] When they fail or, as it is known, 'blow up', they are quickly replaced by keen newcomers, which can mask the fact that there has been a major loss and the former 'star' is now a 'has-been'. This focus on apparent achievers at the height of their success rather than through their overall career skews our view of who to look up to and measure ourselves against. In order to remove the fear of failure it must be named and managed.

Murder suspect 2—fear of taking risks

Iconoclasts versus phobics

A childlike ability to take risks and risk failure without fear can itself lead to successful innovation. Innovation requires breaking out of the standard ways of thinking and behaving, and innovators are iconoclasts—people who break the rules. We all start as iconoclasts as small children, doing what we want to do, breaking 'the rules' without knowing it, until someone explains them to us and socialises us into acceptable behaviour.[45] In our school video *Hands Up*, teacher Anthony Lennon remarks that 'kids are fearless—they just push buttons, not worrying what might happen next'.[46]

33

You might imagine that rules are just part of the game in business and need to be accepted as such, but psychologist and entrepreneur Roger Schank challenges this notion, arguing that the willingness to take risks and fail is fundamental to innovation. Although most big organisations are typically risk averse—as he says, 'Wall Street hates risk'—the organisations that allow originality and failure will be the ones that will progress the most.[47]

When economic realities hit, many people become afraid of losing their jobs, and therefore they take fewer risks. Sometimes people also fear offering creative input in group situations or to other people in the organisation in case their ideas are rejected or disparaged. But developing the confidence to step out and take risks can make all the difference between long-term success or failure.

Murder suspect 3—fear of the unknown

Naked fear

First they came at night, when we didn't know what was out there in the dark beyond our home territory; when the forest was still a mystery they were there waiting for us in the forest depths; once we understood the land they moved to the oceans; and now we have sailed the seas our monsters and associated fears have moved into outer space and the supernatural. We have always feared what we don't know.

Of course, you don't know what you don't know, and many people will simply avoid taking a risk if they imagine there could be a negative outcome. Current economic conditions have conjured up exceptional and often unreasonable fears in the individual that has had a significant impact on workplace conditions and culture. 'The current level of hostility at work simply reflects naked fear about the future and the belief that whatever firms may say about there being no more redundancies, the axe will continue to fall,' says Jane Clarke, director of the business psychology consultancy Nicholson McBride. She believes the ruthlessness of today's work environment stands in stark contrast to the many prettily worded mission statements that claim to put employees' rights and teamwork at the centre of their business philosophy.[48]

From 1940 Roosevelt's health started to deteriorate. By 1944, when he turned 62, his health was in sharp decline, and tests revealed that the physical exertions of dealing with his paralysis, work stress and years of smoking had all taken their toll. On the afternoon of 12 April 1945 Roosevelt said to his butler, 'I have a terrific pain in the back of my head', before slumping forward in his chair unconscious. He died soon after from a stroke—a massive cerebral haemorrhage. The man who had shown no fear during his long term of leadership, who had so courageously borne the additional weight of his disability, was finally beaten by the pressure, the next assassin in the murder suspect line-up ...

Have no fear of robbers or murderers. They are external dangers, petty dangers. We should fear ourselves ... The great dangers are within us. Why worry about what threatens our heads or purses? Let us think instead of what threatens our souls.

Victor Hugo

Investigator's report

Have you seen this Fear profile in your neighbourhood or workplace? Profile characteristics can include:

\ suppression of confidence to try new things ☐
\ inability to take risks ☐

The impact on victims can be:

\ panic—an inability to think clearly and creatively about options ☐
\ paralysis—an inability to take action ☐
\ a tendency to run away from challenges ☐

CRIME SCENE DO NOT CROS

Stage 2: restriction — the use of pressure and insulation to restrict ideas

The second stage of the murder process limits thinking and includes the '**Pressure Pack**', assassins that apply unreasonable tension and stress, and the '**Insulation Clique**', killers that isolate and confine.

Murder profile 3: the Pressure Pack

Those fitting this profile are driven by creating unrealistic expectations and pushing their victims to the limit. With the faster pace of life and greatly increased communication speeds, the 'pressure' profile is apparent in every part of society. This seductive assassin dispatches its victims by exercising a stranglehold on real or perceived expectations. The first sign that the killer is at work is stress, as revealed by a broad range of potentially deadly physical and psychological symptoms. The vicelike grip on its victims often panics and paralyses them, sapping their energy and denying them the time to save themselves through creative strategies, so that they eventually asphyxiate. Associated personality disorders are *histrionic, borderline personality* and *addictive*. The preferred weapon is *strangling stress*.

Rock star suicides and death by asphyxiation

Michael Hutchence, the charismatic lead singer of the internationally successful group INXS, died a tabloid-worthy death just as he had lived a sensational life. In 1997, aged 37, the raunchy rock singer was found hanging from a self-made noose in the Ritz-Carlton Hotel in Sydney. It was widely rumoured at the time that he had been intentionally trying to restrict oxygen to his brain for the purpose of sexual arousal—a behaviour known medically as autoerotic asphyxiation. When the major arteries on either side of the neck (the carotid arteries) are compressed, the resulting loss of oxygen to the brain induces a lucid, semi-hallucinogenic state called hypoxia. The 'rush' of this hallucinogenic state combined with the dopamine high produced by orgasm is said to be highly addictive, not unlike the effect of certain powerful drugs.

If the rumours were true, and Michael Hutchence did indeed leave this world in pursuit of an insatiable craving for erotic pleasure, he wouldn't have been the first and sadly will not be the last to follow this path. It's an impulse we apparently share with other animals. In one well-known experiment, rats were wired up to receive an orgasm every time they pressed a lever.[49] [50] The rats that discovered the pleasure the lever could provide became addicted to the dopamine reward; they began neglecting to tend to their physiological needs and eventually died from the experience. One of our workshop participants once exclaimed on hearing this story, 'Yeah, but what a great way to go!' This seems to epitomise the addictive nature of pressure and the intense love/hate relationship we have with it.[51] [52] Pressure can also gain a stranglehold on those who enjoy the rush of adrenaline it can bring, and many people become addicted to the 'buzz' it provides.

Death through strangulation is a dramatic way to die, as is frequently exploited in TV shows and movies. The victim gasps for air as the blood is blocked from the brain and carbon dioxide levels build to toxic levels. Similarly, when commitments and expectations lead to intense pressure, our creative energy is blocked and our regular brain functioning can be impeded. This sort of murderer can only kill when close to the victim and will often leave no visible marks.

People today experience pressure in a number of different ways. The exponentially increasing pace of life has led to higher demands at work, with individuals expected to juggle longer working hours with greater personal commitments. The result is that we are all running faster just to stay on the same spot, struggling to keep ahead of these commitments. More deadlines, overwhelming amounts of communication to deal with through email, Facebook, mobile phone and Twitter, longer and longer task lists to get through, greater parenting expectations and involvements—all are inescapable, defining areas of the 'rat race' that we must adjust to and deal with.

Increased productivity demands on employees are leading to a crisis in job satisfaction levels. In a 2010 study, 36 per cent of employers revealed that their workload had increased over the previous year, and 40 per cent of employees reported experiencing an increased workload over the same period.[53] At around the same time another survey found that only 45 per cent of Americans were satisfied with their work, which was the lowest job satisfaction result in the whole 22 years of the survey's history.[54] It can be assumed that the lower job satisfaction was partly due to the recession itself, but it has nonetheless been a growing trend over the past 20 years.

Pressure is the type of killer that, once allowed in, is a constant burden, like being stuck in a horror movie where you can't escape a terrifying sense of foreboding, at first it may seem like good company. It can even be stimulating and fun spending time in pressure's presence. But before long it will begin to dominate and stifle. Pressure may appear harmless enough: a familiar presence, an old friend just popping in every now and then for a chat. Research shows that the more familiar we are with something, the more we start to see its features as attractive, but in the case of pressure this only makes it more dangerous. Before you realise it, pressure has moved in like an unwanted mother-in-law and becomes so overbearing that there is room for little else in your life. When pressure seizes total control, there simply isn't room (or time in the day) for creativity. A holiday may offer temporary relief, but often pressure is waiting for you, welcoming you home the minute you get back into your regular routines.

Under pressure, the body's instinctive response is 'fight, flight or freeze'. The constant adrenaline produced can lead to irritation and anger management issues—the fight reaction. The flight response offers only a short-term solution, as eventually pressure will catch up to you and confront you when you least expect it. Most pressure needs to be dealt with rather than simply escaped. Obviously if you freeze up, your life will be significantly compromised and you will become a victim to pressure sooner than you might otherwise anticipate.

When the brain is under stress, the primal emotional 'shutdown' response is triggered as a coping mechanism, moving you rapidly into what has been called 'the red zone'.[55] People in this state are less likely to be aware of the implications of negative emotions and less likely to be able to manage them, and there is often associated anxiety, fear, anger, distress and/or guilt. When 'red zone' emotions are expressed, they often have a negative impact on personal and working relationships, shutting off the relaxed and open state required for creative thinking. We need to learn how to control these brain responses more effectively so we can access the prefrontal cortex more easily and ensure we remain in the freethinking open 'blue zone'.

The Pressure Pack suspects we will cover here include:

- excess stress
- multi-tasking and tech addiction
- increased expectations.

Murder suspect 1 — excess stress

The flirtatious socialite at work

Stress is a like flirtatious socialite. She is a hugely active but under-recognised killer, working effectively through an often subtle and charming approach. Stress is always hanging around the others in the Pressure Pack, linking up with them for the kill whenever she has the opportunity. Most people enjoy hanging out with her until they realise it takes too much energy to keep her entertained, at which point she has already taken over their lives. Her constant presence will induce a raft of physical and emotional symptoms. These will start with apparently

THE PRESSURE PACK

X. S. Stress

MURDER SUSPECT

insignificant symptoms such as sleep loss, headaches, stomach problems and joint pains, but ultimately will lead to cancerous diseases, strokes and heart conditions as well as mental disorders such as depression, bipolar syndrome, addictions, neuroses and psychoses. Stress can kill in any number of ways.

If we were to personify stress in psychological terms, we might equate it to the 'histrionic personality disorder' (HPD). As defined by the American Psychiatric Association, HPD is characterised by a pattern of 'excessive emotionality and attention-seeking, including an excessive need for approval and inappropriately seductive behaviour. These individuals are lively, dramatic, vivacious, enthusiastic, and flirtatious. Associated features may include egocentrism, self-indulgence, continuous longing for appreciation, and persistent manipulative behaviour to achieve their own needs'. People with this disorder usually have good social skills and are able to function socially and professionally at a high level, but they tend to use these skills to manipulate other people and become the centre of attention.

It is now common for people to open a conversation by asking how busy you are, and the commonly accepted response will be a roll of the eyes and an indication that you are currently experiencing extreme stress (and this will be the same response every time you are asked). Stress is often worn as a badge of honour by busy executives, who are proud to admit they are captivated by her. Indeed they thrive on communicating that they are constantly busy and under pressure.

So why and how does stress kill creativity? Modern pressures can actually drain the brain, sapping the energy and resources that might otherwise be available for creative thinking. Creative thinking needs to be processed through the more sophisticated, reflective frontal lobe of the brain, and when we are stressed or anxious, when we feel insecure or not listened to, our brain resources are reduced to dealing with the immediate needs of the more primitive survival functions of the base stem of the brain. According to neuroscientists, continuous or intense stress can damage brain cells, brain structure and brain function, causing side effects such as memory problems and depression. Stress also inhibits brain cell replacement in the hippocampus, which is one of the few areas of the brain that can create new cells throughout one's life. Both phenomena can affect brain cell communication and memory.

According to Maslow's hierarchy of needs, we can only attend to higher level thinking tasks such as creativity when our basic needs are met. In his hierarchy, esteem needs have to be met before 'self-actualisation' can take place. 'Esteem' is where excess stress lives. In our culture, esteem needs are often work and money dependent, and many people (once their fundamental needs are met, and irrespective of where they start or progress to) strive ever harder to build esteem through ascending the corporate ladder and making more money. However, it is in self-actualisation that creativity dwells. The paradoxical nature of this form of pressure means stress keeps you circulating on the esteem needs escalator. Self-actualisation is achieved when you can ignore all the nagging distractions of stress and pressure to focus on the values you esteem, and then put these into practice in your life. In other words, self-actualisation means actively *creating* your own life.[56]

Prolonged stress can also lead to structural changes in the brain. The ongoing release of corticosteroids can change neurons and their synapses in the hippocampus and medial prefrontal cortex.[57] These produce impairments in working and spatial memory, and can lead to increased aggression. They can also lead to deficits in the striatum, which can bias decision-making strategies and decrease flexibility—a critical quality for creative thinking.[58] Under stress the brain will return to more conservative patterns of thinking and rigid habitual memory functioning at the expense of more flexible 'cognitive' memory.[59]

Stress has become a prevalent and costly problem in today's workplace. According to recent US statistics:

- one-third of workers report high levels of stress in their job
- one-quarter of employees view their job as the number one stressor in their life[60]
- three-quarters of employees believe workers experience more on-the-job stress than a generation ago.[61]

Evidence in the US also shows that stress-related costs are a major expense for organisations.[62] Health-care costs for workers who reported high levels of stress were nearly 50 per cent greater than for those who reported low levels of stress at work. Those who experienced depression along with stress had health-care costs that were 150 per cent greater—an annual increase of more than US$1700 per person. Stress is strongly related to occupational burnout.[63] Similarly, stress is identified as the major cause of turnover in organisations.[64]

Workplace stress is such a significant killer in Japan that they have coined a word to describe it: *karōshi*, literally 'death from overwork', covers sudden workplace killers such as heart attacks and strokes. *Karōshi* is such a recognised cause of death in Japan that it is reported in a separate category in national statistics. In a popular multi-platform arcade game, also called *Karōshi*, players face death as they move through each of the levels!

The DC (demand control) model predicts that the most adverse health effects of psychological strain occur when job demands are high but the ability to make decisions is low. A high level of job control is associated with increased job satisfaction and decreased depression. High demands without adequate control may lead to increased anxiety.[65] The effort–reward imbalance (ERI) model is based on the findings that emotional distress and adverse health effects occur when there is a perceived imbalance between efforts and occupational rewards.[66]

Despite all these dangers, stress can be productive if it is managed in the right way. Eustress can stimulate motivation and action. Sometimes people work well to deadlines—some writers, for example, set themselves specific goals, such as producing a certain number of words per day, or maintaining a disciplined focus for a certain number of hours. Students may focus better when they know they are preparing for an exam. But there is a fine line between productive stress, which the body can sustain for only short periods of time, and destructive stress, which is often a prolonged state that the body cannot handle over the long term.

Murder suspect 2 — multi-tasking and tech addiction

Addiction and multi-channeling

It can be stressful for parents to watch how teenagers study these days. Where we once would have sought out a quiet place to study, kids are now constantly bombarded by multiple communication opportunities through myriad electronic gadgets that they literally can't switch off. When Zoe was in her last year of school studying for her final exams, we would often find her in front of the TV with a study book in her hand, music in her ears, and her smart phone buzzing in her pocket alerting her to social media contacts that must be urgently attended to. To us this level of input would be overwhelming, but young people today appear to be already rapidly evolving to deal with multiple simultaneous sources of information.

THE PRESSURE PACK

Mull T. Tasker

MURDER SUSPECT

New technology undoubtedly saves us time, yet it can create additional pressures, as both work and leisure activities come to revolve around the overwhelming demands of technological communication. Of course it is possible to master multi-tasking, but more often than not we end up unwittingly being enslaved by it. With faster communications technology, much faster response times are expected, distracting us from opportunities for creative thinking.

Some people are comfortable with this technology and feel in control, but many others feel overwhelmed and out of control. Some suffer from 'Infomania', a new term used to describe an addiction to email or texting.[67] Not only can email and texting addiction be dangerous for your mental health, but it can actually lower IQ twice as effectively as addiction to marijuana![68] Psychologist Dan Ariely explains the potential for email addiction: 'If you think about it, e-mail is very much like gambling. Most of it is junk and the equivalent to pulling the lever of a slot machine and losing, but every so often we receive a message that we really want. Maybe it contains good news about a job, a bit of gossip, a note from someone we haven't heard from in a long time, or some important piece of information. We are so happy to receive the unexpected e-mail (pellet) that we become addicted to checking, hoping for more.'[69]

Each day a typical office employee checks their email 50 times and uses instant messaging 77 times.[70] Like the rats in B.F. Skinner's behavioural psychology experiments, these variable reward schedules (along with the fear of not responding quickly enough according to expectations) get us and keep us addicted. More than half of 1100 people in one research survey indicated that they always responded to an email 'immediately' or as soon as possible, with 21 per cent admitting they would interrupt a meeting to do so; 62 per cent indicated they checked work messages at home or on holiday; and 10 per cent of people say it's even okay to text while they're having sex! As with many other forms of dependency, your brain is being rewired or sculpted differently with rises in dopamine from tech addiction.[71]

Breaking away from a task by way of interruptions or distractions can have the same impact on intelligent functioning as losing a night's sleep.[72] The average desk worker loses 2.1 hours of productive time a day jumping from one task to another. Your brain needs to focus to be really productive, and when your brain loses focus it can take 25 minutes to get back to full productivity. One experiment revealed that when people read a section of text with no distractions, 92 per cent were able to provide correct answers to questions about information in the text. However, when asked to listen to something at the same time as reading the text, only 31 per cent could answer the same questions correctly.[73] Our brains are simply not wired for dealing with multiple sources of input. In order to process information we need focus, and it is difficult for the brain to take in too much if it is required to constantly shut down, reset and refocus on a new message. Every time we shut down from one task to open up a new one, we lose data from the first task and also lose information from the second. Similar experiments have reproduced these results over and over.

Each additional input into our brains diminishes our focus, and each additional form of output we try to focus on decreases our total concentration. Too much in and too much out leads to a lower quality of work and non-productive mental 'wheel spinning'.[74] The problem is that the human brain operates more like hyper-threading than true multi-threading. We maintain multiple contexts, but although the brain can quickly switch between 'channels', it can effectively process only one channel at any given moment. The energy needed to switch between contexts is considerable.

Imagine how frustrated the advertising industry must be that we can't take in all the masses of information we are constantly bombarded with wherever we go! Over 24 hours, the average young person takes in 26 hours of content, which they can't possibly process. To try to push their message in edgeways, advertisers have learned to cut the word count, compress the message and ensure all input is aligned—in effect, 'dumbing down' the information we're passing on to the next generation. The more advertisers try to compete for children's attention, the more overwhelming the assault on our overstimulated kids becomes. Their brains have already started to adapt to the 'multi-channelling phenomenon', but perhaps at a cost to their attention spans and their mental and emotional health, and certainly at a cost to their ability to be creative. With no space for their brains to breathe, and with no room for creative ideas to flow and grow, any brave creative shoots are quickly cut off and left to die.[75]

Murder suspect 3—increased expectations

The inter-role bloodbath

A chronic lack of time becomes a significant problem in a fast-paced society. We all complain there are never enough hours in the day. But if the day were longer, we would probably still fill up the available time with all the 'urgent' activities imposed on us or that we ourselves had created.

One of the greatest sources of pressure in modern life is inter-role conflict. We all play a number of different roles in our lives, and the higher the expectations in each of

THE PRESSURE PACK

X. Pectations

MURDER SUSPECT

these roles the greater the overall pressures we will experience. Various personal and professional roles compete for our time and attention. At home we struggle with family and social roles and responsibilities, while in our jobs, too, we may need to juggle competing official and unofficial roles. One of the greatest problems is struck when our work roles are not clearly delineated, so expectations and boundaries are uncertain. This can lead to role confusion and frustration, resulting in job dissatisfaction and increased pressure.

Inter-role conflict has been defined as 'incompatibility between the role expectations of different roles'.[76] Most surveys measure inter-role conflict in terms of time pressures[77] or the interference of working hours with other roles.[78] A significant correlation has been found between inter-role conflict and family stress and conflict, along with increased cognitive difficulties. Naturally this impedes creative thinking, which depends on a lack of stress and conflict.

Often inter-role conflict can erode an individual's feelings of personal connection and psychological identification with the job, which in turn affects their work attendance and staff turnover, both of which are costly for an organisation to deal with.[79] The more clearly we delineate our roles, integrating them in a meaningful way and/or simplifying them, the less pressure and stress we will experience, and the more room we will give ourselves to grow creatively.

Michael Hutchence's second last phone call was to leave a voicemail message for his personal manager, Martha Troup: 'Marth, Michael here. I've f----ing had enough.' When Troup returned the call there was no answer. His last call was to his former long-term girlfriend, and in this call he sounded distraught. His body was found by the hotel maid not long after.[80] In the end the hedonistic rock-star lifestyle may have claimed another unwitting victim. When we fail to deal with the stresses that assail us, the pressure can become overwhelming. We unknowingly let the wolves in the door, and what may have once been intensely pleasurable suddenly becomes intensely painful. So creativity is snuffed out. But there are other killers out there that may be even more masked and furtive but are just as menacing.

Investigator's report

Have you seen this Pressure profile in your neighbourhood or workplace? Profile characteristics can include:

\ works on the compulsion to reach unrealistic expectations ☐
\ creates unreasonable stress ☐

The impact on victims can be:

\ confusion ☐
\ frustration ☐
\ difficulty with managing time and prioritising ☐

Murder profile 4: the Insulation Clique

Also known as isolating killers, those fitting the insulation profile employ a lethal combination of segregation and homogeneity to beat their victims into biased conformity. They quarantine their victims from different ideas and information, denying them exposure to a diversity of opinions and therefore access to potentially life-saving devices. Victims have their options limited without their realising it. They are bruised and hammered into submission, dying through accumulated injuries including often concealed blows to their ability to think differently and independently. Because the murderers fitting this profile create prejudiced cliques even within apparently diverse societies, they can get away with their crimes in broad daylight. Killers of this type tend to be *narcissistic*. Their preferred weapon is *bludgeoning bias*.

Solitary confinement and malignant self-love

In some countries solitary confinement is the most extreme sanction that can be legally imposed on prisoners short of the death penalty. The physical and psychological impacts can be severe, and many human rights advocates consider it to be a form of torture. Input restriction and sensory deprivation can, over time, produce long-term changes in brain physiology and lead to mental illnesses such as depression.[81]

Insulation is a creativity murderer that can inflict isolation on individuals within an organisation, although many choose willingly to embrace these restrictions. In the same way that placing prisoners in solitary confinement limits their experiences and restricts their brain capability, Insulation confines the victims' experiences and limits their capabilities over the long term. The psychopathic profile of this murderer can be likened to that of the narcissist. With a hyper-dependence on the views of others, a strong sense of entitlement, a manipulative and exploitative nature, and delusions of grandeur at odds with real achievements, Insulation is a self-absorbed killer. 'Self-love helps survival—it is a prerequisite,' says Sam Vaknin, author of *Malignant Self Love*, but when derived exclusively from the outside, he explains, this sort of self-focus can become malignant—it will kill emotionally.[82]

This obsession with the self and interests directly related to the self limits creative potential and stunts creative growth. Insulation is a sly murderer, its victims unaware that their options have become limited, and that they have developed a strong bias in the process. Also a seductive killer, Insulation appears attractive but hides its sinister secrets.

Consider the lure of Sydney's Northern Beaches, where we have lived on and off for a number of years. Some of the best beaches in the world, they stretch for 30 kilometres from Manly to Palm Beach, close to the city yet a million miles away. Lining a narrow isthmus between the ocean and the Pittwater inlet, the strip gets narrower the further you travel from the city. The area officially starts at Spit Bridge, which separates the Northern Beaches from the wealthy suburbs of Mosman, and ends at the billionaires' retreat of Palm Beach. Although a range of socioeconomic groups are represented, the region is generally fairly monocultural—frustrated schoolteachers have been heard to refer to it as the 'insular peninsular'. Conservative politically and ruthlessly parochial, the locals here are very protective of their idyllic existence and are happy there are no easy public transport connections, as this keeps away the tourist hordes. There are very few hotels and only one camping ground. The multifaceted area of Bondi wholeheartedly embraced the popular TV show *Bondi Rescue*, but when the actors and crew of the US TV hit show *Baywatch* turned up at the Northern Beaches' Avalon Beach, they were sent packing. David Hasselhoff and friends were almost lynched by the local community, who wanted no part of the international attention.[83]

As a child, our daughter Zoe lived and travelled with us overseas before we moved back to live in the Northern Beaches area during her later teenage years. When she started at a local school at age 14, the students were told she had just moved schools from Indonesia. One exclaimed, 'But I thought Indonesian children had dark skin and dark hair?' (Zoe is fair-skinned and blonde!) She was horrified to discover that some of her schoolmates had no idea who US President Barack Obama was, and professed not to care as they believed this was not important information to know. In geography tests students would do such astonishing things as mistake India for Africa on a map and name Jamaica as one of the seven continents.

Research has revealed that people who have travelled and lived abroad are more creative than those who haven't across a number of different measures, including measures of insight, association and generation. This startling finding reveals just how important it is to be exposed to a wide range of information and ideas over our lifetime. If we are not exposed to diverse ideas and people, we can become protected from the need to think creatively. As we grow older we continue to isolate ourselves from new ideas. To gain a feeling of security we gather around us like-minded people, which further insulates us from new experiences.[84]

Historically the development of cities vastly increased the diversity and range of human ideas, creating an important evolutionary advantage. Cities offer a proliferation of educational and cultural opportunities, and can provide the wealth to support them, but this growth can have a downside. In capitalist societies, in which innovation can flourish, economies need to keep growing. 'Open-ended growth' is in many ways positive, but although in biology sigmoidal growth eventually slows down and stops, in capitalist economies growth cannot stop or the system will die, which means that eventual economic collapse is inevitable, as identified by Geoffrey West.[85] Mathematically, this sort of open growth will use up all resources and lead to collapse (the 'finite times singularity' principle). In the past we have avoided this through constant innovation, which has enabled us to 'reset the clock'. With each major new discovery or invention, such as the discovery of penicillin or the invention of computers, we have found a way to reinvent the cultural and economic paradigm and in effect 'beat the system', ensuring that we can keep the innovation process alive.

Beating Insulation, then, will involve careful growth strategies that ensure openness and access to new ideas to enable ongoing innovation, but also to continue to question and reinvent the system that might otherwise ultimately destroy it.

The Insulation Clique we focus on here are:

\ biased information sources (such as the media)
\ sticking to like-minded people (homogeneity)
\ lack of diversity.

Murder suspect 1 — biased information sources

Reality TV and ADD

We once decided to refer to a reality TV show as a case study in a seminar on creative thinking we were running (as an example of non-creative thinking). Browsing the internet to see if we could capture a short clip to use, we discovered that someone had uploaded a 3-minute version of the 24-minute show. It struck us as hilarious that you could edit 24 minutes' worth of content down to 3 minutes and keep the storyline intact![86] Even news shows have become diluted and sensationalised to

seize our attention and entertain rather than educate, as was once the news services' noble intent. Twitter epitomises the problem of rapid, instant information generation and recycling of a kind that will eventually give us all epilepsy as we are hurled from celebrity to crisis and back again. The media often cater to the lowest common denominator in order to win advertising dollars, with the result that we are presented with very limited information and are effectively insulated from what's really going on in the world around us.[87]

Given the current state of the mass media, it's no wonder that a researcher at the University of Texas in Austin, Elizabeth Vanderwater, has found that children's creativity drops about 10 per cent for every hour they watch TV.[88] That's a pretty dramatic impact. For the average child, who watches up to three hours of television a day, this means a 30 per cent reduction in creativity. And what about the kids who watch more than 10 hours? Imagine how destructive the impact of modern technology could be on adults, as both work and leisure pursuits revolve around the demands of the constant, overwhelming presence of technology. Of course it is possible to master it, but more often than not we end up unwittingly becoming enslaved to it. As communication technology improves, faster response times are expected and opportunities for creative thinking are further disrupted.

The media are closely allied to multi-tasking and other Pressure Pack co-conspirators. Combined, they can make their victims feel busier than ever, and yet ironically there has never been a time that humans have been so sedentary. As Professor Paul O'Brien, of the Centre for Obesity at Monash University, puts it, 'new technologies enabled us to indulge our human instinct for laziness and productive procrastination'.[89] As though suffering from ADD, these characters move from one thing to the next at lightning speed, and together they distract their victims, making sure there is never any time for creativity to get a look in. While the Pressure Pack are usually attractive, invited guests and the Control Crew are obvious thugs, the media gang are often deliberately scheming manipulators. In terms of psychotic behaviours, the media we are most often exposed to are narcissistic (exhibiting a pervasive pattern of grandiosity, a need for admiration and a lack of empathy, and including pervasive attention-seeking, inappropriately seductive, and shallow or exaggerated behaviours). The media are demanding with an expensive, insatiable appetite that needs to be constantly fed. Through smoke and mirrors (Botox and airbrushing along with clever editing and camera work), the media are able to create an image of reality based on entirely artificial perfection. We are often left feeling inadequate and inferior, unable to meet the unrealistic expectations.

The media are kept alive only through their puppeteer, Advertising. TV advertisers collectively spend about $70 billion each year in the United States. In his subversive film *The Greatest Movie Ever Sold*,[90] Morgan Spurlock gave 23 sponsors the opportunity to peddle their wares shamelessly throughout the film. By making an entire movie about the power of advertising that was itself funded by advertising, he cleverly brought this sinister, inseparable relationship out of the closet. Spurlock reveals how advertising has become so ubiquitous in films and life in general that people often fail to notice it. As consumer advocate Ralph Nadar points out, 'There is advertising now in public rest rooms, on the floors of supermarkets, in elevators, even on the walls of schools and the sides of school buses'.[91] The BBC documentary *Secrets of Super Brands*, presented by Alex Riley, highlights the seduction of the big brands. Riley describes the stampede prompted by the launching of a new Apple store: 'The scenes I witnessed at the opening were more like an evangelical prayer meeting than a chance to buy a phone or a laptop!' Indeed, Riley reported, neuroscientists have found that super brands have encroached on the region of the brain that was previously reserved for religion.[92][93]

Another interesting case study of the way super brands have come to limit our thinking is the now-infamous Coke/Pepsi taste test of the 1970s. Many people will remember the original story, in which, after Pepsi had conducted blind taste tests across America and convinced a generation that Pepsi tasted better than Coke, Coca-Cola tried to copy their rival's successful formula—and failed dismally. Not so many will know this follow-up story. In 2003 neuroscientist Read Montague set up an experiment to try to gauge the appeal of Coke's 'brand influence'. To do this he repeated the original experiment with a slight difference: this time he announced which of the samples were Coke and which Pepsi. Astonishingly, almost all the subjects said they preferred Coke—and their brain scans revealed more activity in the prefrontal cortex, which is responsible for high-level cognitive powers. The Coke brand had been so internalised by the subjects that it had actually changed their brain patterns and created a blinkered 'love' for a product brand.[94]

The great challenge we face is where to allocate that most valuable resource, our attention—and subsequently our 'affection'. When our information sources are limited in content but overwhelming in quantity, the brain simply can't cope. The beauty of the media is that to a degree we can just turn it off, or we can choose positive programs that open our minds to new ideas and information and stimulate creative thinking. As long as we are in control of the quantity and quality of what we are exposed to, and as long as we maintain a healthy scepticism about the motivations behind the media's point of view, it can provide a positive window to the world and can be an ally rather than a killer.

Murder suspect 2—sticking with like-minded people

Mediocre monotony

Leaders who deliberately surround themselves with people of like mind create environments where there is little diversity in ideas. If group members are too much alike they will find it hard to keep learning, because each member is bringing less and less new information to the table.[95]

Teams made up of different sorts of people (heterogeneous teams) are the most creative. In *The Medici Effect*, Frans Johansson describes how he found that creativity is most likely to occur at the intersection between different cultures, disciplines and backgrounds, where there is maximum diversity. In one experiment, researchers took two types of groups: homogeneous (similar behavioural, thinking and learning styles) and heterogeneous (mixed behavioural, thinking and learning styles), and gave them a problem to solve. The homogeneous group solved the problem much faster than the heterogeneous group, but the results were always mediocre. The heterogeneous group took longer but delivered an outstanding result. There was more friction in this group, but the issue was how effectively this friction was managed and channelled. When heterogeneous teams discuss an idea they are more likely to move away from extremes to the centre and average of the group, providing a more balanced outcome. Diversity of opinion is the single best guarantee that the group will reap benefits from face-to-face discussion. The absence of debate and minority opinions is dangerous for a team.[96]

Groups are smartest when there is a balance between the information that everyone shares and the information each of the members of the group holds privately. It is the combination of all those pieces of independent information that keeps the group wise. Heterogeneous groups that can manage their diversity have a better chance of problem solving than homogeneous groups or individuals. When properly combined, teams are capable of coming up with potent, dynamic solutions. A good team strategy will focus on:

❧ team perceptions (the way the team feels)
❧ team processes (the way the team thinks)
❧ team actions (the way the team behaves).

When Peter Karolczak was engaged by HP to form a new software venture he said that the first principle he would use was to gain multiple perspectives with divergent expertise — to harness the power of team creativity. Once individuals have had the opportunity to develop their creative potential, teams then need to be prepared for the process of creative innovation and, ultimately, implementation in the organisation. Creative ideas and possibilities will always be enhanced by a team, providing the structures and strategies are put in place to support team processes.

When there is an appropriate connection between individual creativity and team processes, it is possible to make the transition from simpler individual concepts to complex solutions. Creative processes can benefit enormously from the input of a range of perspectives and ideas. Through the input of different people, and through integrating their different perspectives effectively, you can build a creative hothouse of ideas. Team creativity utilises the creative talents of individuals and integrates these to produce an outstanding combined result. Not everyone is creative, in the sense of being able to make something out of nothing or designing and creating unusual new concepts through art, but everyone can contribute to the creative process through using their strengths. When people organise to solve a problem they form a coalition. Each member brings his or her own unique energy and ideas.

Murder suspect 3 — lack of diversity

The tendency towards sameness and tunnel vision

Lack of diversity at the leadership level in organisations can also lead to problems.[97] A limited range of thinking styles seems to be the key culprit. As leaders tend to choose, support and promote like-minded people, over time organisations can become insulated from thinking styles and ideas that are more likely to lead to innovation. As leading innovation blogger Chuck Frey has explained, 'Without diversity of thinking and perspective in its leaders, a company is less likely to identify creative employees,

THE INSULATION CLIQUE

Lacko Di Versity
MURDER SUSPECT

less likely to embrace the conflict inherent in breaking and making connections, and quite likely to lack the range of vision needed to make the best use of whatever creativity it is able to stimulate... Leadership is naturally often the least diverse group in a company... The tendency toward sameness, which many leadership teams unknowingly exhibit, puts a company in danger of tunnel vision right where an organization can least afford it—at the top'.[98]

There is very strong evidence from universal scaling laws that dimensionality leads to innovation. This holds true across cities, countries and time periods. Companies inevitably shift from dimensionality to unidimensionality because they have to, and thus they eventually die.[99]

The longer you work for an organisation, the further removed you risk becoming from real life (how customers think, feel and behave) and the more likely you are to adopt groupthink. When there are too many people together thinking they are experts, the possibilities are narrowed and creative problem solving ability is reduced. In a work situation, this can also mean that there is pressure to conform and that a person may change his or her opinion not out of agreement but because it is easier to conform than to go against the group. Many different organisations develop a similar culture of leader dependence, which ultimately hampers development.

A banker from Lehmann Brothers has described the impact insulation had in the dying days of the company: 'Just before the crisis we felt insulated from the whole market reality. It was an out-of-body experience. We just sat and watched the people pass and talked about what might happen next. How many of these people were going to lose their jobs. We fed the monster until it blew up.'[100] A lack of openness to new ideas and information will ultimately lead to implosion.

Inclusion of diversity can be scary. It can even be downright risky. On the other hand, a failure to accept diversity will lead to decline. Part of Geoffrey West's theory is that cities need to be exceptionally tolerant of diversity, even supporting crazy people, which is why they continue to grow. Unlike the organisation, which will only tolerate people who toe the line and can easily fire those who are considered crazy, cities breed acceptance. As West puts it, 'If you go to General Motors or you go to American Airlines, you don't see crazy people. Crazy people are fired'.

Extended or forced sensory deprivation, such as is experienced in solitary confinement, can result in extreme anxiety, hallucinations, bizarre thoughts and depression. It is an effective form of torture. Short periods of sensory deprivation, however, are described as a relaxing form of stress release and conducive to meditation. Isolation or flotation tanks are sometimes used as a form of tension relief, lowering the blood pressure and increasing blood flow. After an initial stage of restlessness and compulsive itching (a sensation also sometimes noted during the early stages of meditation), a person in a flotation tank will typically transition from alpha or beta brainwaves to theta waves. These waves most often occur between sleeping and waking and can induce a creative dreaming state. It is also possible to use isolation tanks to generate intense visualisation and creative thinking. So it's important to use these opportunities for individual seclusion in a positive way, ensuring they do not become insulating or counterproductive, and do not become a permanent state of mind.

Investigator's report

Have you seen this Insulation profile in your neighbourhood or workplace? Profile characteristics can include:

\ isolation from a broad range of opinions and ideas ☐

\ a tendency to ignore or put down differing opinions and ideas ☐

\ the forming of cliques ☐

The impact on victims can be:

\ closed-mindedness ☐

\ a tendency towards unhealthy bias, bigotry or discrimination ☐

CRIME SCENE DO NOT CROS

Stage 3: degeneration — inhibition of growth driven by apathy

The third stage of the murder process indicates the impact 'oppression' and 'restriction' will have on the individual and focuses on the '**Apathy Clan**', indolent individuals who end up tormenting others to compensate for their own detachment and lack of interest.

Murder profile 5: the Apathy Clan

Murderers fitting the 'apathy' profile lack motivation and drive. These villains are often themselves victims of systems that have deadened their will to succeed. With no stimulus or incentive to progress or achieve, and with the desire to see others suffer in the same way, these menacing killers often significantly stunt growth. They cut down the 'tall poppies' and undermine all efforts towards development. The profile can often be detected in cutting sarcasm and acerbic cynicism. Disdaining those who help to save life and promote progress, these killers can stab their victims deeply, piercing the heart and other organs vital to survival. Victims may either die suddenly or bleed to death slowly as the will to live drains out of them. Apathy types are often *schizoid*. Their preferred weapon is *lacerating lethargy*.

Producing gold from urine

In 1675 a German named Henning Brand convinced himself that gold could be created from distilled human urine. Every night Henning would collect his urine in a bucket. He stored 50 buckets of this urine in his cellar for months at a time. After a while the substance began to glow, and when exposed to fresh air it burst into flames. This substance came to be known as phosphorus. Eventually it was used for a multitude of purposes ranging from fertiliser and explosives to toothpaste and detergents. Once its usefulness was recognised, soldiers' urine was collected in buckets and stored (it took 1100 litres of urine to produce about 60 grams of phosphorus). Later more efficient production processes were developed.

Was Henning creative, lucky, mad, intelligent, delusional or all of the above? Do we have to come up with a mad idea such as transforming our pee into gold to invent something worthwhile—to be creative? This story illustrates the role luck and determination can play in creativity. It also prompts the question: are creative geniuses born or made? The simple answer is that creative development requires a little of both. It needs a creative spark or at least a willingness to learn and practise creative techniques, but it also usually takes a lot of dogged perseverance to come up with real creative success.

A reflection on creative genius by Malcolm Gladwell[101] reveals just how important both elements are: 'Did you know that we may never had heard of Virgin or Richard Branson if it weren't for the musical hit song *Tubular Bells*, or if just one of his bank managers decided one morning to not extend his credit or Branson decided not to beg for an extension? If Thomas Edison didn't invent the light bulb would someone else have? If Steve Jobs hadn't remained at Apple would we not have had the electronic 'Swiss army knife' iPhone and apps store concept that revolutionised both mobile phones and the music industry?'

Apathy kills creativity by extinguishing any initial creative spark that may be ignited or by smothering the will to persevere if that creative spark has had the opportunity to catch. Real innovation requires a long period of committed creative thinking, so it can easily be killed by the apathy murderers. They tend to work by either cutting down victims in their prime or striking at them relentlessly, draining any creative motivation they might have. Those who can beat apathy develop the will and passion to continue to be creative despite ongoing challenges.

Murderers who stab or slash their victims usually do so in a purposeful, planned way, and this distinguishes those fitting the apathy profile. An apparent lack of motivation, concern or passion can be twisted into a deliberate 'stab in the back' or a 'cutting remark'. Apathy, characterised by sarcasm and cynicism, can inflict terrible damage in an organisation where a passionate culture of commitment is not supported.

The impact of apathy on the organisation can be measured by levels of employee engagement. Engagement can be measured by:

❧ the extent to which employees commit to something or someone in their organisation
❧ how hard they work
❧ how long they stay as a result of that commitment.

Employee engagement is recognised as a major factor in individual and team success in the organisation. It relates directly to morale and productivity, and ultimately influences business success. A study of 50 000 employees around the world[102] revealed how important employee engagement is. It found that organisations low in employee engagement are most vulnerable to talent loss and underperformance. As well as being disruptive, employee disengagement can also be very destructive. It has been found that while the majority of employees in an organisation are neither highly committed nor uncommitted, the more than one in 10 employees who are fully disengaged (actively opposed to something or someone in their organisation) can have a wide influence on others and can affect the culture of the whole organisation. Consider these powerful facts: 11 per cent of the workforce is highly engaged; 76 per cent is neither highly engaged nor highly disengaged; 13 per cent is highly disengaged.

Employees with a high level of engagement perform 20 per cent better and are 87 per cent less likely to leave the organisation. Workplace apathy that results when there is low engagement, on the other hand, is undoubtedly a huge cost to business. A British survey[103] found some employees surf the internet for up to three hours a day.[104] Other analysts have found that up to 40 per cent of workers suffer from a big slump in productivity in the afternoon.[105]

No direct correlation has been found between specific groups within the organisation and levels of engagement. Gender, tenure and function, for example, do not appear to predict employee engagement at all. In fact, none of the top 25 drivers of employee engagement identified in the survey were shown to potentially affect employee engagement levels. Company culture, strategies and policies, however, do seem to have a strong influence. Significant differences in employee engagement between companies reveal how important this dimension can be. If individuals within the organisation feel linked to a positive master plan, it seems, there is buy-in and commitment. Not having a positive vision, and not being able to connect to this vision—or, better still, take ownership of it—can lead to a downward spiral.

Apathy can cause mortal wounds to an organisation. An apparent lack of motivation, concern or passion can soon be twisted into something worse. An organisation plagued by apathy will have a destructive culture characterised by bitching and bullying, and the wounds inflicted by these weapons will not heal easily. Where the wounds are deep, permanent internal damage may result, and no amount of surgery can repair the damage. The organisation also becomes vulnerable to infection, which can easily spread.

From ancient through to medieval times it was believed that a physical wound could indicate a wounded heart or soul. The wounds that apathy inflicts may be targeted at hurting people psychologically, but ironically they often reveal the deep psychological wounds of the apathy murderers themselves.

The areas of Apathy Clan suspects covered here include:

- ⚔ lack of motivation
- ⚔ lack of initiative
- ⚔ lack of drive.

Murder suspect 1 — lack of motivation

Secrets of the über-successful

In his book on creativity *Element*, Sir Ken Robinson interviews a number of creative people in an effort to learn the secrets behind their success. From the star-studded celebrity line-up some might mistakenly conclude that you have to be a school dropout in order to become creative,[106] but Robinson's key point is that we should all be looking for our 'element' (or, according to Csikszentmihalyi's[107] more original and more scientific thesis, finding our 'flow'). The importance of natural talent meeting personal passion, both critical ingredients in finding your element or flow, does stand up in research, but 'luck' also needs to be factored in as a major contributor to success. The key differentiator is drive, or lack of it.

In searching for the best way to become creatively successful and to innovate wisely, it is more important to focus on the process than the result, as results can be biased. For example, most businesspeople would never call a decision 'foolish' if it ended up making money, even if it was the result of a 'lucky break'. But stories of those who have 'made it' and discovered something great are usually skewed.[108] It is not possible to usefully assess the particular path someone has taken in life *in isolation* without taking into account other people who have taken a similar path. So where does that leave us when trying to identify the attributes of creative geniuses? Things always seem more obvious after the fact, and hindsight bias looms large in many case studies, so to look at someone who has come up with a creative idea and reverse engineer the whole experience to a simple step-by-step process can be dangerous.

Some of those whose success was based on often madly risky decisions were exposed during the global financial crisis and 2008–09 credit crunch. After the crash some bankers admitted that they didn't really have a clue what they were doing and how they had become successful, but that because people continued to come to them for advice they continued to give it. Looking back at the crisis after his empire had fallen apart (hindsight bias), Wall Street banker Michael Lewis observed, 'To this day, the willingness of a Wall Street investment bank to pay me hundreds of thousands of dollars to dispense investment advice to grownups remains a mystery to me. I was 24 years old, with no experience of, or particular interest in, guessing which stocks and bonds would rise and which would fall. The essential function of Wall Street is to allocate capital—to decide who should get it and who should not. Believe me when I tell you that I hadn't the first clue'.[109]

It's not pure luck that makes one successful in developing creative ideas and making creative decisions, but small inputs persistently pursued over time can lead to often disproportionate results and events. The lucky fool might benefit from winning a lottery once (or gain from an upward cycle on the stock market), but let him try to do it repeatedly in all circumstances. Unlucky people who keep trying, using the principles discussed below, are likely to benefit from some luck over the long term. In real life, each of us is likely eventually to revert to our long-term tendency towards optimism (which keeps us persisting) or pessimism (which leads us to give up). We need to look at the process that generates long-term success rather than short-term media headline events.[110] Most long-term über-successful entrepreneurs hedge their bets, taking small risks while keeping one foot on secure ground, but this modest approach can't compete in the media with the flamboyant Bransons who fly into our lives in red hot-air balloons surrounded by sexy girls and feel-good logos. Branson has branded his creativity commercially (now that's clever creativity in action!) but he is the exception rather than the rule. We may be inspired by him and other entrepreneurs like him, but we rarely hear about those who were less 'lucky'. If creative success is based on a combination of talent and luck, then what's needed to be creative is motivation, and what stops people being creatively successful and 'lucky' is lack of motivation and drive.

So how do we 'persistently pursue' opportunities to make our own luck?

Murder suspect 2 — lack of initiative

Beyond dumb luck

If you have that initial creative spark to explore a new idea, the next step to ensuring you are not simply waiting for success to come your way through 'luck' is to actively seize opportunities for success. This is the next junction in the journey where creativity may be killed by apathy.

THE APATHY CLAN

Lacko In Itiative

MURDER SUSPECT

> *Chance favours the prepared mind.*
>
> Louis Pasteur

Luck often plays a part in whether your success becomes known and recognised, but not necessarily in the creative thinking process itself. To come up with a truly creative idea or solution you need a positive 'creative break' — a breakthrough 'Eureka moment' that comes about only with disciplined perseverance through careful trial and error. Yes, we can be inspired by lucky creative people, but we also need to recognise that not all innovators have lucky breaks. It is only by looking at the *processes* behind the work of successful creative people that we can start to distil the factors that we ourselves can use to produce the conditions for our own creative breakthrough. No-one can guarantee success by following certain steps, but we do know that you definitely won't succeed if you don't try. As the saying goes, 'You will always miss 100 per cent of the shots you never take', and this is the main difference between people who exercise creative thinking successfully and those who don't. In other words, those who succeed in achieving 'lucky' creative breakthroughs will invariably exhibit a dogged determination that creates the opportunities for success.

'Lucky' people have been found to be particularly open to possibility. This is also in line with research about the mindset of creative people. Without an optimistic mindset it's easy to become paralysed by fear and to give up before a solution is found. But this sort of optimism is not simply dumb luck. 'Most people are just not open to what's around them,' says psychologist Richard

Wiseman.[111] One way is to be open to new experiences. Unlucky people are stuck in routines (*bureaucracy*). When they see something new, they want no part of it (*fear*). Lucky people always want something new. They're prepared to take risks and are relaxed enough to see the opportunities in the first place. You don't want to broadly say that whenever you get an intuitive feeling, it's right and you should go with it. But you could be missing out on a massive font of knowledge that you've built up over the years if you fail to recognise and assess these opportunities adequately.

'Survivorship bias' (elevating the successful celebrities and ignoring the failures) presents us with a distorted view of the facts. As our brains are set up to detect patterns, we tend to look for the common features of 'creative success stories', hoping they will provide us with a secret miracle formula. But the reality is that we often try to detect patterns where there are none, and the secret formula may be little more than optimistic determination. It is more likely that people end up being successful simply because the more people there are aiming for a creative breakthrough or innovative success, the greater the likelihood is that at least one may get 'lucky'. If Thomas Edison hadn't invented the light bulb or Bill Gates a worldwide software product, we can be sure that someone else would have solved these problems at some stage. We need to extract the creative principles, rather than elevating the individuals.

Murder suspect 3 — lack of drive

Conquering cancer

The third point of the creative process at which creative thinking can be mercilessly attacked is at the stage where developing ideas need to be pushed towards specific applications and through to completion.

We have a friend who epitomises the positive mindset and hard work that is essential for creative breakthrough. A high-powered, successful lawyer who became an Olympic-level coach after battling with terminal cancer, John Harvey knows what it takes to persevere when faced with great challenges. Andrew had been surfing with John for a number of years before he discovered the real capabilities of this quietly spoken man. After learning more of what John had faced and how far he had come, we decided to invite him to speak to some of our corporate clients about his personal journey. The first group he faced with us was a sceptical bunch of burnt-out stockbrokers with low attention spans. His challenge was to inspire and motivate them to develop an optimistic mindset. To get their attention, John sat in a chair at the front of the room and attached himself to a heart monitor, projecting the resulting graph onto a screen. To the group's amazement, within minutes John was able to raise his heart rate from its normal resting rate of around 70 to over 160, then a few minutes later he had lowered it to under 50. Now his audience sat up and took notice, obviously hoping that if they listened attentively enough they too might learn the secret of John's control. Some exclaimed afterwards in admiration, 'Wow! I wish I could be like you'. This was a typical reaction to John's amazing stories and demonstrations (he has several other clever demonstrations up his sleeve), but whenever we hear this response we think to ourselves, 'If only they knew what he has had to go through to get to this point'.

John had no choice but to try to conquer the cancer that threatened to defeat him. So he subjected his mind and body to disciplined research to find ways to fight the tumours that had riddled his body for 20 years. For all those years he astounded doctors and specialists with his mental resilience and ability to go on fighting and surviving. He learned to create natural cortisone in his body and to control his lactic acid levels when playing a sport. He learned to target the cancers with his mind and to reduce their size merely through creative visualisation exercises. During this time John reached the finals of the indoor world rowing championships (against former Olympic champions) and set several Australian records in the sport. He has since coached world champion sportspeople, celebrities and even the odd prime minister.

At the end of that first motivational keynote session the stockbroker participants nicknamed John 'Lucky'. Indeed he has been one of the fortunate ones to have survived such trials, but John's daily routine is incredibly disciplined and focused. Most people who know him don't realise just how hard he works to keep the cancer at bay. His whole day/week/month is carefully planned, with short-term goals leading towards long-term visions. John exercises up to eight hours a day, and he 'trains' his mind an additional six hours a day, on average. At one stage the bone cancer in his shoulder became so painful he could not physically row his machine, so instead John would sit for hours at a time visualising the rowing process and his body, including his pulse, would respond as though he actually was rowing. Despite not being able to train on his machine, John went on to win at the titles a second year—through positive visualisation alone. So it is not luck but hard work and a clear vision that has kept John focused and, ultimately, alive.

The central conclusion that Gladwell reached through his research was that, rather than simply a genetic inheritance, successful genius is cultivated through a potent mix of lucky circumstance and sheer hard work.[113] By analysing birth dates in children's sporting teams Gladwell was able to show that those who are born closer to the cut-off date and are therefore the oldest in their cohort will have a much higher chance of succeeding than their younger, often smaller and less physically developed peers. As the older children in the peer group physically mature faster, they are more likely to be chosen for sports teams, which builds their confidence and motivation, which in turn enhances their performance. Gladwell suggests you're better off being the oldest guy in the younger class than the youngest guy in the older class. There is certainly often an element of luck here that can't necessarily be controlled

When Pink Floyd's album *The Dark Side of the Moon* was released in March 1973 it became one of the biggest selling albums of all time (45 million copies and 741 weeks in the charts), and with this release many thought the band was emerging as an overnight international success. But in reality, as band members reported in a documentary, its success was due to the thousands of hours leading up to the recording: 'it was really ten years in the making'.[114] In the latter part of his life Michael Jackson was better known for what happened off stage than on it, but the movie *This Is It*, a tribute based on footage taken of the rehearsals leading up to his final concert, shows the intense preparations and many hours of practice that went into his trademark smooth and slick performances. Clearly a lot of work went into channelling the creative genius behind Jackson's mesmerising performances and highly successful marketable product. Branson's autobiography reveals the lucky breaks he had in his life, and these helped pave the way to his entrepreneurial success, but it also shows the sheer drive and effort that went into this success. His strong will and determination to succeed helped him bounce back from failure and forge through the obstacles to reach his desired goals.

What about Bill Gates? Did he get a lucky break? Was he simply in the right place at the right time? He was certainly born at a time when opportunities opened up for him. He was able to gain unusual access to more advanced computers than previous generations or even the majority of his peers could have dreamed of. His mother happened to have the connections that helped him get his fledgling business off to an unusually good start. But he was also prepared to put in the long hours of practice needed to master the required skills (often working through the night, when the computers were more readily available). If circumstances had been even slightly different we might not be reading about Bill Gates today but about someone else who stepped up instead. Whoever that person might have been, like Bill he or she would most likely have put in thousands of hours as a teenager learning code and developing the skills.

Henning Brand was undoubtedly an optimist. He believed he could make something special out of 'nothing'—to produce wealth (gold) from waste (human urine). In this regard he was wrong, very wrong. His house must have become smelly (it's hard to imagine anything worse than the stench of 'curing' human urine wafting up from the cellar!), but his drive to follow his instincts and his single-minded determination to persist with the experiment meant that eventually he stumbled across something completely unexpected but incredibly useful—phosphorus. Would someone else have discovered phosphorus over the course of time? Very likely. So again it is not the discovery itself that is the major lesson here. Rather, it is the process that is important. We can recognise the pure dedication and commitment it takes to come up with creative new ideas and solutions, and we can learn again that only those who try succeed.

Rather than letting hostility build up inside and then turning this antagonism outward, the best way to fight apathy is to convert that energy into a will to persevere. Like Henning Brand, you may not find gold, but you may yet be surprised by what commitment, drive and dogged persistence produces. Water to wine...urine to phosphorus... Transformation from the ordinary to the extraordinary doesn't always need faith in the supernatural or smoke and mirrors; it may be just a matter of being motivated, taking the initiative to begin the search, and having the focus, determination and commitment to see it through.

Investigator's report

Have you seen this Apathy profile in your neighbourhood or workplace? Profile characteristics can include:

- a tendency to give up easily (a lack perseverance) ☐
- cynicism and sarcasm ☐
- the tall poppies syndrome ☐

The impact on victims can be:

- disengagement ☐
- lack of interest in growth ☐

CRIME SCENE DO NOT CROS

Stage 4: destruction — destructive narrow-mindedness and pessimism

The final stage of the degenerative murder process can also lead to irreparable damage. This stage includes the '**Narrow-minded Mob**', who have become intolerant of other opinions and ideas and therefore target innocent victims mercilessly, and also the '**Pessimism Posse**', who have given up hope themselves and poison others with their noxious negativity.

Murder profile 6: the Narrow-minded Mob

With a stubborn and often headstrong approach, killers fitting the 'narrow-minded' profile ensure their dupes remain trapped in their standard, familiar patterns of behaviour. Victims are unwitting casualties of their own habitual ways of thinking and behaving. Often closely related to the 'Insulation' profile, those fitting this profile will usually have had restricted input and exposure to varied ideas and ways of thinking. As a result, they tend to have a developed rigid mindset and a blinkered approach and impose this rigidity on their victims. Their victims are persuaded to look in only one direction, unaware that the grip of narrow-mindedness is becomes tighter and tighter, and failing to recognise they are dying a slow death. Once they see this, it may already be too late to escape. The Narrow-minded Mob commonly manifest *avoidant personality disorder*. Their preferred weapon is *intractable intolerance*.

Formula One battles and constraining channels

Before World War II, Formula One motor racing was domin-ated by the great industrialised European countries of Germany and Italy. Most years, the World Championship was fought out between Mercedes-Benz, Maserati and Ferrari. The received wisdom was that winning races was all about building stronger cars and bigger engines. Horsepower was the measure of a car's worth. By the 1960s, however, a new breed of racing team from Britain arrived. Not backed by any manufacturer or state, they scraped together the cash, tools and manpower to build cars in modest suburban garages. They were designed intuitively and inventively, and tested mainly on the track during a race. When they turned up at a race weekend they were derided by the established teams. Enzo Ferrari, the founder of the great Italian marque, jokingly called them the *Garagistas*—the 'garage cars'—scorning their lack of pedigree and resources. But then an amazing thing happened: they won races! And they kept winning. Right through the 1960s and 1970s, the *Garagistas* won races nearly every year of the World Championship.[115]

What was different about the *Garagistas*? They represented an open approach to innovation. Without the resources and fixed ideas of their competitors, they were free to take a different path. Starting with a clean sheet of paper, they experimented with new ideas, cheerfully improvising and unafraid of failure.[116] For a start they moved the engine from the front of the car to the back. This gave the car far better handling, making it faster on track and more predictable in corners. They used new materials to make the car lighter and stiffer. The engine was part of the strength of the car, rather than just being bolted inside the body. The established teams, entrenched in their ways and sure of their pedigree, stuck to their assumptions about the fastest way around a track—more power. Meanwhile the *Garagistas* kept winning races.

Narrow-mindedness is usually not evident to those who are already blinkered. The less you take the time to look around, the less you are aware of what other options there may be, and the more your thoughts and behaviours become stuck in the specific groove you have chosen. Before you know it, your vision is fixed firmly in one direction only, and you simply fail to see alternative possibilities. By restricting ability and perspective, narrow-mindedness traps and crushes creativity.

A limited perspective and an inflexible approach to life can lead to psychopathic behaviour, which as already discussed, is all too common in organisations today.[117] Psychopathic behaviour is often confused with talent in today's organisation, say the authors of *Snakes in Suits*. Just as you will find psychopathic elements in controlling behaviour such as bullying (as discussed in the first murder profile section), you will also find them in narrow-mindedness. Individuals with personality disorders often exhibit a restricted outlook, which characterises a certain type of working professional. This can become a very real concern when it threatens the death of creativity. Narrow-mindedness also leads to convergent thinking, but the full creative process requires divergent thinking before a specific focus is chosen.

To illustrate how the mind can become trapped in this way, try to imagine a table on which a number of small balls are randomly positioned. Now imagine you are required to ensure these balls line up in two neat rows. Rather than physically positioning each ball one behind the other, though, picture in your mind two gutters on the table, so that as you drop the balls onto the table they naturally fall into these gutters and form the two neat rows. Reach further back into your imagination, and picture that these grooves have been formed by the impact of continuously dropping balls. In this way these grooves have effectively become a 'self-organising' system. This can be an advantage for the process of organisation, but it can become a disadvantage for human creative thinking.

There are many such naturally occurring self-organising systems. Streams, rivers and valleys, for example, become self-organising systems as a result of geology and rainfall patterns. Future rainfall will automatically be channelled into these naturally carved features of the landscape. Strangely enough, our minds also develop these self-organising systems. As our brains develop over time, they tend to build 'catchment areas', which encourages them to push all ideas into standard channels or ways of thinking. Brain scans show how certain neural pathways can become more developed than others — they form 'freeways' along which information passes rapidly and readily, or 'paths through the jungle' that have opened up over time and are easier to use. Increasingly, it takes a lot of effort to force future thoughts off this well-used freeway or path and to think in new ways. The brain's network of neurons conveys thoughts using electrical impulses, and the more these impulses are fired the more the neural pathways will develop, so that they often become thicker and heavier than the neural connections that are not often fired.

Edward de Bono first came up with this idea of a self-organising mind after researching self-organising systems in the body, including the heart, circulation, respiration and glands.[118] From there it was a natural progression to investigate the brain's neural networks. He deduced from this that the brain is good at forming patterns, and because patterns are often asymmetric, the brain should be able to develop lateral thinking.

Human thought patterns tend to slip into these standard channels, or set ways of thinking, if they are not regularly challenged. The brain seeks to organise its thoughts — often in response to incoming information — into temporarily stable states that succeed each other to give a sequence. When a sequence or pattern is repeated, it becomes a thought-pattern or mindset that channels future thoughts more easily along the same path. It thus becomes a standard way of looking at a situation or problem.

The sixth approach to individual creative development emphasises the need to explore all possible avenues and paths – even if at first they seem irrational. Probably the most commonly used expression in relation to creativity is 'thinking outside the box', but what does this really mean? Often when we look for solutions we end up getting stuck 'inside the box', which means we access the place we store all the ideas that fit into our current system as they come along, and then we put a lid on it to ensure nothing gets out and nothing new comes in. Interestingly, this is the way 'magic' works. Most magic relies on the magician's ability to keep the audience thinking inside the box — to keep them thinking along predictable lines and in predictable ways. To truly innovate you must go beyond this system of normalised thinking to 'break out of the box' and to follow different and new paths. When you make new connections on issues that previously seemed to have limited solutions, it's surprising what outcomes you can discover for yourself.

What it all amounts to is a system in which incoming information sets up a sequence of activity. In time this sequence becomes a preferred path or pattern. Once established, these patterns are useful because they allow us to recognise things easily and also to readily predict what will happen next. As recognition is the foundation for daily action, and as the ability to predict is a foundation for intelligence, this is obviously an essential survival mechanism that enables us to cope with life's challenges. Once a pattern has been established then we can more easily analyse and understand new situations in terms of previous experience.

The difficulty with a simple pattern system, however, is that a huge number of patterns are needed to deal with all manner of situations. Any new situation that does not lead directly into an existing pattern must be analysed and restructured afresh. But the brain handles this problem in a very simple way. Like rivers, the patterns have large catchment areas, which means that any activity within the catchment area will lead towards the established pattern. Computers find this sort of pattern recognition very difficult because it is so flexible, but the brain can do it instantly and automatically. We may better understand how it can end up encompassing such a wide range of situations if we see the catchment area as a sort of funnel. This means that whenever we look at the world we are all too ready to see the world in terms of our existing patterns, which is why perception is so powerful and so useful. But this is also why the analysis of information does not tend to lead to new ideas.

Because the brain sees only what it is prepared to see (existing patterns), when we analyse data we tend to pick out only those ideas we already have. Just as magicians deliberately control the focus of our attention, when our 'tunnel vision' is exploited as we maintain focus on one thing, everything else around us is automatically suppressed by our brain.[119] We expect things to be done in a certain way. Creative thinking requires us to learn to open up new paths for our thinking. To explore different paths therefore means to be aware of, but not limited by, familiar patterns or ways of seeing things.

Our memories, too, tend to be narrow-minded in the way they form a reconstruction of experiences that combines accurate and inaccurate elements. As in a feedback loop, when we allow narrow-mindedness to take over, we reinforce an image of our memories and experiences that fits our existing patterns of thought.

The Narrow-minded Mob suspects who can gain a vicelike grip include:

❧ blinkered expertise

❧ prejudice

❧ groupthink.

Murder suspect 1 — blinkered expertise

Zen and the arrogant expert

Made popular in several Hollywood movies is the story of a student of Zen Buddhism who visits his master to seek wisdom. As was the custom, the master offered the student tea. But when the level of the tea reached the top of the cup, the master continued pouring. 'The cup is full and will hold no more,' the bewildered student exclaimed.

The master stopped and looked at the student. 'Like the cup, you are too full of your own opinions and ideas. How can you learn until you first empty your cup?'[120]

The movie *Avatar* explores this idea in a different way.[121] The mythical Na'vi people, who are invaded by the human race, possess a humility that is born of spiritual connection with their natural world. On meeting the central human character, Jake Sully, who has been sent to the Na'vi in avatar form to negotiate the mining of their land, the Tsahik (Righteous One or spiritual teacher) of the Na'vi tells Sully, 'It is hard to fill a cup that is already full'. It is the inability to be open to new ideas, to listen and learn, that defines the worst traits of the human race in the movie, and in the end it is only through 'emptying his cup' that Sully is able to take on new ideas and skills and succeed in a completely new area. We often think of ignorance as a sign of weakness or stupidity, and that is unfortunate, as it encourages the *appearance* of being knowledgeable, which can cut us off from real learning. The Zen tradition calls this the 'expert' mind. It is our frame of mind when we feel we already know everything. We hold onto our ideas and close the door to learning others. To resuscitate creativity it is necessary to distil the style of thinking that can bring ideas back to life. Reviving creative thinking ultimately involves the humility of becoming a beginner.

The belief that experience in a field equates to expertise and therefore to greater competence has been challenged in a number of case studies.[122] One study, for example, compared psychotherapists with high qualifications and decades of experience with novice psychotherapists with only three months of limited training. Test results showed very little difference between the two groups in their ability to accurately assess and treat patients. Doctors are actually less able to diagnose unusual diseases after a period of time following their training, as they are rarely exposed to them. In another interesting case study, the 'Judgment of Paris' wine-tasting exercise of 1976, a blind tasting of a number of French and Californian wines was arranged. The wine 'experts' had trouble distinguishing between the Californian and French wines offered, and gave the American wines the highest scores. The authors of the study concluded that the judges who had a greater knowledge of wines were in fact no more expert in distinguishing wines than regular wine drinkers might be. What's more, they went on to confirm this finding through their own laboratory tests.[123]

The closed perspective of many experts makes it difficult for them to be open to creative new ideas. The expert's mind lives in the past and the future, while the beginner's mind lives in the present. The expert feels he has seen it all before; the beginner sees each detail as if for the first time.[124] The expert mind is closed to the idea of different possibilities — it has lost its creative innocence.[125] The expert mind becomes that of the realistic pessimist. The beginner, in contrast, is willing to keep learning. The beginner is open to trying, failing and starting again. The creative beginner's mind must be that of an eternal optimist.

Research shows that 'expert groups' can end up sharing an illusion of infallibility and a tendency to rationalise away counter-arguments.[126] Experts can also be poor at calibrating their judgement, routinely overestimating the likelihood of being right. A recent study of foreign exchange traders found that they overestimated the accuracy of their exchange rate prediction 70 per cent of the time. So areas that can be influenced by expert 'illusions of invulnerability' include narrow-mindedness, poor judgement and groupthink.[127]

Many organisations today are starting to experiment with moving away from the more experienced 'expert' as the exclusive gatekeeper to knowledge. At an executive meeting of one of the largest auto companies in the world, for example, 35 executives were asked when they had last bought a car. The idea was to gather information—not just from the targeted market segments—on what car buyers were looking for from the people who made the big decisions about car design, construction, marketing and distribution. But it was found that these people had not bought their own cars for years. Having been provided with company cars for as long as they could remember, not a single one could remember what it felt like to choose a car. In contrast, the younger employees who were not given company cars had a solid grasp of reality and were able to make significant contributions to the research.[128]

By exploring different ways of gathering information, this company had identified a problem that had not been previously recognised, and this provided fresh insights. There are plenty of reasons why the most innovative people in any organisation are likely to be the newest recruits. Young people tend to have the most energy and the most confidence. As 'outsiders' they have less respect for tradition and orthodoxy. Their lack of experience can be a positive asset because they're not restrained by history or preconceptions. Older employees, on the other hand, believe they know it has all been tried (and has failed) before.

Information has become very complex. It's not possible for one expert to know everything. Instead leaders need to tap the collective knowledge of the team they lead. Research has shown that experts can be 'spectacularly narrow' in their knowledge, rejecting creative alternatives or new perspectives on issues.

In the beginner's mind there are many possibilities, but in the expert's mind there are few.

Shunyu Suzuki

Murder suspect 2 — prejudice
Poisoned preconceptions

When you think of creativity, do you think of 'vomit', 'poison' and 'agony'? An interesting research project has found that while people tend to explicitly desire creativity, unconsciously they associate creative ideas with such incredibly negative concepts as these. Perhaps surprisingly, as humans we have developed a natural bias we are most likely unaware of against creative ideas. Creative ideas are commonly rejected by organisations at all levels, including academic and scientific institutions. In education institutions, too,  although teachers promote the importance of creativity, they can unconsciously shut it down. Even in organisations that champion their paramount importance, creative ideas are often rejected. And this natural bias against creativity actually interferes with the ability to recognise a creative idea! The researchers recommend that, in the face of this clear bias, creative thinkers shift their focus from 'generating more creative ideas to discovering how to help innovative institutions recognise and accept creativity'.[129]

The word prejudice is derived from the Latin *praejudicium* (*prae* meaning 'in advance' + *judicium* meaning 'judgement'). Prejudice, then, is a bias towards making advanced judgements rather than waiting to judge a situation based on its merits. Unfortunately, because many of the habitual triggers that activate prejudice become ingrained in our thought patterns over time it is difficult to shake off its power and influence. This stalker has accompanied us since we were young, so we do not readily recognise it as a criminal. Born and brought up in a particular culture, we tend to be victims of its constraints, which can limit our ability to think openly and creatively, even about creative thinking itself.

Dr Jason has recently demonstrated in his own research that an area of our brain called the anterior temporal lobe appears to be important for perpetuating our prejudicial associations. In one experiment, when he effectively turned off this area using brain stimulation, he found that the subjects were less likely to associate 'Arabs' with 'terrorism'.

Prejudice will keep you prisoner 'inside the box' of your own volition. Only when you recognise the restrictions of this box—its specific dimensions and characteristics—will you have the chance to glimpse the 'big wide world' beyond and move out into the freedom of creative thinking.[130]

Murder suspect 3—groupthink

The illusion of invulnerability

As discussed in the Insulation section, many leaders deliberately surround themselves with people of like mind, thereby creating environments in which there is little diversity of ideas. Groups whose members are too much alike or too 'knowledgeable' will find it hard to keep learning, because each member is bringing less and less new information to the table. The longer you work for an organisation, the further removed you risk becoming from 'real life' (how customers think, feel, and behave) and the more likely you are to adopt groupthink. When there are too many people together thinking they are experts, the creative possibilities are narrowed and creative problem-solving capacity is reduced. Under increased pressure to conform, individuals may change their opinion not because they agree but because it is easier to conform than to go against the group. A culture of leader dependence will also hamper development.

American foreign policy fiascos, such as the doomed Bay of Pigs invasion and the failure to predict the Japanese attack on Pearl Harbor, illustrate how easily decision makers can fall into the groupthink trap when they are too much alike in their worldview. As expert groups of like-minded thinkers become closer, they become more isolated from other ideas and opinions, and their judgement is increasingly impaired as a result. Convinced that their narrow view is the best or only view, the 'illusion of invulnerability' kicks in and they stop looking for alternative ideas and actions.[131] The Bay of Pigs invasion strategy was developed within a closed group at the CIA, the Pentagon and the White House, with little external advice sought or included. The people who planned the operation hadn't even considered important background information such as the popularity of Castro and strength of the revolutionary forces in Cuba at the time (1961), let alone the logistics of taking over the mountainous island with only 1200 troops. And these were to be the same people who would judge the success of the operation!

The man who follows the crowd will usually get no further than the crowd. The man who walks alone is likely to find himself in places no one has ever been.

Albert Einstein

In the world of Formula One motor racing the established teams stuck to what they knew and continued to develop along the same pathway they always had: They built bigger cars while the *Garagistas* built lighter cars. They focused on horsepower while the *Garagistas* focused on brainpower. Convinced they would beat the upstarts in the end, the established teams trusted in their expert opinions and their tried and true methodologies. But in the end open innovation won over closed-minded expertise.

Investigator's report

Have you seen this Narrow-minded profile in your neighbourhood or workplace? Profile characteristics can include:

\ restricts thinking ☐

\ limits ability to see beyond the 'usual' ☐

\ maintains conservative thinking ☐

The impact on victims can include:

\ the conviction that they are right and
others are wrong ☐

\ the tendency to be suspicious or critical
of others who are different ☐

Murder profile 7: the Pessimism Posse

Another stealthy killer, this profile type subtly perpetrates destruction through a toxic mindset that inflicts nerve impairment. This debilitating process spreads insidious disease, incapacitating its victims. Sufferers of the disease initially communicate in negative ways, and eventually undermine their own and others' attempts at positive survival. Pessimism kills through stifling positive new thoughts and ideas. Pessimists tend to be *self-defeating* and *masochistic*. The preferred weapon of these twisted tormentors is *noxious negativity*.

Chemical warfare and the pessimism porthole

Chemical weapons as a form of warfare were first introduced on a large scale during Word War I. The Germans deployed chlorine gas, a by-product of dye manufacturing, against the Allies on the Western Front in early 1915. The grey-green gas that was released caused death through asphyxiation when in strong enough concentrations. The chlorine turned to hydrochloric acid when it dissolved in the water in the victims' lungs, and this destroyed tissue in the lungs. Chlorine gas was also a powerful psychological weapon: whenever the troops saw the distinctive grey-green gas clouds they were filled with dread.

Despite condemning the weaponising of gas as a blatant violation of international law, Britain soon came to accept that they would have to use the same weapon if they were to survive, but the first time they deployed gas in September 1915 it literally backfired on them. As this form of warfare relied heavily on favourable wind conditions, unexpected wind changes could mean the gas failed to reach the enemy. Worse still, it could blow back over their own lines, which is what happened on this occasion. Compounding the disaster, the wrong turning keys were sent with some of the canisters, and the unopened canisters were hit by German shells, spreading more gas across the British lines. Although the soldiers dispensing the gas had been issued with flannel masks to protect them, the small eyepieces fogged over with the heat, and eventually, in order to see or to gulp in some fresh air, many of the soldiers opened their masks and were themselves overcome by the gas.

Next French chemists developed a new chemical weapon, phosgene, which had the advantage of being colourless and relatively odourless so it couldn't be easily detected. Phosgene, in turn, was superseded in 1917 by mustard gas, which inflicted horrific chemical burns on its victims, blinding many of them and causing respiratory distress and vomiting, leading to eventual death. Heavier than air, this 'yellow gas' settled on the ground, lingering and remaining active for up to months at a time, depending on weather conditions. Mustard gas became the widest used and most notorious chemical weapon of the Great War.[132]

Death by gas is often slow and painful. Like gas, pessimism initially causes irritation, eventually inflicting emotional and psychological pain that will subject creativity to a slow and painful death. Using the noxious weapon of negativity, pessimism is a neurotic, pathological killer that ultimately drives people away. It can also easily backfire on those who use it, eating away at them so they too become its unintentional victims. Pessimism's negativity is a dangerous weapon that cannot easily be subdued, since the conditions under which it is dispersed cannot always be controlled. Unlike some of the more subtle killers, pessimism's motives and impact are obvious. No-one enjoys hanging around pessimists—their company isn't pleasant. You can often see them coming, but they impose their will relentlessly and it's easy to get drawn into the negative gloom they spread.

Pessimism and optimism are now recognised as distinctive traits that characterise individuals, determining their outlook on life. In one study,[133] researchers divided children into optimists (self-mastery) and pessimists (helpless). They then gave them a series of exercises—first impossible tasks, then possible ones. Before the failures there was no difference in performance. After the failures the following differences were found: Among the pessimists, problem-solving skills deteriorated from fourth-grade to first-grade level. They began to hate the task. When they were all then given a task that was *not* impossible to complete, the helpless kids discounted their previous success and simply gave up. The optimists, on the other hand, stayed at their fourth-grade level and kept focus, and they expressed the confidence to keep trying. This research demonstrated that children or adults who believe they are helpless stop trying and their performance drops. When people stop trying, they no longer look for new ideas and ways to solve problems—they cease to be creative. Because uncreative people are stuck in routines, when they see something new, they want no part of it. Pessimism can cripple creativity in this way.

Some psychiatrists now claim that 'defensive pessimism' is a constructive coping mechanism, as it ensures a realistic outlook. People with a naturally pessimistic outlook can find ways to work through 'worst-case scenarios' and come to terms with the demands of modern life. Indulging in negative thoughts like these actually helps many people go on to do their best by being prepared for the worst.[134] But extreme pessimism is never healthy (just as extreme, unrealistic optimism is dangerous). Defensive pessimists are similar to moderately depressed subjects in that they report negative expectations and high levels of anxiety. Extreme pessimists also fall more easily into depression, although the antithesis can also apply: depression can cause a person to develop a more pessimistic outlook.[135]

For creative thinking, optimism encourages an openness to more possibilities.[136] Although there's an old belief that pessimism and depression foster creative thought, in fact the opposite is true.[137] Researchers have long recognised that negative emotions give people a kind of tunnel vision or filter on their attention, and that people are at their most creative when they are optimistic and happy. An upbeat attitude makes people receptive to information of all kinds. As psychologist Adam Anderson, co-author of a University of Toronto study, says, 'With positive mood, you actually get more access to things you would usually ignore', so that, 'Instead of looking through a porthole, you have a landscape or panoramic view of the world'.[138]

Pessimists tend to have a lower level of confidence, a lack of interest in activities, and little drive or ambition to go out and accomplish things, so they are less likely to be actively creative. Nietzsche wrote that pessimism leads to resignation.[139] Optimists, on the other hand, tend to do well in life. Optimistic salespeople outperform their pessimistic counterparts by up to 37 per cent. In fact, the benefits can be seen across industries and job functions. For example, doctors with a positive mindset are 50 per cent more accurate when making diagnoses than those who are negative.[140]

The Pessimism Posse suspects we are covering here are:

ϟ negativity (such as negative language and emotions)
ϟ lack of hope
ϟ lack of trust.

Murder suspect 1 — negativity

Insidious self-defeat

Pessimistic language can destroy creativity by limiting thinking. Through rephrasing, it is possible to change the focus to open up more possibilities. Consider some customer service examples. Instead of saying, 'We can't do that', you can say, 'That might be a problem, but we *can* do this instead...' Rather than saying, 'We can't start until we get the information we need from you', it is possible to say, 'Please give us the information we need from you so we can start'.

THE PESSIMISM POSSE

Neg A. Tivity
MURDER SUSPECT

Have a look at how Shell Petroleum was able to play on the problems with negative language in one of their advertisements:

> ... *the real energy crisis lies in the inertia that afflicts all but a few of our species when faced with apparently overwhelming problems. In the willingness of the majority to say, 'no', 'never', 'can't' and just give up. Thankfully, the creative problem solvers at Shell have never taken 'no' for an answer...* [141]

Following are some common examples of self-defeating ways people think about and interpret events in their lives:

- *Dichotomous thinking:* perceiving events in extreme, 'all or nothing' ways (for example, depicting events as wonderful or terrible, with no recognition of the grey areas in between).
- *Excessive personalisation:* automatically concluding that another's behaviour or mood is in direct response to you (for example, 'She's in a bad mood. I must have done something wrong').
- *Overgeneralisation:* seeing an event as having more impact, in more areas of your life, than it truly has.
- *Filtering:* magnifying negative events in your life and discounting positive ones.
- *Emotional reasoning:* concluding that what you feel must be the truth (for example, if you feel stupid, you must be stupid).

To combat pessimism, it is important to identify and deal with all of these tendencies. Some ways negativity can be counteracted include:

- specific thinking
- avoiding unnecessary personalisation and generalisation
- positive filtering
- logical reasoning.

Murder suspect 2 — lack of hope

Learned helplessness

Learned helplessness is the giving-up reaction, the quitting response that follows from the belief that whatever you do doesn't matter. The way in which you habitually explain to yourself why events happen — your personal explanatory style — determines how helpless you become. When innovating, it is important to persevere, to push through failures in order to come up with creative solutions. What's crucial is what you think when you fail. Using the power of non-negative thinking — changing the destruc-

tive things you say to yourself when you experience the setbacks that life deals out to all of us — is the central skill of optimism. 'I always try but sometimes fail' is far better than 'I always fail but sometimes try'.

Pessimists are up to eight times more likely to become depressed when bad events occur;[142] they do worse at school, sports and most jobs than their talents would indicate; they have worse physical health and shorter lives; they have rockier relationships. They tend to blame themselves when things go wrong, becoming more reluctant to try again with each negative experience. They begin to look at positive events in their lives as 'flukes' that have nothing to do with them, and they expect the worst. The benefits of optimism and a positive frame of mind, on the other hand, are huge: optimists enjoy better health and stronger relationships, are more productive and experience less stress. This is because optimists tend to take more risks and blame external circumstances if they fail, maintaining a 'try again' mindset; this makes them more likely to succeed in the future, and less upset by failure in general. In this way, optimists and pessimists both create their own destinies.

According to a dictionary definition, *hope* means 'to look forward with desire and reasonable confidence'. Without hope, there is by definition no desire and no confidence, meaning it is more difficult to initiate and persevere through the creative process.

Possibility is essential for perceptual thinking, creative thinking, design thinking and exploratory thinking.

Edward de Bono

Murder suspect 3 — lack of trust
Misanthropy and nihilism

According to some Muslim scholars, pessimism can lead to a destructive mistrust of others.[143] This can limit thinking about possibilities and reduce the levels of openness needed for the creative process. The problems with a distrust born of pessimism, these scholars say, can include:

\ It destroys the roots of harmony among people.

\ It leads to withdrawal.

\ It affects reason and the ability to judge others fairly.

\ It is contagious.

When this sort of pessimistic mistrust becomes generalised, it is called 'misanthropy'—a dislike, contempt or hatred of people in general. According to Plato, misanthropy stems from continually thwarted expectations or excessively naive optimism. Again, when you close the door on people and opportunities, you close the door on positive potential input for creative thinking.

Sociopaths and serial killers often have misanthropic tendencies. American serial murderer Carl Panzram exemplified this.[144] Panzram, who confessed to 22 murders and to having sodomised more than 1000 males, expressed his nihilistic outlook in his famous final words, spat into the executioner's face as the noose was tightened around his neck: 'I wish all mankind had one neck so I could choke it!'[145] Fortunately, few organisations experience this level of misanthropy, but we do all need to be careful that we don't let mistrust grow.

The US renounced biological warfare and first use of chemical weapons on 25 November 1969. The decree issued at that time is still in effect today. Chemical weapons have since been disposed of by sinking shiploads of weapons, and later by incinerating them in mountainous regions. Most of the chemical weapons stockpile has now been destroyed.

Perhaps it is possible to reduce or dispose of pessimistic ways of thinking and pessimistic language in the same way. Perhaps, more significantly, we can learn to 'sink' or 'incinerate' language and actions that perpetuate the problem—or, better still, 'neutralise' this mindset where possible. Then we can ensure that creative thinking has the fresh air it needs to survive.

Investigator's report

Have you seen this Pessimism profile in your neighbourhood or workplace? Profile characteristics can include:

\ creates a toxic negative mindset ☐
\ stifles new thoughts and ideas ☐
\ instils a sense of despair ☐
\ creates mistrust ☐

The impact on victims can include:

\ learned helplessness ☐
\ isolation ☐
\ lack of will ☐

Where has creativity died?

Probing the possible murder sites

Imagine you're walking towards a playground park bench to eat your lunch. Suddenly your phone buzzes with a secret ring tone, alerting you to the fact that you are about to sit next to a registered sex offender, or maybe even a murderer. This is not a scenario from a horror or science fiction movie. The technology has been around for a while. It's already possible to download an iPhone/android app that tells you how many criminals there are within a set radius of where you are. Tested recently at one city location to cover a designated area, it detected two Vs (violent criminals), four Ts (people convicted of theft/robbery), 50 Ms (those convicted of multiple crimes) and about 12 Os (people with traffic offences or other legal black marks against their name). This could make you feel quite paranoid. What are all these criminals up to? One blogger commented, 'After living here nearly 15 years I'm probably going to start locking my door at night … Good heavens! My city is overrun with rapists and paedophiles. I've got to stop looking at this map!'

In the UK a group called Charity Crime Stoppers has compiled a map of 'hotspots' where Britain's most hardened criminals live. Perhaps unsurprisingly, the busy cities are the top hotspots. According to shadow home secretary Chris Grayling, 'The most persistent offenders often come from the most challenging and deprived areas of our biggest cities. It underlines how those areas are disproportionately affected by crime'.[1] Police use these stats when deciding where to allocate resources and focus on prevention and education programs.

In the same way, the more we know about where our creativity murderers can be found, the better prepared we will be for finding ways to prevent and deal with their activities. So it will be helpful to find out if there are any particular places in the organisation that are likely 'hotspots' where the villains hang out.

Locating the crime hotspots—from the boss's office to the coffee shop

Most burglars are lazy and will use the easiest way to get into their target location.[2] Their preferred method of entry is the same as ours—walking through the door. Creativity murderers also prefer to simply walk in through the front door of our living rooms or workplaces and then happily park themselves in their favourite spots. As they can be well disguised or quite charming, they will often get away with this.

An interesting (often entertaining) exercise is to go through the murderer section of this book and to speculate whether each murderer has entered your organisation undetected—and, if so, where his favourite hangouts might be. You can also try to match the murderer and the weapon with the most likely location. You will first need to consider 'whodunit'—was it, for example, X.S. Stress using Drowning Dread in the boss's office? Or Beau Rock-Racy with Crushing Coercion in the accounting department? In our workshops we use our simulation board game with these characters to spark discussion on this, then groups vote on the most likely culprits, weapons and places—which can vary greatly from organisation to organisation, and even team to team.

In considering the places where the creativity killers are most likely to be found, it is interesting to think back to your school days. Do you remember where the tough kids used to hang? In our case, thinking back, it was not in the most glamorous or desirable of locations—they actually used to congregate in the toilets! The junior students would often hold their bladders all day rather than risk having to face the smoking and swearing seniors in the lavatories. On the other hand, the school library, quiet and boring but peaceful and calm, where the timid could escape (especially if being bullied), was reserved for the nerds. In our research we have found that in work organisations creativity killers tend to skulk in those areas that are more rigid and structured and less open and playful.

Our online survey has uncovered some of the major environmental factors involved in the death of creativity, according to the participants. Many indicated that the higher up one goes in the organisation (for example, the CEO, boardroom, executives, accounts and HR), the more likely it is that creativity will be killed. Comments have included: 'HR and finance have been the two most regulated fields in my line of work that have restricted creativity' and 'creativity is killed anywhere where people are listened to and valued because of their rank rather than their talent and ability.'[3]

The other important environmental factor to consider is the social environment. In school you have the bullies or tough kids (we'll call them toilet culture kids to give you a specific image) at one extreme and the nerds (we'll call them the library culture kids) at the other, but most kids sit somewhere in the middle. These kids are often easily influenced one way or the other by the toilet culture or the library culture. It's up to the school to set a positive tone and create a constructive culture, establishing places that are conducive to their mission. Like the swinging voter, the influence of the swinging student can be immense if tapped effectively. Peer pressure doesn't finish when we leave school. We like to please the people we hang with, and if this means being controlling or cynical or narrow-minded, many of us will do it. If it means encouraging others, we'll also do this—as long as the incentive is there. If creativity is shut down by those around you, it's hard to entertain new ideas, but if it's encouraged, all will participate enthusiastically. There are toilet and library cultures everywhere.

In the organisation too it is possible to create a positive environment that ensures there is a constructive bias towards creative thinking and away from the creativity killers that can dominate. Malcolm Gladwell's concept of the 'tipping point'[4] is as relevant to team dynamics as it is to other areas.[5] Sometimes a small change in personnel in a team can change the whole environment. Underlying any organisation is a culture that will encourage either the criminals or the resuscitators to thrive.

Consider the NAB and ANZ banks. Both institutions have publicly stated they are keen to change the way their organisation functions. Both are using a similar approach to change (NAB's program is called 'Breakthrough', ANZ's is called 'Breakout'). Both programs have been designed directly or indirectly by management consultant McKinsey. And both are focusing on the social behaviours that need to adapt to bring about a positive cultural change. As identified by NAB program architects, the sorts of influential values that will set these behaviours and establish a positive cultural change include trust, transparency, accountability and empowerment.[6] Where this doesn't happen, or where destructive competition and distrust dominate the organisation, creativity cannot survive.

So how to deal with the toilet culture in the school or work organisation? Try taking your meetings there, and turn them into an object lesson! One creative regional executive for Greyhound decided to turn up at a problem bus station unannounced and hold an impromptu staff meeting in the toilets to highlight the fact that they needed to place more emphasis on keeping the toilets clean.[7] A clear object lesson with undoubtedly high impact. In another, similar object lesson, a private school conducted a meeting in the toilets with similarly spectacular success. A group of 12-year-old girls had been regularly congregating in the toilets and leaving lipstick imprints on the mirrors. Whenever the cleaner removed the prints, more would appear the next day. The Principal's efforts to discipline the girls failed, and the lip prints continued to appear — until she finally came up with a creative solution. She called the girls into the bathroom with the cleaner, and explained how much effort it took to clean the mirrors. And then she asked the cleaner to demonstrate. The cleaner took out a squeegee, dipped it in a toilet bowl, and cleaned the mirror with it. The problem ceased after that!

This chapter will navigate some of the general areas you will find in most organisations and institutions, government and private, at all levels. See if you can work out where the creativity killers may be hanging in your organisation!

Potential murder site 1: the boss's office

The killers have definitely left their marks here. CEOs and other high-level managers are generally struggling to keep up with increasingly volatile and complex business environments, and they need to focus on bottom-line business issues. The IBM study[8] revealed that fewer than half the global CEOs surveyed believe their organisations are prepared to handle the massive shifts in the way business needs to be run. They are challenged daily with trying to deal with such major areas as new government regulations, changes in global economic power centres, accelerated industry transformation, growing volumes of data and rapidly evolving customer preferences. Creativity is undoubtedly needed here, but with the need to conform to such broad expectations there is often simply no room to think creatively.

One CEO of a large organisation we surveyed described the frustration of having to run a company according to board mandates, and the impact it had had on his own creative confidence. He explained how the more creative outlook he started with had fallen by the wayside as he had been required to meet ever stricter guidelines. 'When I was young,' he said, 'I had no barriers, I did not know any better, I was not programmed, I did not care what people thought, I had no downside — the world was my canvas. But now I realise that although I have much more to offer and much more drive, I am limited by board mandate.'[9]

Bosses at every level and in every organisation are having to deal with the pressures from above and below, and will need to come up with creative ways to reshape the future.

Potential murder site 2: the boardroom

Many employees don't realise that *everyone* has a boss. Gossip and scorn are often directed upwards, and most assume that the buck stops in the CEO's office. But CEOs have one of the loneliest jobs in the world, as they too are accountable. The CEO needs to direct a company and keep it profitable *and* report to a board. The board, in turn, has to ensure that the decisions made satisfy their stakeholders. So almost everyone is accountable to someone else. The Pressure Pack, the Fear Family and the Pessimism Posse tend to frequent board meetings. You will also often find the Insulation Clique and Narrow-minded Mob there. With such a heavily weighted crowd holding court, saying something out of line or suggesting something new and creative is often not worth risking. Creativity is entertained only if it can offer short-term gain and bottom-line financial benefits. There's usually too much pressure to even think about radical innovation and transformation that might rock the boat.

Potential murder site 3: accounts/finance

There once was a business owner who was interviewing candidates for a division manager position. He decided to select the applicant who could best answer the question: 'How much is 2 + 2?' The engineer pulled out his slide rule, shuffled it back and forth, and finally announced, 'It lies between 3.98 and 4.02'. The mathematician said, 'In two hours I can demonstrate it equals 4 with the following short proof...' The attorney stated, 'In the case of Svenson vs the State, 2 + 2 was declared to be 4'. And the trader asked, 'Are you buying or selling?' The accountant looked at the business owner, then got out of his chair and went to see if anyone was listening at the door and pulled the drapes. Finally he returned to the business owner, leaned across the desk and said in a low voice, 'What would you like it to be?'

The term 'creative accounting' is frequently used to describe how individuals and companies utilise accounting practices to minimise their tax and overstate their assets or understate their liabilities. An accountant has been defined as 'someone who solves a problem you didn't know you had in a way you don't understand at a price you can't afford'. And yet accountants don't consider themselves to be creative!

Enron is frequently cited as epitomising creative accounting and is a good example of what happens when the practice is taken too far. The company's auditors, Arthur Andersen, were at the time one of the most respected accounting firms in the industry, so everyone was surprised that the fraud had gone so far. Those who know how widespread this sort of accounting fraud is believe they were just unlucky to get caught.

Apart from this more dubious form of creativity, 'accounting' and 'creative' are not often used in the same sentence. The accounting department must be 'precise' and rigorously 'correct', so it must follow rigid systems and procedures within set guidelines. And it must diligently serve the god of profit. Business consultant Jim Collins believes that while profit is critical for the survival of an organisation over the long term, it's like oxygen—something we need to live but not what we live *for*.[10] The potential rift between purpose and profit as the main motivation must be effectively resolved for creative thinking to survive and thrive in this part of the organisation.

Potential murder site 4: executive offices

Powerful people have difficulty seeing from any perspective other than their own, according to a recent study.[11] When the study asked participants to use a finger to draw a capital 'E' on their forehead, it was found that the most powerful people were drawing the letter from their perspective and had trouble imagining how others might see it. It was concluded that power leads individuals to assign too much weight to their own viewpoint.

Executives need to be careful that their language doesn't alienate others and prevent them from contributing to the organisation. Here's how philosopher Sam Keen sees one of the problems:

> *Every institution and profession ... has its lingo. It is the nature of professions and organizations to invent special languages that are understood by insiders but are otherwise opaque; to be a professional is to speak in code. For the uninitiated, reading internal documents is like deciphering code. It is not uncommon for professionals of all kinds ... to use obfuscation, complexity, and mystification to claim knowledge—and thereby power—unavailable to the layperson.*[12]

Potential murder site 5: research and development

The movie *Fast & Furious 5* (or *Fast Five*)[13] was highly successful financially, breaking several box office records with a new type of 'car chase' plot focusing less on car racing and more on a heist—the target a corrupt police station. As the criminal team watch the police station and ponder whether they can break into it, most of them believe it impossible. But our trusty hero Dominic Toretto (Vin Diesel) explains to them that most police stations and jails are designed to keep people in, rather than to keep them out, and he believes this weakness can be exploited. Naturally the criminals eventually achieve their goal and do drive off into the distance in a high-speed chase (the whole purpose of the movie). The film reverses the good guys/bad guys archetype by locating the bad guys in the police station, offering the interesting message that sometimes the criminals will be found where you least expect them.

In the business organisation, the R&D department would probably be the last place a CSI team would look for the creativity killers. After all, creativity is supposed to originate there. The death of creativity in the R&D labs may seem unlikely, but maybe that is the department's greatest weakness—no-one would pick it as the crime scene. Imagine interviewing an R&D person who declared she was not creative. It would be like a hotel saying they don't have beds!

We expect the R&D department to be an incubator for creativity (and sometimes even that it will be the only place creativity thrives). But murderers such as apathy and insulation can still easily strike here. One problem with keeping R&D as a separate department is that it can be divided into the 'rainmakers', who come up with most of the creative ideas, and others not assigned this role, who can be overlooked and not encouraged to develop creative ideas. Also, in a sense the creativity here can dampen creative enthusiasm in other parts of the organisation. If the average person believes that creative thinking is the role of R&D, they'll continue to battle on inefficiently in their own work. So while creativity may not have been killed in the R&D department, it may have been snuffed out surreptitiously and unknowingly elsewhere because of the mere existence of the R&D role.

Another problem is that although the R&D department may breed fabulous ideas, these ideas are not guaranteed implementation. Many of those who work in this department complain that they are only a single isolated department and their creative ideas are frequently cut down by others. All the people in R&D we have interviewed felt constricted by other departments. Because the department's success is difficult to evaluate by standard measures such as turnover or revenue, when there are strong financial pressures the department as a whole can be depleted in terms of resources and reach. The sporadic nature of this function and the fact that it is not driven by standard market factors are significant issues to be taken into account in this respect.

If R&D want creativity and innovation to flourish and to influence the whole organisation, they will need to ensure they are not simply buried in their own projects. They may need to pop over to PR and sales to pick up a few pointers on how to 'sell' their new ideas internally, ensuring there is buy-in for them. Many salespeople can tell you about great ideas that never made it past the cutting-room floor because of poor communication or persuasion skills. R&D needs to master the power of influencing, which may be the very thing they were trying to avoid in their research role!

One research person we spoke to explained that R&D need constant resourcing and creative development, rather than being just shoved in a room and told to produce results. But if they want to be a bastion of creativity, and if R&D want to ensure that their hands are clean when it comes to creativity murder location, they will need to make sure their doors are wide open for ideas to flow in as well as innovations to flow out. They will also need to ensure that others in the organisation don't feel threatened by their expertise in the area and instead are welcomed as creative collaborators.

The *Fast Five* movie heroes broke into the police station so easily because no-one had expected or planned for such a stunt. Be careful that the murderers don't just as easily get into R&D.

Potential murder site 6: sales and marketing

Creativity murderers in sales and marketing have a clever method for killing it off here. They simply pit different S&M teams against each other or against other departments in the organisation and eventually, like in an old mob movie, everyone kills each other off.

S&M are often creative in their sales approaches and marketing ideas, but time and time again they hit a brick wall when it comes to execution. When the finance department puts the pressure on to meet financial targets or to cut spending, inevitably the enthusiasm in S&M is dampened and creative ideas die. The paradox is that any S&M people worth their salt need to make the numbers, but it can end up being a constant weight around their necks. In a typical scenario sales blames marketing for failure yet takes the credit for success. Fifty-four per cent of sales teams believe they could reach their sales targets more easily if marketing was able to produce more compelling marketing messages; 34.4 per cent of marketers, on the other hand, believe their sales teams need to follow up on leads more consistently, and 26 per cent feel the messages and tools they create are under-utilised by the sales teams.[14] The rivalry and lack of trust within S&M teams is such a problem that 80 per cent of marketing expenditures and sales collateral is often wasted.[15]

Who killed creativity in the S&M department? This was a clever murderer who set the stage and then sat back and watched. The murder scene can easily turn into a full-on brawl with a bloody outcome. Where this is not controlled, brainstorming can easily become 'blamestorming'. Team members will start to find it is easier to critique than to create.[16] When the opposite happens, though — when S&M and the other departments can get together and share creative ideas — then revenues increase and blue oceans appear.

Wal-Mart, for example, came up with some creative ideas about supply and demand. By taking time to examine their databases in 2004, for example, they noticed that a large number of torches and batteries were sold, which was not a surprise, but at the same time sales of the sugary sweet American breakfast snacks called 'Pop-Tarts' went through the roof. The retailer never would have expected to stock up on an item like this before a hurricane (and associated blackouts), but some creative analysis utilising the sales team in collaboration with the supply chain and analysis teams helped to identify a sales opportunity.

Perhaps it is no surprise that with creative ideas like this Wal-Mart has a revenue of around $400 billion — more than the GDP of many entire countries. With more than 2 million employees handling over 200 million customer transactions each week and more than 8400 stores to keep track of worldwide, it's a small miracle that they are able to keep track of such data, but it's obviously a great contributor to their success. A simple creative idea assisted by modern technology changed a whole business model and benefited the business immeasurably.[17]

Potential murder site 7: the coffee shop

A coffee shop can be a focal point for meeting and sharing ideas. In a busy city, where there are many opportunities for the cross-pollination of information, the coffee shop has become the hub. Some coffee shops are too open and exposed for the creativity murderers to hang around, and many actively welcome creativity. The problem can be that many people will be too influenced by members of the Pressure Pack to even make it to the coffee shop. When we are too busy to meet and catch up, we miss out on opportunities to get together to share creative ideas.

The communal coffee pot at break times used to provide an opportunity to connect with work colleagues and friends during the day. Casual gossip and tasty titbits of organisational information were important to keep communication open and foster relationships within the organisation. But as people now make their single cup of coffee, grab a cup of water from the water dispenser or duck out to Starbucks to pick up a convenient takeout drink, they are rapidly becoming socially disconnected. A sign of the changing times came when Microsoft in the US threw out all their coffee filter pots in 2010 and replaced them with single-cup coffeemakers. So bringing back the communal coffee get-together could help to foster collaborative creativity.[18]

This 'soft issues' agenda has become so important that executives in the organisation are starting to sit up and take notice. More than 20 years ago American psychologist Edgar Schein, in his book *Organisational Culture and Leadership*, first noted that these hidden subtleties of the corporate culture need to be recognised.[19] Global managing partner for McKinsey Ian Davis has also emphasised that leaders need to understand how to use this 'soft power'. If they can learn to manage the complex internal and external issues inherent in today's contemporary organisation, they can also foster creativity and innovation. Perhaps it's time for more people to wake up and smell the coffee!

Potential murder site 8: the lecture room/classroom

When it comes to learning, or to training and development, we need to change expectations to recognise the fact that life is ambiguous, to accept the reality that there may be many 'right' answers depending on what you are looking for. The 'one correct answer' approach kills creativity because people stop searching as soon as they have found that answer. So the curiosity that should spark an ongoing love for learning is quickly snuffed out. And like an old house that has been gathering mementoes for years, our minds will become cluttered with useless information, and we will not have the mental space or energy to break out and explore. As creativity consultant Roger Von Oech says in his book *A Whack on the Side of the Head*, 'We never have an opportunity to ask the questions that lead off the beaten path in new directions. If we're repeatedly successful, we're tempted to believe that we've found the formula for success and are no longer subject to human fallibility'.[20] Tim Harford describes this approach as taking 'predictable steps along a well-chosen pathway' and laments how educational institutions such as Harvard have become bastions of 'short-term gratification'.[21]

Becoming a true learning organisation is not a passive process. As company structures become more established, the drive to learn and grow will die unless there is an active initiative to ensure it continues.[22] And if there is only a single-loop learning approach, problems will continue to re-emerge in the future if they are not dealt with properly in the short term.[23]

Unfortunately—perhaps shockingly—many participants in our survey indicated that HR also kills creativity. Instead of supporting and promoting creative development, which you might expect to happen in the HR/training arena, there can be a focus on jumping through the hoops to keep up rather than thinking and planning ahead for future growth opportunities.

Potential murder site 9: the playground

When the next generation of kids arrives on the office floor we may be in for a shock. According to Susan Linn (author of *Consuming Kids*), children are now taught that what will make them happy is what the big corporations produce. Young children have no interest in carving their own Harry Potter wand from a stick but demand the cleverly branded plastic wands they have seen advertised on TV, she says. Linn believes they are now learning about the world based on what's best for corporations rather than what's best for them, and that can't be good. Play has changed dramatically from the time when children invented their own play world—an age when Plato's famous words, 'Necessity is the mother of invention', rang true—to a world invented by adults with often insincere motives,[24] where children no longer need to create.[25]

The playground should be a hothouse of creativity, an open environment for exploration and free experimentation, but it may no longer be providing that opportunity. Free play should create a mental state in which it is possible to feel safe and secure and to explore ideas without restrictions. But 'free play' is being transformed into 'controlled play'.

Research clearly shows that individuals who had less play time as children are less creative as adults. Children (and animals) who do not 'free play' when they are young may grow into anxious, socially maladjusted adults.[26] Free play is one of the conduits needed to ensure brain resources are diverted away from dealing solely with the primitive survival functions so they can access creative thinking. Today our organisations may not be providing that opportunity. When the life of 'Texas Tower' mass murderer Charles Whitman was studied in detail, it was found that he had been severely deprived of play as a child, which was deemed to be a significant factor in making him vulnerable to the crime he committed. Such deprivation has also been found as a critical factor in a number of other similar crimes, including the Virginia Tech massacre.[27]

Opportunities to take work breaks, to make time for free thinking and 'play'—and designing places of learning and work to encourage these—will be critical for future creative development. In fact, there is unexpected evidence that this shift may already be happening. A new theory highlights an interesting social trend. It is believed that adults are now hanging on to the behaviours and attitudes traditionally associated with youth as a survival mechanism.[28] This immaturity is thought to be enabling adults today to think and respond creatively to changing contemporary demands. Where maturity, wisdom and experience were once valued qualities in a predictable 'fixed' environment, an open, youthful mindset seems to be a better coping strategy for dealing with a rapidly changing environment. 'What is required in the new economy is child-like receptivity and cognitive flexibility,' writes Jennifer Viegas regarding this theory. 'In other words youthfulness and playfulness may be adaptive responses to change where jobs, skills and technology are all in a state of flux. This could certainly explain the apparently adolescent behaviour of innovators like Richard Branson and Steve Wozniak and, if true, has profound implications for everything from HR policy to office design.'

Professor of theoretical medicine Bruce Charlton believes society no longer formally prepares young people for 'adulthood' through rigorous initiation ceremonies, so it is not unusual for children to retain many of their childlike habits into adulthood. The 'psychological neotony' of ongoing education encourages a certain flexibility of the mind and openness to new ideas. Those who continue to maintain an open mind after they have finished their formal education are generally surviving and succeeding best.

Any time, any place

Of course the murder sites are not limited to single offices, departments or locations. It would be too narrow-minded to assume that the death of creativity is restricted to a particular place. Any number of them can turn up in any location at any time, frequently moving between them, sometimes settling into the one place, and sometimes making a casual visit only; sometimes accompanying specific people or situations or systems, and always drawn by a combination of different factors.

Often specific locations or departments will finger-point, blaming other departments for the death of creativity. Those in the field, for example, will often say the killers are found at head office, and this 'blame game' can erode team effectiveness. More than 50 per cent of virtual teams fail to reach their objectives, usually because they feel constrained or shut down by a function they perceive to be out of touch with real needs and experiences.[29]

Many organisations eventually develop 'silos', where others can be easily 'boxed in' or 'walled in' by prejudices and expectations, and blame can then be more easily hurled 'over the walls'. Some say that Sony lost the music industry race to Apple after such an incredible head start because it developed silo departments with no common positive vision. 'Sony has long thrived on a hyper-competitive culture, where engineers were encouraged to outdo each other, not work together,' reflected one employee. Meanwhile at Apple the more a positive, collaborative culture was established the more creative they became, and the boundaries between departments soon evaporated. An Apple employee highlights the contrast: 'We were all working together late at night, and it was highly energized. It was just an incredible team project. There were no boundaries. The software guys, the hardware guys, the firmware.'[30]

British burglar Stuart McCormick was recently convicted and imprisoned for a single offence, but then owned up to a further 505 previously undetected crimes! By finding where criminals like to hang then isolating and dealing with these offenders, it may be possible to uncover and deal with a range of deeper, previously unnoticed issues. It would be nice to have an app that alerts us with a secret ring every time we walk into a place that is a hotspot for creativity murderers. In the absence of this technology (and the paranoia it would generate) we must rely on our instinct, or at least ensure we engage in good healthy discussion on the topic so we can identify the killers in any area of the organisation.[31]

Why save creativity?

Emergency response

A new rescue squad is being trained to deal with critical emergency situations. Perhaps the most unlikely of saviours, the knights in shining armour we are about to describe are not chosen for their physical strength or expert medical knowledge. They are painstakingly trained but will never set foot in the training room. Dispatched to the most dangerous of scenarios, these rescue squads have very high rates of success, yet they are not receiving the bravery awards or recognition you would think they deserve.

The rescue squad is, in fact, a team of furry rodents, a miniature army of rat risk-takers ready to step out into the unknown and sniff out danger. Trained by psychologist Alan Poling, the rats are helping to deal with two major, very different problems in the developing world—land mines and tuberculosis. More than 25 000 people a year are killed or maimed by landmines, which are considered one of the leading sources of suffering in the developing world. In Mozambique, for example, where land mines are still a major problem after a 16-year civil war, the livelihoods of thousands of civilians are threatened. If the people return to the land that is seeded with mines, they risk losing a limb, but if they cannot grow food on the land they risk starvation. After eight months of meticulous lab training, African pouched rats, which have a very keen sense of smell, have been taught to detect mines in the field with 100 per cent accuracy. Rats are now also being trained to detect tuberculosis, which still kills around two million people a year according to World Health Organization statistics. The rats have been found to be 44 per cent more accurate than standard smear microscopy in predicting the presence of TB.

Ironically, then, while we tend to associate rats with disease, danger and death (think of the bubonic plague, a disease spread by rodents through the fleas they carry, which has claimed more than 200 million lives worldwide), they may themselves now become a saviour in our fight against disease, danger and death.[1]

There are undoubtedly many who would prefer not to know too much about these squeaking sewer dwellers, but despite their gruesome reputation rats are actually clever animals that will often find creative ways to deal with challenges. To demonstrate the rat's high level of creative intelligence, a couple of bloggers put together a list of rat attributes, suggesting a few good reasons to take the rat seriously when it comes to creative thinking and problem solving:

- the ability to learn to navigate a maze by trial and error
- the facility to venture into the unknown and to learn from their mistakes
- the ability to retain information and apply it in specific situations (for example, utilising information about what food is good and tasty, and what is poisonous and induces illness)
- the ability to develop organisational structures at an early age and to learn to stay in their place within that system (usually) in order to benefit the group as a whole.

The rat is said to have won its position in the Chinese zodiac through its creativity, rather than through great physical or intellectual skill. In one story the Chinese tell, Rat found a way to compete and win the Jade Emperor's race through guile. He succeeded in outwitting his friend Cat to enter the race, and during the race he rode on the back of Ox, considered the most tolerant, courageous and hardworking of all animals. Just when the finishing line was approaching, Rat leapt over Ox's head to take first position. By working smarter, not harder, Rat was able to stay ahead of the pack. The image of this race between animals of different sizes and strengths is humorous. But the story may offer a lesson to individuals or organisations facing economic or political challenges. Creative thinking allowed Rat to focus on and achieve his goal. This is the approach that will help us navigate the challenges of the future.

Innovation is no longer a luxury but rather a necessity. The visionaries understand they have no choice but to be creative and innovate. Perhaps we should start to believe in our ability to make our own luck or, more accurately, to create our own opportunities through intentionally creative decision making. It's a lesson that can be well learned from the rat!

Innovation is a necessity, not a luxury

The necessity of human and organisational ingenuity is undisputed. Yet it's not just about sustaining economic growth and supporting the capitalist system for its own sake. There are a myriad important life-changing decisions we can make and actions we can take. All around us there are problems of local, national and international importance — from saving the environment to bringing peace to Afghanistan to ending the scourge of poverty — that are begging for creative solutions. We will be able to draw the solutions that are needed only from individuals and communities committed to the creative thinking process.

Difficult economic times or tough market conditions usually dictate that areas perceived as non-essential 'extras' are the first to go. The individual will forgo the desire to develop in creative ways and simply do the job that brings in the cash. Organisations will slash their discretionary spending to focus on the areas that are considered to be core to their business. In times like these, innovation is considered to be the icing on the cake — a luxury you can afford to support only in times of plenty, when you are seeking ways to get a step ahead of the rest. But the pace of life has changed so much that innovation is actually now a core survival skill — a necessity, not a luxury.

In order simply to stay up with the rest, to avoid being culled by the latest cost-cutting measure, people at all levels need to be able to think and act creatively, and organisations need to live and breathe innovation. In an evolutionary twist, new adaptations must now emerge, not over thousands of years or at least generations, as they once did, but many times in a lifetime. We must be thinking ahead and moving ahead in cleverer and nimbler ways in order to save ourselves from obsolescence.

Take, for example, the trend towards downsizing when times are tough. Sometimes known as 'rightsizing' (after organisations have become overconfident and employed beyond their real needs), the general idea is to take dramatic measures to reduce an 'overweight' or even 'obese' organisation to a healthy and sustainable size. Rather than looking at ways to modify diet and exercise, and to become fitter and more capable through the process (to sustain the metaphor) most organisations will panic and resort to dramatic surgery to slice off the perceived 'excess fat'. However, further down the track the real problems will still be there and are likely to re-emerge like a cancerous growth, with potentially more dangerous consequences. This is quite apart from the fact that the 'amputated body parts'—the people treated as unwelcome surplus—and the remaining body itself will experience deep pain and trauma.

Any team or organisation that needs to 'take off some weight' or 'cut the fat' must ensure it doesn't remove vital limbs that may hold major arteries supporting healthy organisational functioning. It is essential to determine where creative changes can be made and costs can be trimmed without having to resort to major surgical amputation.

Creative thinking and innovation are no longer buzz words for the more adventurous, but are instead recognised as skills and approaches that are fundamental to any proactive organisation strategy. Innovation can be the essential survival tool that enables positive progress. If you fail to innovate, or simply make a token gesture towards it rather than ensuring it is integral to daily functioning, the consequences will soon become clear. All individuals and organisations will need to make sure that innovation is used to build the future and that this is communicated clearly.

We have discovered that in times like these maintaining the status quo—simply working the treadmill with no real goals—is no longer enough. Survival means staying ahead of the pack, no matter what the external pressures. No excuses. Proactive team innovation must be seen as a core competency. What was acceptable last year may not even get you to the start line this year. Before you know it, the lead your organisation may once have enjoyed is as useful as a typing pool in an age of computers. Western Union, for example, started off in the 1800s transferring money on horseback from city to city, but they have managed to constantly adapt to rapidly changing conditions. For more than 100 years they have built on their strengths through drastically adapting the products and services they offer, while maintaining their core values. It is creative thinking that has enabled them to thrive through all the challenges.

'Trimming the fat' is a proactive process that will continue to be necessary to keep the organisation lean and ready for high performance at all times. But sudden reactive cuts, triggered by the fear of a recession or a one-off crisis, only frighten employees, adding to the negative media fear frenzy, and leading to even lower motivation levels and paralysis. How can employees come to work each day ready to give their best when they are uncertain what will become of their jobs or whether their employment conditions will change?

Innovate, don't amputate

Creativity must be fostered as an essential work skill in our contemporary competitive environment. According to brand designer Bruce Haddon, consumers quickly tire of yesterday's innovations, and because rapid change environments constantly demand new ideas, successful organisations must come up with better ideas before their competitors.

A six-star, $1000+ per night hotel company we have worked with shared with us how for years they had enjoyed great success. Without much extra sales and marketing effort, guests simply continued coming through their door. But although they benefited from high occupancy rates and fees, no-one stopped to ask what had made them so successful. It took a crisis and a sudden drastic reduction in business for them to start asking the important questions and to recognise how important it was to *continue* to innovate.

Another company we worked with recently was also stuck with a major problem. This leading machine lubricant producer had a great new product, but its customers weren't using it properly, with detrimental results. It was really a user rather than a product problem, but customers would inevitably blame the product. The best client machines were becoming damaged and breaking down because the users failed to replace the lubricant often enough. As the lubricant aged the machines wore down, and the lubricant company's reputation was in danger of becoming permanently tarnished. Through our 'creative collaboration' team workshop process we encouraged the project team to look for creative solutions. Within a few hours the team came up with a new design for the product that effectively eliminated the user problem. As we took them through the creative thinking process we discovered that the principle of toothbrushes changing colour when they became old could be applied to these machines. The solution was to have the lubricant change colour, or even smell, when it needed to be replaced. The team had produced an outstanding practical solution to a problem that had been very costly both financially and in terms of reputation.

In yet another simple example, an airline saved hundreds of thousands of dollars when their flight attendant team discovered how much caviar was being wasted in first class. They simply designed a new process that reduced this unnecessary waste but still kept the passengers happy.

Alan Nobel, of Google Australia, believes that Google's success can be attributed to innovation. 'Innovation should just be there, it's like the air you breathe—you innovate to survive, there's nothing to systematize, it's just what you do.' It takes a great vision, a clear and focused company culture, and empowering leadership to reach Google's level of success, but you have to start somewhere. You can't simply bet on 'hope' and 'luck' to stay ahead.[2]

The people most likely to have creative ideas are those at the coalface with direct customer contact, as they are the first to recognise what is needed. But those few companies that understand the need for creative development usually start the implementation process from the top levels. At this level, if there is no specific practical focus, creative development can end up as a 'groupthink' exercise in which established ideas are simply reinforced. This process rarely reflects what is really going on in the organisation or reaches the whole organisation.

Trying to be 'better', 'faster' and 'cheaper' without making clear links to the creative process can also be counterproductive or even destructive.[3] NASA found this out the hard way during the ill-fated shuttle disaster of February 2003. The left wing of the shuttle was damaged by debris that had broken off the shuttle on take-off, tearing a hole in the body of the spacecraft. The shuttle exploded when it re-entered the atmosphere. Even though the problem had already been identified by the NASA space team, debris having damaged the shuttle only two launches previously, NASA failed to resolve the issue.[4] In this case, the pressure to keep the space program on track without taking the time to really analyse the problem from all angles led to disaster.

In the introduction we described the destruction of our favourite beach community on the island of Bali. Over a period of time we saw it slowly die, accelerated in the end by a terrorist bombing. The stakeholders in Jimbaran village did not deliberately set out to destroy it, yet it was nonetheless devastated over time. But that is not the end of the story, for the community survives and the people live on. One response was that the local Hindu Balinese priests conducted a major cleansing ceremony. Searching for explanations, they looked at the deeper issues, recognising that the Balinese people as a whole had been seeking short-term gains at the expense of long-term principles.

We have set out to make strong cases for the prosecution of potential creativity murderers, but we know that no-one deliberately sets out to destroy creativity, and our survey suggests the crime scenes are evenly spread across most organisation areas, with no clear single suspect. So moving forward may mean laying down the hatchets, and looking for ways to rescue and reform rather than take revenge. And it may mean looking deep within ourselves to see what principles we may have lost sight of in our race to the future.

We will finish this first section with a story from another part of Indonesia, another beautiful but very remote island beach not yet taken over by tourists. Here the hotel general manager had created a lovely internal environment for his guests, but there were problems with random attacks and thefts from locals in the nearby villages. The staff had to warn guests that they ventured up the beach at their own risk, which must have disconcerted many. People were talking, and negative reports on the travel website TripAdvisor were also discouraging tourists from coming, which meant the marketing department was losing its spin. People who did dare to venture out to the beach too often came back minus their cameras, pale despite the tans they had worked hard to build up that morning, the fear of having been robbed in plain daylight clearly etched on their faces.

But the GM was creative. He knew that the thieves who preyed on tourists had their own personal needs: they needed to have enough to live on and to feed their families. (It must be hard to watch a tourist who casually carries around a camera worth three years' salary while your children go without food.) Understandably the local people were upset that a foreign owner could plonk a hotel in their village and take all the profit elsewhere. They had lost their power and their pride, and now the gap between the haves and have-nots was excruciatingly clear. So some formerly unoffending, peaceful villagers turned to crime. Of course not many of the tourists knew or understood this context—most saw only criminals who ambushed and robbed helpless tourists as soon as they stepped out of the resort.

The manager knew he had to address the real problem, and he decided he could not do this by simply increasing security as other GMs might have done. Instead he met with the villagers to find out what their specific needs were. When he understood their situation better, he came up with what may in hindsight sound like a simple solution (but that's often creativity for you!): to put the same men who had been robbing the tourists in charge of security for the beach, paying them to protect the guests instead of isolating and disempowering them as had been done previously. This gave them a decent income and at the same time gave them back their sense of pride. By making these people feel valued and giving them a purpose, the problem was solved. The once-hostile villagers became a part of the solution, and almost overnight the signs were pulled down and the hotel, its guests and the villagers coexisted in harmony. 'Whenever you can, bury the hatchet with an enemy,' advise Robert Green and Joost Elfers in *The 48 Laws of Power*,[5] 'and make a point of putting him in your service.' Abraham Lincoln also famously said, 'The best way to destroy an enemy…is to make them your friend'.

When you get to the heart of the matter and identify the deeper needs and drives, and when you look for solutions from which everyone can benefit, you can effectively deal with negative influences without resorting to harsh measures and creating enmity. The creativity killers can be dealt with in the same way. With the murderers isolated or reformed, and with the weapons identified and laid aside, people are free to welcome creativity back into their lives and organisations.

Part II

...And how can we get it back?

The forensic lab report

Off-piste innovation and training the brain

Your heart skips more than a beat when you see your precious child strapped tightly to an emergency first-aid snow sled that is shimmying its way down a steep Swiss mountain slope with a first-aid officer at the helm. For a keen snowboarding family it is not uncommon to see these snow sleds, and it is usually a sobering reminder of the inherent dangers of a sport that is just asking for trouble. Think about it. Standing on a highly waxed plank and hurtling at high speeds down the sheer side of a mountain through a white mass of slippery ice crystals has to be crazy!

But this was the closest we had come to thinking that Kallen, then an active 12-year-old, might be critically injured. Our hearts probably simultaneously clunked back into beat when the sled arrived and we saw that our son was smiling. 'That was such a cool ride,' he said. 'Can I do it again?!' In the end the only thing he had suffered that day was sore and battered legs and a bruised ego, but luckily no broken bones. As the story came out little by little we discovered that he had gone 'off-piste', as he loved to do, and had not seen a sudden cliff drop in the afternoon shadows. The paramedics who came to Kallen's aid on the snowfields not only helped him recover physically, they also gave him valuable advice on mountain safety, ensuring that he would thereafter treat wild off-piste runs with respect while enjoying the ride.

Usually the first professionals on the scene of an accident or violent crime, paramedics regularly handle life-or-death situations. Historically, the first known paramedics were probably aging Roman Centurions. No longer fit to fight, they were often required to carry out serious medical procedures, such as suturing wounds and performing amputations, on

117

wounded fighters. The concept of 'triage', which originated in the American Civil War, enabled paramedics to increase the chances of survival of the injured significantly. The principle of triage is to sort patients into three categories, according to the severity of their condition.[1]

Where creativity is the victim, the same principle may be applied. The resuscitation of creativity will need to consider three factors:

- saving individual creative thinking—the first casualty of the crime
- finding team solutions—the conduit for resuscitation
- establishing innovative systems—the life support system for ongoing innovative intervention.

Rather than limiting the rescue process to creativity (that is, the ability to use the imagination to develop new and original ideas or things), we need to take it a further step by reviving creative thinking through giving strategies for ongoing growth. Creative problem solving is the process of devising a solution to an issue, problem, opportunity or a challenge, and this is the natural outcome of creative thinking. As they are outcomes focused, creative thinking and problem solving are not mere navel gazing. They are *productive*. The practical application of the creative thinking process is innovation. But here's the catch: solving school-assigned homework problems or recalling information in training assessments does not usually involve creative problem solving, because such problems typically have well-known solutions, and yet that is exactly how our society has attempted to revive creative thinking.

We let Kallen continue with snowboarding as a sport, naturally with many stern instructions and dire parental warnings, and he went on to compete, even winning a few gold medals and reaching national-level competition. When he progressed to risky jumps and acrobatic tricks, much to our anxiety, he remembered the advice of the paramedics: 'Know what's ahead, travel at a safe speed if you don't know what's ahead, and practise a new move until you know it back to front—until it becomes second nature.' Soon we discovered the most wonderful of all snow-sport inventions that enabled Kallen to do just that. Around this time huge inflatable airbags, designed to catch you gently as you landed after attempted aerial stunts, first came into use. With the aid of one of these bags Kallen could practise and perfect the most outrageous gymnastic aerial contortions, jumping as high as he liked, over and over again, and still land safely on the massive bubble of air.

We have told you this story because we are about to take you on an off-piste adventure. We want to stretch and challenge you in ways you might not have believed possible, and you may well end up feeling completely out of your comfort zone. But don't worry, we have found ways to make it a pleasurable rather than potentially painful experience—and we are introducing the paramedic rescue patrol, which not only will help stitch up any wounds and mend broken spirits experienced in creative thinking battles, but can also provide you with strategies to develop to new levels. After years of experimenting we have found ways to make possible the stretch without risking the snap. We have developed a series of exercises to enable you to practise (safely) until you have built up the skills and confidence to trial the most unlikely of creative experiments and come up with the most fabulous ideas. We can save you from having to take the big (dangerous) risks that might cost you your reputation or cost your company significant amounts of money. In this creative thinking adventure you'll be unlikely to suffer much more than a bit of a shock in the areas of the brain least utilised.

Exercising the brain: stretch, but don't snap

Just as getting to the stage where you can do aerial jumps and tricks on a snowboard requires a lot of disciplined practice, effective creative analysis and innovative development also takes discipline. It is important to mentally prepare for the challenges before embarking on the journey of reviving the creative process. Like many other talents and skills, creativity does not always come quickly or easily; it usually needs to be developed through sheer perseverance and experience. So where to get started with the creative stretch?

There are more than 630 muscles in your body—in fact, on average your body weight comprises 40 per cent muscle. The expression 'move it or lose it!' can be directly applied to muscle fibre. A sarcomere is a segment of a striated muscle fibril, tiny pieces of muscle. If you don't exercise these muscles by contracting and relaxing them, you will in fact lose some 100 sarcomeres a day. Think about the brain as a muscle. Through this book we want to work on brain muscles you may not have used for a long time, perhaps even since childhood. The brain is made up of different areas that approximately correlate with different functions; each has a different purpose, but a well-rounded person uses all parts of their brain.

'Use it or lose it' can also be applied in the context of keeping our minds active. Physically fit people aim to build all their muscle groups then focus on specific areas they would like to develop. Mentally fit people do the same with their brains. Studies in creative thinking show that children with low divergent thinking scores who continue to exercise these creativity 'muscles' can outperform others with higher scores who do not. Einstein said, 'When the mind is stretched by new ideas, it never returns to its original dimensions'—in other words, it grows to accommodate the new capabilities.

Another area of brain research that reveals our capacity for learning creative thinking is the growing evidence that the brain is in fact plastic. Apparently the brain is not completely wired with location-specific neural pathways that are preset according to genetic coding and then established for life. Accumulated research supports the idea that it is possible to 'rewire' the brain at any stage in life to form new and varied connections.[2] The brain has also been found to be plastic enough to allow specific areas to be strengthened and built up over time. This should give us hope that even if we feel we have established ingrained patterns of thinking and habitual ways of perceiving and behaving, we are not stuck with these habits for life.

The good news from neuroscience on brain plasticity, psychotherapist Richard Hill noted in a Creative Skills Training Council Forum (CTSC) discussion,[3] is that 'the human brain has a preference to integrate, socialise and creatively expand', and, even better, 'we are phylogenically organised... to be socially engaged and creatively seeking personal meaning as a default setting, i.e. when all is going well'. It is interesting that decades after Maslow observed these tendencies in human behaviour, neuroscience is starting to provide an empirical base that supports his theories.

For hundreds of years educators have focused on drills and exercises that strengthened brain connections.[4] After the method became unfashionable in the 1960s, when teachers concluded that these approaches were too rigid, many students started to have difficulties with basic reading, writing and numeracy skills. An almost fanatical approach to rote learning, for example of languages (rote learning actually strengthens auditory memory and thinking in languages) and a strong focus on handwriting (which helps to strengthen motor capabilities, and adds speed and fluency to speaking and reading) were abandoned. But the pendulum is now starting to swing back again. A great deal of recent research has gone into identifying the specific connections that can be developed and the benefits of developing these connections. Targeted exercises allow weakened neural links to be strengthened, not unlike the way targeted physical exercises can quickly strengthen specific physical muscles.

What is the impact of specialised brain training? Animals raised in enriched environments (surrounded by other animals, with opportunities to explore and play) have been found to learn better than otherwise identical animals that have not spent time in the same sort of enriched environment.[5] The animals from enriched environments have:

- higher levels of acetycholine, a brain chemical essential for learning
- increased brain weight (5 per cent greater in the cerebral cortex and 9 per cent greater in the area that is targeted for training)

\ 25 per cent more branches of 'trained' neurons with greater size, more connections per neuron and greater blood supply.

Post-mortems have also shown that people who have been educated in specific areas develop a greater number of neural branches, which is linked to a general increase in the volume and thickness of the brain in those particular areas.

To what extent can creative thinking be taught?

So can creative thinking be taught? Is there an environmental basis underlying creative thinking? University of New Mexico neuroscientist Rex Jung believes approximately 40 per cent of our creativity comes from our genetics and 60 per cent from environmental influences.[6] All people, he says, have the capacity for creative thinking, which is influenced by their interactions with the environment. Even if not encouraged at an early age, this capacity can still re-emerge later in life. When the brain is most relaxed and considering a multiple of possibilities—that is when developed creative thinking becomes possible.

HBS professor Teresa Amabile argues, 'One myth about creativity is that it's associated with the particular personality or genius of a person[7]—and in fact, creativity does depend to some extent on the intelligence,[8] expertise, talent, and experience of an individual. Of course it does. But it also depends on creative thinking as a skill that involves qualities such as the propensity to take risks and to turn a problem on its head to get a new perspective. That can be learned'.

Dr Jason points out that creativity has been found to be linked to the following personality variables:

\ intelligence (according to findings from IQ tests)
\ cognitive flexibility (for example, as measured by the Wisconsin card sorting test)
\ extreme perseverance—often to the point of obsession (a personality dimension)

❧ openness to experience/extroversion (according to the Big 5 Inventory)

❧ divergence and fluency (from Guildford's alternative uses test).

Apart from these personality and intelligence dimensions there are, arguably more importantly, a number of environmental factors that can significantly influence creative development. To develop creative thinking you can learn to align the circumstances that best foster it. Rather than trying to induce a lightning strike, developing creativity is more akin to fostering the right opportunities for it to prosper. As Scott Berkun says in *The Myths of Innovation*,[9] if you wait around for a Eureka moment to happen 'you are just going to get bored'!

The challenge of 'being creative' can be intimidating for those who don't feel they are that way inclined. Because we often associate creativity with artistic or musical ability, many people without these talents assume they therefore can't become more creative, yet although everyone is certainly not an artist, everyone can be creative. Creative thinking focuses on changing ideas, perceptions and concepts rather than developing aesthetics or working harder with the same ideas, perceptions and concepts. The good news is that creativity is also a *mindset*. Natural ability does play a part, but a positive attitude and determination can compensate for any lack in this department.

We are all born with creative ability, but many of us have forgotten how to use or apply it. Most research in this field shows that anyone with normal intelligence is capable of creative thinking — what most stifles creativity in us our failure to exercise it.

Michael Michalko[10] identifies the following key characteristics of creators:

❧ Creators have the *intention to create*, and act and speak in a positive and joyful manner.

❧ Creators *look at what is and what can be instead of what is not*. Instead of excluding possibilities, creators consider all possibilities, both real and imagined.

❧ Creators *interpret the world for themselves* and disregard the interpretations of past thinkers. Creators *are creative because they believe they are creative.*

❧ Creators *learn how to look at things in different ways* and use different ways of thinking.

To teach creative thinking, then, we first need to provide the environment for encouraging creative development in these areas. We can, for example, act on the following (which form the basis of our seven strategies):

❧ *Encourage the intention to create.* Make the creative process fun, interesting and relevant, and provide time and dedicated opportunities for creative development.

❧ *Teach optimism and self-belief.* Reveal the thought–patterns that can lead to open rather than closed thinking. Establish a culture in which employees are treated with respect.

❧ *Build confidence and independent thinking.* Provide a platform for creative ideas where all ideas are encouraged and supported, where individuals can feel proud of what they achieve and can learn to present these ideas confidently. Draw on the experience as a learning opportunity, not just a moment to praise or reprimand.

❧ *Show individuals how to see different possibilities.* Utilise exercises that encourage divergent thinking.

The brain workout

Dr Jason argues that 'there is no single creativity nucleus of the brain', but rather that creativity is almost always a very complex task that integrates all of the different brain faculties we use for normal thinking. In our snowboarding example, although people assume the sport involves only the leg muscles, it in fact involves an intricate combination of muscles all over the body—from the neck muscles to the stomach muscles and the arms. Creativity too is a complex, integrated process.

Four modes of creativity identified by neuroscience (see table 5.1) reveal how we can actively develop creative thinking through a 'front to back' system—recognising the need to deliberately develop creativity in the prefrontal cortex, which is capable of conscious thought, and then passing this back to either the cognitive or emotional areas of processing.[11] In fact, simply by being aware of these different processes it is possible to increase access to different ways of solving problems. The model shows that as well as the spontaneous creativity that can occur simply when we are placed in the right environment, we can also deliberately shape the brain to generate creative solutions.[12]

Table 5.1: four modes of creativity

	Cognitive	Emotional
Deliberate	*Deliberate cognitive* *'Left brain'* *Prefrontal cortex (PFC) to temporal parietal occipital (TOP)*	*Deliberate emotional* *'Right brain'* *PFC to limbic structures*
Spontaneous	*Non-conscious processing* *TOP to PFC*	*Non-conscious emotional* *Limbic to PFC*

Target exercises or other interventions can be used to enhance brain functioning in relevant areas and encourage creativity. These can help to establish previously unexplored pathways, strengthen weak pathways and open up new possibilities. In one method that is often used in high-performance training and rehabilitation, for example, an individual is placed in a new situation that mimics the desired outcome. Through this exposure, new connections are formed in the brain that can then be mentally rehearsed to strengthen the neural pathways that will create the opportunity for pattern recognition and support development in that area. Finally actual physical rehearsal can follow. When this approach was used with swimming sports teams, swimmers were dragged through the water at high speeds (faster than they were able to swim themselves). This enabled the swimmers to get the feeling of high-speed movement, in order to stimulate the brain to make the connections needed to simulate this movement, and finally to know how to practise the skills required to reach high speeds in swim racing.

The concept of 'brain training', once thought to be a niche market for people with Alzheimer's or other cognitive problems, is now so popular that 'brain gyms' have become multimillion-dollar businesses. Companies such as Lumosity have designed games and other products to improve brain performance for which there is a universal demand across all demographics. Some 14 million people in more than 180 countries now either subscribe to Lumosity's website or have downloaded its iPhone apps. A market research firm that specifically tracks development in the area of brain 'fitness' predicts that this market will grow to at least $2 billion by 2015.[13]

Rex Jung has concluded that those who diligently practise creative activities learn to recruit their brain's creative networks quicker and better. When this is done over a lifetime, the neurological patterns of the brain are gradually changed. Although tall individuals obviously have an advantage in a game like basketball, it doesn't mean that people who aren't so tall can't train to become very good basketballers. In the same way, naturally creative individuals will have an advantage in creative thinking and may be more likely to develop careers in this area, but that doesn't mean it is not possible for everyone else to develop their creative thinking. As well as areas of brain activity that are innate, there are also specific areas that can be developed, such as convergent thinking and focused attention. The ability to rapidly shift between convergent and divergent thinking is also critical, and the good news is that this too can be learned. Through developing training programs that alternate periods of intense convergent thinking with maximum divergent thinking repeatedly over stages, a number of studies have shown that brain patterns have changed and greater creative thinking capacity has emerged.[14]

Studies of jazz musicians improvising have been particularly interesting in this area. Well-trained musicians are able to deactivate their right temporoparietal junction, which is usually engaged in reading incoming stimuli and sorting it for relevance. By switching this off and therefore blocking out distractions, they are able to achieve superior levels of concentration and therefore work with the music more spontaneously. Other trained individuals who have also shown an ability to shift into this higher gear of concentration include dancers, comedians and orators—and athletes too. Learning to deactivate this part of the brain can therefore help with creative development.

Slowing down for the synaptic fire-up

A number of years ago some family friends of ours were told when their daughter was in kindergarten that she might need special help. She seemed to have difficulty focusing on activities, to be slow in responding and slow in learning. When the other children were busy preparing their equipment at the beginning of the day, their child would be absent-mindedly staring out the window. When other children had finished changing their clothes and were out the door for the morning break, she was still on the floor trying to tie her shoelaces. Naturally her parents were very concerned so they took her off to get proper psychological testing. As it turned out, this child was not intellectually delayed at all—quite the opposite. She had an unusually high IQ. She was, they soon discovered, simply taking time to reflect on and process information at a higher level, ultimately coming up with superior connections and outcomes.

Let's head down to the forensic lab to dissect the brain a little and find out what happens there when we get creative. As groundbreaking new research on the brain continues to emerge, we are learning more and more about the way it processes information, as well as new scientific ways to revive creative thinking. It is increasingly recognised that neural pathways are established early in life, and that the development or lack of development of specific pathways can be critical to our ability in specific areas and to our general intelligence. It has been found that it is possible to deliberately build up the strength and capability of particular neural pathways and in the process increase specific intelligence through training. Since intelligence is arguably about making fast predications, which in brain-speak equates to fast-responding nuclei and well-established neural pathways, such training can increase intelligence in specific areas that may contribute to general IQ. There is, however, another significant newer finding that has come to light recently that appears to run counter to this idea.

As neuroscientists seek to discover the scientific basis for creative thinking, diverse research teams are now finding that slower minds may better nurture more creative ideas.[15] When divergent thinking scores increase, the amount of white matter, myelin, in certain regions of the left frontal cortex actually decreases.[16] This may mean that these people have slower neural transmission, because this white matter is a fatty insulating sheet that wraps around the neurons, enabling the electrical impulse that travels along nerves to move faster. Less myelin means information is transmitted more slowly. The more divergent thinking ability an individual has, the more the 'integrity' of the white matter is found to be reduced. In particular, Rex Jung has discovered that the most creative people have lower white-matter integrity in a region connecting the prefrontal cortex to the thalamus, which lies at a deeper level.[17] It is arguably these distant brain connections that underlie diverse cognitive functions and may support thinking processes that are not specialised and direct, such as creativity.

This experimental finding has given rise to an unexpected idea: although it might be assumed that an efficient-performing brain would enhance creative thinking, it may be that people who have brain synapses that fire *slower* than usual have more of an ability to think creatively. This may be because, in that fraction of a millisecond between the firing of an impulse and the reception of that impulse, the message has the opportunity to make other new connections. In creative thinking, the pathway from one thought to another is not a straight line. This means that highly creative people can not only make original new connections more easily, but are also not limited by the standard approaches. They do not simply fit into established thinking grooves or follow standard pathways.

This theory remains speculative, and there is a lot of contrary evidence that correlates speed of neural transmission with intelligence, and intelligence with increased creativity. On the other hand, Paul Thompson, from the University of California in Los Angeles, argues that the fast transfer of information through the synapses may not be vital for creative thought, as was once expected. He believes that, 'Sheer mental speed might be good for playing chess or doing a Rubik's cube, but you don't necessarily think of writing novels or creating art as being something that requires sheer mental speed'.[18]

So when considering the question of how we can foster creative thinking, perhaps we need to think about how we can help to *slow down* our thinking processes to provide opportunities for new synaptic connections to occur. Which probably means we need to start to slow down our lives.

Triggering the brain's 'on/off' switch

If you couple these interesting new theories with something that has been long known—that stress can 'shut down' or 'switch off' significant areas of the brain so they can no longer effectively be accessed—it becomes clear that inducing a relaxed state is critical for encouraging creative thinking. It is important to be able to access deeper and broader levels of the brain, from the hippocampus through to the prefrontal cortex. The more relaxed the individual, and the more 'open' the mind, the more easily these broader connections can be made. In effect, it enables conscious awareness to be freed from pressing and direct tasks to more open and divergent thinking.[19]

The brain appears to be capable of temporarily shutting down connections where there is significant stress, as often happens after a trauma when there is short-term or long-term memory loss, perhaps to reduce pain and ultimately protect the individual. Some have argued that this is an atavistic trait that is, for example, highly functional in animals when they are being eaten! Have you ever noticed that at the moment a gazelle starts to be eaten by a lion it appears to give up the struggle and become quite calm, with a glazed look in its eye? It may be that by entering a dissociative state, the animal can escape the pain and horror. Not that we recommend this brain state for productive work, even if there is creativity murderer lurking in the hall!

Equally, it seems, stress can shut down an individual's receptiveness and openness to learning. This can be especially significant for creative thinking, which requires a relaxed state, the ability to think through options at a slow pace and the openness to explore different alternatives without fear. As Richard Hill points out, when someone suffers stress or trauma, the brain shuts down the social and personal meaning systems that affect creative thinking in order to help focus brain resources.[20]

There appears to be a specific gene that enables us to be more relaxed under stress and more able to cope with the potential impact of stress through creating more cells in the hippocampus. This gene can be 'switched off' early in life when there are stifling environmental factors. It has been shown that where stress has reduced a specific protein — the brain-derived neurotropic factor (BDNF) — neurons in some parts of the hippocampus shrink and the hippocampus as a whole decreases in volume. Because the hippocampus plays a key role in mood, cognition and memory, stress is obviously detrimental to the development of creative thinking. Interestingly, one study showed that baby rats are born with this gene already switched off, perhaps as a protective mechanism, and the gene is triggered only when the baby is nurtured by its mother through grooming and feeding.[21]

To encourage creative thinking, then, it is important that there is no undue external stress and/or that effective mechanisms for coping with stress are in place. This ensures that the areas of the brain that access personal meaning are engaged, and the individual flourishes.

New paths to superior thinking

Just as Kallen learned to carve out fresh new paths across the untracked snow, so all individuals can learn to develop creative new ideas that stretch and challenge them. And just as he needed the discipline to practise his new skills while he taught himself to jump and spin, so you too can practise using the strategies that will lead to superior creative thinking. The following rescue principles and strategies will set out the simple steps you will need to take, and the exercises we introduce will ensure you have that big inflatable bag to launch into as you try out your new aerodynamically challenging or brain-stretching moves. This will save you from embarrassing yourself in the process — and possibly even help to protect you from making that million-dollar mistake!

How can creativity be saved?

Profile of a paramedic: the seven creative thinking strategies

We were with a group of 'at risk' school students, on a government-funded wilderness expedition that would, we hoped, help them get their lives back on track. The most troubled of them had run afoul of the law; for others their families had given up hope. This was a rescue mission for many of these boys—the last stop on a long road that had been leading to almost certain destruction. The expedition involved taking them into the wilds, far from all their regular negative influences, and allowing them to learn the consequences of their behaviours. It was a tough trip: the boys ended up having to camp on the side of a cliff when their navigation skills went awry, and they had to eat cold food scraped out of cans when they wasted rations in a food fight and got their matches damp in the process. They often had to set up camp in the dark, battle inhospitable terrain and deal with unfamiliar wildlife.

The biggest and final challenge of the trip was to be a long abseil, a 400-metre drop down a massive cliff. There was only one way to get out of the wilderness, and it involved scaling that cliff, but even the most intrepid of expeditioners would have been terrified by this precipice and the sheer drop to the distant valley floor below. The night before the students were to take the big plunge we took 10 of them across to the other side of the valley to view the challenge they would face the next day. As the sun set over the mountains, casting a rugged shadow across the valley, we looked over in awe to what was actually the biggest abseil in Australia, Mt Banks. Silence fell over the group of students as they contemplated dropping off the overhang. Although we had been preparing for and

131

building up to this final challenge all year, all the students, even the toughest of them, went pale at the sight of the steep cliff face.

Fiery red-haired Jack was the first to ask what was on everyone's mind: '*%#@! How do we get down this f---ing drop? We don't even have a rope that's 400 metres long, do we?' 'Yeah,' agreed Robert. 'We couldn't carry a 400-metre rope — it'd be too heavy.' 'What other choice do we have?' countered Dennis. 'It's the only way out.'

As evening descended on the valley, spirits sank and a deathly fear fell over the whole group, almost paralysing in its grip. Most students crouched on the edge of the cliff and grappled with the fear of the unknown, trying to imagine what they would be doing and how they would be feeling in 12 hours' time.

The only way to get these kids down this mountain would be in small, achievable steps. Robert was right, we didn't have a 400-metre rope, but what the students didn't know at that time was that we wouldn't actually need it. What we did have in our supplies were two 50-metre ropes that we could use to make the descent, one pitch at a time. What it was not possible to see from a distance was that the sheer cliff face actually had several levels of ledges that could be used as separate pitch points as we descended. These students had already successfully completed numerous 55-metre abseils, so it would be a matter of helping them understand that they need face the challenge only one step at a time, in manageable stages. Looking at the whole mountain, the students believed the task was impossible, but when the process was broken down they began to believe they could do it.

The next morning every student took the plunge. The first few were lucky as the fog had not cleared, so they dropped into cloud without being confronted by the scale of the drop, but when the cloud disappeared and the full pitch was revealed it took far more coaching from us to prepare the children psychologically. We finally got them all over the top, and eight hours (and seven pitches) later, all had reached the valley floor without incident.

Once they found they could break the problem down, we were able to help them to see how they could apply that principle to other parts of their life, including dealing with problems at school. Suddenly the paralysing fear of the apparently impossible had gone, and a whole new world of possibilities was opened up for them. Many of these students were dramatically changed by that moment, discovering a new confidence that they could face whatever challenges came their way. They saw the world from a new perspective.

No matter how creatively challenged people may feel, or how much damage the creativity killers have already wreaked, it is possible to achieve the apparently unachievable and to rescue creative thinking. Some individuals and organisations find the process hard to get started; others start off enthusiastically but then feel overwhelmed or get stuck somewhere along the way. The more this happens, the less optimistic and persistent they become. We have found it's better to break the process down to make the jump easier, providing people with clear, incremental steps they can take. Even then some become impatient and try to skip crucial steps, and as a result fail to reach the solution they'd hoped for.

When you go 'off-piste'—or take a leap off a mountain!—there may not be a clear path for you to take. But no matter how challenging the terrain, with the right skills, equipment and planning, you can be ready to face anything, one step at a time. The process we will share in these next sections should help you to explore pathways to creative development in a way that provides specific practical and useful outcomes. We have broken the process down into seven strategies so you can confidently take one pitch at a time.

Creativity starts with the individual, but individuals often don't allow their creativity to develop. Time pressures, deadlines, an unsupportive environment, fear of failure and bureaucracy can all paralyse creativity. What threatens it most, however, is lack of exercise. Because you are in control of your life, you can actively develop your creativity. When was the last time you actually set aside some time to try something creative?

Once there is individual buy-in and commitment to creative development, there can then be organisational change. People who don't think they need to be creative will stifle creativity in a team, allowing the organisation to chug along inefficiently.

133

A lack of individual creative competence will also inhibit customers' requests, which will prompt them to go elsewhere. Customers and clients (internal and external) will innovate with or without your organisation, so you will need to proactively pursue creative development opportunities to stay ahead.

Developing creativity involves taking on a new thinking style. There are many different ways you can practise this style and release your creative potential. Just as there are four stages of degeneration in the death of creative thinking, there are four corresponding stages of regeneration we have identified as necessary in the rescue process:

⟩ Stage 1: liberation
⟩ Stage 2: initiation
⟩ Stage 3: motivation
⟩ Stage 4: transformation.

There are then seven strategies we recommend to assist with the rescue process (as illustrated in table 6.1):

Table 6.1: the Creative Thinking Life Cycle Model™ — the regeneration of creativity

RESCUING CREATIVE THINKING: the stages of regeneration		
	Rescue process	Rescue strategy
Stage 1	**Liberation** *The FREEDOM and COURAGE to step out and think freely*	
	Freedom	1 Cultivate curiosity.
	Courage	2 Accept ambiguity.
Stage 2	**Initiation** *The INDEPENDENCE and OPENNESS to let go and grow*	
	Independence	3 Unleash the imagination.
	Openness	4 Access all parts of the brain.
Stage 3	**Motivation** *The PASSION to drive transformation*	
	Passion	5 Reconstruct common concepts.

Stage 4	Transformation	
	The FLEXIBILITY and POSITIVITY to make real changes	
	Flexibility	6 Explore different paths.
	Positivity	7 Embrace optimism.

Stage 1: liberation — the freedom and courage to step out and think freely

The first stage of the rescue process provides the platform for potential creative growth. It recognises the need for **freedom**, which opens up thinking in readiness for accepting new possibilities, and **courage**, which is the launch pad for stepping out on the intrepid journey.

Rescuer profile 1: freedom

This probing pioneer creates a mental state in which it is possible to feel safe and secure and to explore ideas without restrictions. Freedom encourages humble leadership and accessible work environments. It is a profile that is not restricted by preconceived ideas or concepts and is able to unlock challenges and open up possibilities. As a rescuer, freedom is ready to face any challenge at any time. Constantly finding new paths, and travelling cross country rather than on the beaten track, freedom is extremely resourceful and self-sufficient. It always wants to see what's around the next bend, over the next mountain, beyond the next deadline, over the new horizon. The preferred rescue strategy of the pioneer is to *cultivate curiosity*. Freedom helps

135

rescue you from control murder suspects whose main weapon is *crushing coercion*.

Consider Jason Kilar, who is not your typical CEO. Rather than enjoying the benefits that his status could provide or flaunting his power, he goes to considerable lengths to communicate modesty and humility. Instead of taking the grand corner office with the best view, Kilar is out with everyone else, sitting at a desk made partly from empty boxes. He takes a personal interest in all his new employees, taking them out to lunch to get to know them better and to find out from them what they would like to see happening in the organisation.

Writer and educator Gregory Ferenstein describes this revolutionary new approach to organisational structure that supports innovation, and explains the ideas this company and others like it have introduced. He explains how, as CEO of the multimillion-dollar video streaming giant Hulu,[1] Kilar is taking some unorthodox steps. In his position he would have the right to enjoy the benefits of success, yet he sees a very important principle at stake here. He believes, 'You will not attract and retain the world's best builders in a command-and-control environment'. Andrew Mason, CEO of the similarly successful internet phenomenon Groupon, explains this concept further: 'We assume that people are fundamentally good and people are responsible adults. The policies we have reflect those beliefs.' Most organisations focus on setting up rules and regulations to deal with difficult employees, but Mason says, 'The cost of creating bureaucracy and red tape that assumes the other 90 per cent of people are also bad is creating rules that encourage people to live up to the edge of those rules ... Because the company is not showing them the respect and autonomy to get the work done in the way that they know it will actually get done, they're treating the company with the same lack of respect'. Ferenstein explains that in these companies:

 ⹋ Sales agents have access to real financial progress data so they can craft their own sales strategies rather than being set external targets.

136

✝ Employees work and sit together at interconnected desks of threes and fours, which removes the need for close managerial supervision and encourages ongoing discussion and open sharing of information.

It's not surprising that Hulu and Groupon have both recently received awards for their exceptional commitment to workplace empowerment. (Pioneers of this empowering leadership style, which ensures freedom in the organisation, are the twentieth-century union movement and the Kibbutzim in Israel. Ricardo Semler introduced the concept of self-set salaries and employees voting for new managers nearly 30 years ago.)

Creating freedom in the organisation should not involve simply a superficial makeover; it needs to be built up from the foundations. Through establishing flatter management structures that help everyone to feel they have the potential to create, through establishing models of modest leadership, and through designing more accessible work environments that give the opportunity for employees to connect and collaborate, the kind of freedom that supports collaboration can be established. When it is, we'll see more CEOs mixing with those who will ultimately make the difference in the organisation.

As we've discussed, children (and animals) who do not 'free play' when they are young can grow into anxious, socially maladjusted adults.[2] Free play is an essential conduit to divert brain resources from dealing with the primitive survival functions so they can access creative thinking. If creative thinking is not exercised regularly, strong pathways in the brain cannot be established, and the ability to think creatively can actually wither. People who have enjoyed free play from an early age are better prepared to develop the creative confidence needed to thrive in later life.

Rather than allowing authoritarian, mafia-style management to take over, freedom creates opportunities for all to be empowered and to thrive. In contrast to the controlling bully boss and his weapon of choice, coercion, the guiding or facilitating leader who is able to encourage and bring out the expertise, confidence and creativity in others is increasingly valued.

Rescue strategy 1: cultivate curiosity

The important and difficult job is never to find the right answers,
it is to find the right question.

Peter Drucker[3]

The terminal at Denpasar International Airport in Bali is an unusual architectural building, and sadly we are not using the word 'unusual' here in a positive way. The airport sits at the northern end of Jimbaran Bay, just far enough away from the smoky seafood cafes, the runway jutting out between two crystal-clear blue lagoons with white sandy beaches. A single small wire fence separates the famous rolling surf of tourist hotspot Kuta on one side and the quieter cove of Jimbaran on the other. Most of Bali's 2.75 million tourists pass through this airport twice — either looking forward to their tropical beach holiday or looking back fondly on memories of their experiences. It's a beautiful waterfront setting. The roof (if you could get to it) would offer 360-degree views of the spectacular island beach vistas. There's just one big problem, though: the long queues and interminable waits (up to three hours) see travellers locked in a rather dull room with bright lights and expensive shops, and almost no chance of enjoying the major assets of the site. Apart from a few small windows that look out onto the runway tarmac rather than the open panorama on either side of it, the airport is completely walled in. The architect evidently failed to ask questions that would have produced creative solutions on how to take advantage of this prime location.

When architects design buildings, says former architect Lloyd Irwin, first they need to go to the site and ask questions to open up its creative possibilities. Questions should include:

ᚷ What is special about this site?
ᚷ What does the site need/cry out for?
ᚷ What response does it demand from me/the building?

It seems unlikely that the Denpasar airport architects asked these questions when designing their building.

The architect of the famous Sydney Opera House won an international competition launched in 1955 because he answered these questions most completely. To Jørn Utzon, the site was saying two things that produced revolutionary creativity:

⟨ *Sails*. The waterfront location, great weather and popularity of sailing on the harbour inspired this symbol.

⟨ *The fifth elevation*. Given the city-front location, Utzon was aware that the building would be viewed from above (from skyscrapers) as much as from the side, so he used the term 'fifth elevation' to describe the view of the roof, which needed to be as beautiful as the other four elevations.

Answering questions of design, location and purpose led to the famous sails solution — and an iconic building of creative genius.

The brain is innately creative and curious. Illusions work only because the brain will fill in the gaps to 'create' reality. It is up to us to unlock this capability, and the best way to do so is through learning to ask questions. A questioning mind stimulates curiosity, and curiosity fosters the desire to make new discoveries. The creative process can be triggered only by an insatiable appetite to explore and discover — an open and innocent curiosity. But this first step in the creative development process is often hampered by the inability to get past established assumptions and practices.

Geoffrey West (whom we encountered earlier in relation to his work on innovation in cities) spent most of his career studying high-energy physics, grappling with concepts such as quarks, dark matter and string theory. He started to get interested in the application of physical principles to the biological and social sciences around 15 years ago, and he was able to introduce some fascinating new concepts through asking critical questions such as: Why is it that human beings live around the order of a hundred years? Why don't they live a thousand years, ten years or a million years? Where does that number come from? What is the mechanism of aging?[4] Asking questions such as these opened up a whole range of new possibilities. This first step of *cultivating curiosity* is essential because we usually don't see the world we live in as it actually is, but rather as we think it is. We see reality based on a set of:

\ assumptions
\ beliefs
\ experiences
\ prejudices.

These constitute our worldview, colouring or distorting what we see. Organisations (and societies) tend to have a collective worldview that the majority of its members buy into. To be creative is to see beyond this worldview, and the first significant creative tool is targeted questioning. As George Bernard Shaw famously said, there is a big difference between seeing things as they are and asking 'Why?' and dreaming things as they never were and asking 'What If?' By focusing on how you can disrupt familiar patterns or current systems, you can find completely new and creative solutions.[5]

Understand: the power of curiosity

Asking good questions is a learned competency based on motivation, know-how and experience.[6] We need to learn to ask even 'dumb' questions that come from a desire to search for possible solutions, rather than from expectation. If creativity originates with a question, then the art of asking 'dumb' questions can lead to enhanced creativity. Sadly, as we move from childhood to adult status we stop asking questions and start wanting to provide answers.

Simply acting based on assumptions can be detrimental to creative problem solving. The aviation industry provides an interesting example of how this can happen. On 24 August 2001 an Air Transat flight en route from Toronto to Lisbon in a one-year-old Airbus A330 got into difficulties. A warning light indicated the plane was losing fuel fast. The captain, who knew it was a new plane, assumed it was simply a computer glitch. Later in the flight another warning light indicated a fuel imbalance between the two fuel tanks. The captain opened the crossfeed valve to transfer fuel from the full tank to the empty one, but the empty tank had a hole so the fuel was simply draining out into the air. Suddenly the plane ran out of fuel. Luckily, because of congestion over North America the plane had been rerouted southwards, so that it was now within gliding distance of the Azores, where the pilot guided it to a safe crashlanding without engines. If, however, instead of making assumptions, the pilot had been more curious about the warning lights and had opened himself up to other possibilities, the potentially disastrous incident might have been avoided.

Surveys of more than 3000 executives and 500 other individuals into what has become known as the 'Innovator's DNA' have identified questioning as one of the five key 'discovery skills' that separate true innovators from others.[7][8]

Creativity enables people to:

↘ *Consider different alternatives.* Pierre Omidyar (eBay) talks about how at meetings he pushes people to justify themselves by asking curly questions and playing devil's advocate. Being forced to imagine different alternatives can lead to truly original ideas.[9]

↘ *Create constraints for thinking and open up imagining.* Great questions actively impose constraints on our thinking, which can, curiously, serve as a catalyst for out-of-the-box insights. One of Google's key principles is 'Creativity loves constraints'. This includes utilising 'what if?' scenarios. Many people spend too much time trying to understand how to make an existing process work better; innovators are more likely to challenge the assumptions behind the process.

Unlock: the potential of curiosity through questioning

Questions put us into a ready-to-learn state of mind by stimulating curiosity. When you pose a question you give your mind a target. Asking questions is a powerful way to tap into your creative talents. They can open up possibilities and if used well can also provide focus and direction for creative problem solving. Open-ended questions force people to think beyond their established beliefs and assumptions. A common problem is that people want to jump straight to the answers without considering what they are really looking for. It's almost as though they are too afraid to ask the question if they don't already know the answer—so they don't ask. The important thing to remember here is that the first step is simply to *ask the question*; you don't need all the answers—yet. To ask 'why?'/ 'why not?' and 'what if', for example, can get us thinking beyond the immediate apparent restrictions and open up the realm of the possible.

Next time you have an issue that needs to be resolved, first ask *who? what? how? why? why not? what if?* Perhaps the architects of the Denpasar airport terminal approached the design in purely practical terms—as a processing centre for embarking and disembarking air passengers. No-one provoked them to ask questions beyond this.

When Rembrandt's famous painting *The Nightwatchman* was restored and returned to Amsterdam's Rijksmuseum, the curators performed a simple yet remarkable experiment. They asked visitors to submit questions about the painting. They then prepared answers, and placed the questions and answers on the wall outside the room in which the painting was displayed. As a result, they discovered, the average length of time that visitors spent viewing the painting increased from 6 minutes to 30 minutes.[10] People reported that the questions encouraged them to look longer, look more closely and remember more. Questions can produce dramatic results by:

❯ giving the mind something to aim for
❯ putting the mind in a 'ready to learn' state
❯ helping the mind to focus.

Despite undergoing several large-scale renovations and expansions, Bali airport still ignores the view. Perhaps, to make the wait a little less painful, the tourists should be given the opportunity to write a few questions to post to the architects who designed the 2.5/5 rated airport![11]

Practise: the technique of questioning

Don't simply decide: It is not possible for us to become more creative. Go deeper to challenge the assumptions. Ask questions that will open up possibilities, such as:

❯ *Who* is affected by a lack of creativity?

❯ *Who* should be responsible for bringing creativity into the organisation?

❯ *What* difference might creativity make in our workplace?

❯ *What if* we were to encourage everyone in the organisation to be a part of the creative development process?

❯ *What* can we do to change the status quo and bring in fresh ideas?

❯ *Why* consider different options?

❯ *How* can creative new ideas and approaches help me/ my team?

❯ *How* can we take action?

Apply: cultivating curiosity

Next time you have an issue that needs to be resolved ask *who? what? how? why?*…For example:

❯ *Who* is affected by the issue? Who can take action?

❯ *What* are the issues? What can be done to address the issues?

❯ *Why* consider different options?

❯ *How* can actions make a difference? How can action be taken?

See how creative you can be with solutions!

Rescue strategy summary

\ Build an environment that encourages freedom of thought.

\ Develop a mindset that is open to exploration.

\ Ask questions without expecting specific outcomes or solutions.

Rescuer profile 2: courage

This calm affirmer brings back self-belief. Closely related to confidence, courage helps to deal with fear and neutralise 'fight, flight or freeze' responses to fear. The rescuer creates a positive linguistic environment that allows creative ideas to flow, and a positive emotional state that encourages the launching of daring quests. With no interest in limiting ideas and options to 'black' and 'white', but instead readily accepting many shades of grey, courage stimulates new options and possibilities. Courage's preferred rescue strategy is to accept ambiguity. It rescues from fear murderers such as fear of failure, fear of risk and fear of the unknown, whose weapon of choice is *drowning dread*.

Have you ever wondered why people like to get tattoos? It is believed that tattoos were originally a way for men to demonstrate their capacity to face fear. Such capacity would have given them an evolutionary advantage, as breeding females would have favoured a mate who was strong and bold enough to protect them. Having a tattoo carved into your body with stone or shell would have been a painful and potentially dangerous undertaking. It demonstrated both a tolerance to pain and physical health, so tattooed people were advertising their prowess and vigour.

Similar signals of courage and vitality are seen in the animal kingdom. In many species, adults will form a defensive circle to protect their young from stronger predators. Gazelles will often leap into the air when escaping from lions. The peacock must carry around that ridiculously large tail simply to impress a potential mate.[12]

Rather than such exhibitionist expressions, the kind of courage that helps to save creative thinking is an affirming self-belief that challenges and neutralises fear. Consider again the types of creativity-threatening fear already discussed — fear of the unknown, fear of taking risks and fear of failure. To face the first requires the building of self-belief. The last two fears are in many cases quite understandable. Think about a banking institution, for example, where the wrong decision on a risk could cost the organisation a lot of money — and the individual concerned his or her job! Self-belief alone is not enough in this situation; it will require a combination of self-belief and cautious care.

We've worked with some very conservative Swiss banks over the years, and we usually find in our workshops that creative thinking is one of the last things they want to hear about from us. Being responsible for other people's money is in the forefront of their minds, and that requires a conservative approach. There were harsh lessons learned during the global financial crisis, the fear of taking risks and the fear of failure among them. The country CEO of one insurance company we have worked with believes that insurance companies need to be very careful when they talk about being creative. 'Our company has survived for over a hundred years by being conservative, finding systems that work and sticking with them.' So when introducing creative thinking to a company that depends on conservative reliability you need to tread carefully. Risking failure in this context can be too spectacular.

For Tim Harford, the way to ensure failure is not catastrophic when trying something new is to introduce it on a scale that means failure would be survivable.[13] Learn from your mistakes, and by requesting feedback along the way you can monitor the process. Harford believes that in most cases failure is a price worth paying. We don't expect every lottery ticket to win, but we have to buy one if we want an opportunity to win at all. Research and development is not simply a redistribution of resources, like the lottery. It can generate improvements that make everyone better off in the long run, so it's an area in which it's worth taking risks. Statistically, the chances are skewed towards eventual success, since a lot of small failures will often lead to a few considerable successes.[14] The general manager of the IT company who had refused to acknowledge the value of new ideas failed to recognise that although most ideas would be likely to fail if actually implemented, the one or two ideas that succeeded would make the effort worthwhile. This GM was not prepared to 'fumble forward' in a constructive way, and so shut down his team's creativity in the process.

Many ideas and projects will falter when there is a fear of ambiguity, when fear of the unknown prompts resistance to ideas that do not fit standard expectations. Openness and trust need to be developed in order for creativity to grow.

Individuals report that in ideal school and workplace environments three key qualities stand out[15]:

- Teachers/leaders respect me.
- Teachers/leaders are friendly, approachable and willing to listen.
- Teachers/leaders encourage me and help me to succeed.

Surveys by the Gallup organisation have also found that the best leaders create an environment in which people feel they can build trust and develop solid relationships. Such an environment provides individuals with the opportunity to take risks with learning and to develop in a safe and accepting context. Rather than being restrained by fear, individuals who have been listened to and accepted develop resilience and are therefore willing to take more risks. They are able to accept ambiguity rather than being afraid of apparent contradiction.

Roosevelt had the courage to lead his nation through a world war despite his considerable disability. He insisted that 'there is nothing to fear but fear itself'. Inspired by this example of calm confidence, we can surely face the fears that hold back our creativity and let it flourish.

Rescue strategy 2: accept ambiguity

At the end of day one the organisers of the conference we were assisting with were very upset. The day's keynote speakers had passed each other at changeover time without so much as a nod, one arriving at the podium as the other left. They certainly hadn't taken the time to discuss the perspective each would offer and to coordinate their approaches. Without realising he was doing so, the second keynote speaker began to pull apart everything the first speaker had said. So the day's two keynote speakers had completely contradicted each other, and the organisers thought it made them look bad. As it turned out, though, the apparent contradictions had a positive benefit. Instead of just being 'empty vessels' waiting to be filled, audience members now had to think through the two opposing approaches for themselves and come to their own conclusions. Imagine having to actually think independently at a conference presentation—heaven forbid!

Encouraging diverse, even opposing, opinions and ideas can help the creative process. Being spoon-fed homogeneous opinions and ideas does little for our creativity. Listening to lectures or attending seminars, many people (victims of a poor education system) simply 'bank' the useful information ready to withdraw later if useful. But it's hard to be creative if there is no *reason* to be creative—that is, if we don't see the need to search for new solutions or find new answers.

Paulo Freire argued that reality is an always changing, transitory process with dialogue and critical thinking at its heart.[16] Reality is not static, compartmentalised or predictable, even though some education systems may make it seem so. Freire's key message to educators was to be wary of encouraging the 'banking' of information, by which passive learners have preselected, predefined knowledge deposited into their minds. Freire also saw the danger that people's creativity could be stifled by what he called 'the Culture of Silence', in which individuals lose the means to respond critically to the ideas that are forced on them by the dominant culture. An opposing or oppositional response that struggles with ambiguities is, he believed, at the heart of freedom of expression and free thought. For example, research has shown that in the most successful boards (boards that accept the 'paradoxical pairings ambiguity brings with it'), 'constructive critical dialogue is the single best indicator of board effectiveness'.[17]

Research suggests that highly creative adults have usually been raised in families embodying opposites. 'Parents encouraged uniqueness, yet provided stability. They were highly responsive to kids' needs, yet challenged kids to develop skills. This resulted in a sort of adaptability: in times of anxiousness, clear rules could reduce chaos—yet when kids were bored, they could seek change, too. The space between anxiety and boredom was where creativity flourished.'[18]

Understand: the power of ambiguity

The second approach to individual creative development emphasises the need to accept ambiguities and deal with them, rather than seeing issues in terms of simple black and white and closing off all possibilities when it seems there is no clear option. Remember that accepting ambiguities was listed as one of the keys to successful leadership in innovation and a foundation for creative thinking. Ambiguity can relate to an uncertainty about meaning or application. It can be seeing things that aren't always visible, or even there at all, which can then lead to creative ideas. People like certainty because it's safe, but accepting ambiguity is all about embracing uncertainty.

Jim Collins believes we should embrace 'the genius of the *and*'.[19] We must be able to embrace seemingly opposing extremes on a number of dimensions at the same time. This requires an open, innocent mind—and a whole lot of courage to stand up against the fear that kills flexibility.

Creative leaders don't fear ambiguity; they use courage to learn how to utilise it. The new leadership models are not static but dynamic. The new leader is flexible, adapting readily to rapidly changing needs and demands. Leaders can become limited by their language and lose the ability to approach and resolve important issues creatively. The secret is learning to embrace ambiguity. Many leaders find this difficult. They think they should lead with strong, decisive, unambiguous decisions, but they fail to recognise that before good decisions can be made all options need to be considered carefully. This requires creative lateral thinking, outside of current language norms. Peter Senge[20] believes management teams tend to confront complex, dynamic realities with a language designed for simple problems. It is time, he says, to think and act more creatively as leaders. Creative thinking happens only when people learn to think outside given parameters, when there is a linguistic environment that allows creative ideas to flow.

Unlock: the potential of ambiguity

Few creative ideas are right first time. In fact, innovators have only a 10 per cent chance of starting with the right strategy. What makes the difference in creative organisations is that they start anyway, even before all the pieces are in place. In business it is better to be 'fumbling forward' creatively than not to be moving at all. If we want to function creatively, it often means complete solutions will be unavailable. For example, where others sat back waiting to be sure, Google moved forward to test and rethink their strategy three times before landing on the successful one that drives their business today. Moving forward with creative ideas before there is full certainty means it will be important to face and deal with ambiguity along the way.

We need to encourage dualistic thinking. The most successful leaders are integrative thinkers—that is, they can hold in their heads two opposing ideas at once and then come up with a new idea that contains elements of each but is superior to both. This is the process of analysis and synthesis (rather than superior strategy or faultless execution). They promote multidimensional, nonlinear relationships. They resolve the tension between opposing ideas by generating new alternatives.[21]

When the conference organiser told us that having his two keynote speakers disagree on the same topic was the worst thing that had ever happened in his event-organising career, we smiled. In fact, we were impressed that the speakers had had the courage to express opposing ideas, and the audience had been given a chance to think for themselves. Bring on ambiguity!

Practise: the technique of ambiguous thinking

To use ambiguity as a creative tool you must allow for extremes *on a number of different dimensions* at the same time and learn to synthesise apparently incompatible opposites. Instead of choosing A *or* B, think of how it might be possible to have A *and* B — for example:

ƛ purpose *and* profit

ƛ continuity *and* change

ƛ freedom *and* responsibility

ƛ strength *and* sensitivity

ƛ brains *and* brawn

ƛ drive *and* empathy

ƛ cohesion *and* cognitive conflict

ƛ trust *and* distrust

ƛ independence *and* involvement

ƛ distance *and* closeness

ƛ creativity *and* criticality.

Try this exercise: You are driving along in your car on a wild, stormy night. You pass a bus stop, and you see three people waiting for the bus:

ƛ an old lady who looks as though she is about to die

ƛ an old friend who once saved your life

ƛ the perfect man or woman you have been dreaming about.

Which one would you choose to offer a ride to, knowing you could take only one passenger? You could pick up the old lady because she is closest to death, and thus you could be confident of saving her life. Or you could take your old friend because you owe him and this would be the perfect chance to pay him back. Then again, you might never find your perfect dream lover again...

Apply: to accept ambiguity

Think of two issues that seem to have only either/or solutions and come up with creative ways to allow for both possibilities. The moral dilemma above was actually once used as part of a job application. The successful candidate who was hired (out of 200 applicants) had no trouble coming up with his solution: 'I would give the car keys to my old friend and let him take the old lady to the hospital. Then I would stay behind and wait for the bus with the woman of my dreams.' This answer illustrates how it is possible to come up with creative solutions when ambiguities are accepted and possibilities are not closed off.

Rescue strategy summary

\ Have the courage to face fears of possible failure and uncertainty.

\ Learn to accept and embrace apparently opposing ideas to open up new possibilities.

Stage 2: initiation — the independence and openness to let go and grow

The second stage of the rescue process involves release from pressure and expectation and opening up to growth. It includes **independence**, which frees up the mind to anticipate numerous possibilities, and **openness**, which ensures different perspectives are considered.

Rescuer profile 3: independence

This imaginative liberator offers an objective view of any situation. Independence provides the opportunity for a calmer, non-emotive reflection on thoughts and actions. Independence has a free will that enables it to open up to any number of possibilities without restriction or judgement. It also brings perspective on who really has control by being able to shut out the many high-pressure murderers. Independence's preferred rescue strategy is to unleash the imagination. It rescues from pressure murderers excess stress, multi-tasking and expectations, whose weapon of choice is *strangling stress*.

One of the ultimate tests of courage is the courage needed when facing pressure. In these situations you need to remember that you have free choice, and you can call on Independence to help you through. No matter how powerless or trapped we may feel by pressure, we actually have the means to decide that enough is enough. The insatiable appetite for more and more stress in contemporary life needs to be challenged and confronted head on. Independence enables individuals to recognise the strangling bonds that have held them back and to find ways to release these. It provides an objective view of the situation and gives the opportunity for calm reflection on thoughts and actions.

The first step Independence needs to take is away from constant 'busy-ness' and towards taking 'time out'. Time out can help give perspective, so you can more easily set priorities, assessing which expectations are realistic and which unrealistic. It will also provide the physical, mental and emotional break your body desperately needs. This helps to establish the foundations for learning and creating. An unexpected win to taking time out is that it involves an ambiguity: you can take time out *and* arrive at innovative solutions. This happens because when we take a break from a situation, our brains often keep working on problems through non-conscious processing. Everyone has had the experience of leaving work with a pressing issue unresolved, only to be overtaken by an 'a-ha!' moment during the night, when no longer thinking about the problem. This is the result of non-conscious processing.

What's even more interesting is that it appears that highly creative people are able to utilise non-conscious processing of innovative ideas more than others, and this is what distinguishes them from the pack. Dr Jason found that after a break people came up with more divergent solutions than when working continuously on a problem, and also, in a related experiment, that highly creative people utilise this non-conscious processing time more effectively than others do. A moment's reflection makes it clear that we are consciously aware of only so much at any one time, yet we are able to do many things automatically. For instance, you can drive a car and hold a conversation with a passenger at the same time. So when you are really focused on a work problem, what is happening with the parts of your brain that encode emotion, abstract thinking and visual imagery, for example? Brain scans show they are still active, and in a lot of respects they are doing what they always do; they simply don't have access to your conscious awareness. The bottom line here is that these areas can be called upon to generate diverse ways of thinking about any situation in order to come up with innovative solutions.

Experiments using brainwave scans have measured new neural activity when a rat is exposed to a new situation. When the rat is allowed some down time following this, it is possible to see the new neurons become stimulated through the brain from the hippocampus, which is the brain's memory access point. This establishes a clear basis for learning. If, on the other hand, you don't have down time, there will be a neurological toll, and the damage sustained will significantly reduce your ability to think creatively and learn through the process. Imagine how bad it must be for our brains if we continue to challenge our minds through constant simultaneous stimuli, such as when we are consciously multi-tasking. Instead of taking time out, we tend to 'push through' the work we need to do relentlessly, no matter how tired we might be or how strained our poor brain is. Perhaps we eventually allow ourselves some time off or have a few quiet moments in the day (sitting at a bus stop or walking to work, say). But instead of spending these quiet times simply enjoying the moment, allowing our minds to wander or constructively meditating, we often continue to fill them up with mind-straining activities, such as texting, tweeting, net surfing or gaming. By doing so we are simply not giving our minds the space they need to be creative. Researchers are now beginning studies to see what effect constant technology use is having on creativity and the imagination in upcoming generations.

Innovation consulting firm Brighthouse actively provides its employees with opportunities to think independently and therefore open themselves up to creativity.[22] On top of their regular five weeks' vacation a year, they are all given an additional five days (called 'Your Days') to be devoted to free thinking. Similarly, at the marketing and product development consulting firm Maddock Douglas, employees can bank up to 200 hours a year for pursuing personal interest projects.[23]

You may still have pressure in your work or life; in fact, as mentioned earlier, many people are more creative under pressure, and perhaps that is something that works well for you, but you need to feel in control of it. You need to feel that it is your choice, that the pressure is not externally imposed. That is why independence is so important in dealing with the potential threat of pressure. Within the confines of their regular restrictions and expectations, everyone has a certain amount of choice. For example, are you staying up late to finish a project because you have been told to do so or because you have not organised your time well enough to get it done in normal hours? Should you be blaming someone or something else for the stress you are feeling, or should you be working to develop better coping mechanisms yourself?

To minimise pressure it is important to ensure there is time when there are no deadlines, expectations and commitments. Through thought management and the daily practice of relaxation techniques, it is also possible to face stressors without feeling the stress. After all, lion tamers manage to remain calm when working with lions! By minimising pressure you can encourage independence, activate free, unrestricted thought and unleash the imagination. This is as true for the organisation as for the individual; an organisation that is always stressed, under pressure and behind schedule is extremely constrained in its ability to move forward creatively.

Rescue strategy 3: unleash your imagination

Do you remember the time when travelling used to provide the opportunity to switch off? When you could use this time to dream of the future, to plan a special event or to solve problems in your mind, or even — heaven forbid! — to unwind and relax? Where travelling time used to be unstructured and unfocused, providing opportunities for free thinking, it is now most often used for completing personal and work commitments. How often have you seen people on public transport texting or calling their friends to make social arrangements or using their iPhone or Blackberry to do web research, send emails or make business calls? How often have you seen people on aeroplanes using their laptops to prepare PowerPoint presentations or write business plans? How often have you done any of these yourself? It's a great use of otherwise 'wasted' down time, *but* it can come at the expense of unleashing your imagination.

These days most people's time is strictly scheduled and structured so there is very little left over for 'free thinking', the sort of thinking that encourages creative ideas. 'Free thinking' time allows the mind to wander into new territories and stumble on new ideas (utilising all the different areas of the brain when the mind is not specifically focused). We have developed the mistaken belief that the more time we spend on focused work activities, the more productive we are being, yet sometimes it is only when we switch off that our mind is really free to be creative. Every day, according to de Bono,[24] we should set up 'Purposeful Opportunities — or 'POs' to enable us to let our minds wander. This should be part of our daily routine. Note the famous Google strategy: each employee has one day per week to play with new gadgets/ideas.

Imagination works only in the divergent space in our mind. We know intuitively that down time stimulates creativity: when we suggest that someone 'sleep on it' to help them arrive at a solution, we are allowing their divergent thinking to work and giving their imagination room to breathe. This increases the total space in their brain that is open to new ideas.

Understand: the power of imagination

When do your best, most creative ideas come to you? Common answers are in the shower or just as you are waking up or drifting off to sleep. That's because your mind is at its most divergent and least focused in these moments.[25]

What did the following people have in common?

❧ Manfred Eigen, Nobel Prize winner in chemistry (1967)
❧ Donald Campbell, recipient of Scientific Contribution Award from American Psychological Association (1970)
❧ Freeman Dyson, recipient of Max Planck Medal (1969) — quantum electrodynamics
❧ Kekulé, nineteenth-century chemist — molecular structure of benzene
❧ Archimedes — weight in water theory.

Answer: not one was actively working on his 'discovery' at the time of his breakthrough.[26] Divergent thinking is a major key to creativity. It is the ability to let your mind wander, to go where it has never been before, to dream. When you allow your mind to wander, you utilise your most powerful creative tool, your imagination. As Albert Einstein said, 'Your imagination is a preview of life's coming attractions'.

Remember, 98 per cent of children aged three to five years score at the top of the scale for divergent thinking, while only 2 per cent of adults have similar scores.[27] We tend to lose this capacity with formal education and acculturation, yet divergent thinking plays an essential role in helping us to solve problems creatively.

Unlock: imagination techniques

It is possible to develop your imagination by trialling exercises designed to stretch your mind into exploring a range of possibilities.

The Rorschach inkblot test has been used for around 90 years to help people to explore different ideas and interpretations and supposedly reveal their unconscious desires and motivations. Imaginative ideas don't always have to generate breakthroughs; incremental creativity can be just as productive and frequently more successful.

Mind mapping[28] is an exercise to find connections and generate ideas for problem solving. Try this simple mind mapping exercise to see where it leads you: Write the key word 'happiness' in the middle of a sheet of paper, and draw lines radiating out from that word. Write down your thoughts on what the concept means to you. Continue to follow as many different concepts as you can, radiating out from the central concept.

Now a business application: Write the central question or ambiguous issue to be resolved (for example, 'How can a premium product be sold without discounting?'). Develop into a mind map (for example, look at packaging, changing customer habits, changing product, service, production. Think about where, how, whom to sell it to (for example, only in cities). Are there any ambiguities that can be mapped?

Practise: imagination techniques

⟍ Try seeing shapes in the clouds.

⟍ Think of 101 uses for a billiard ball.

⟍ Come up with different interpretations for words in the dictionary.

⟍ Find funny new explanations for typical kids' questions (for example, 'Where do fairies come from?' 'What makes an aeroplane fly?' 'Why is there lightning and thunder in a storm?')

⟍ Make a symmetrical shape by putting paint in the centre of a page and then fold the paper in half, as in the Rorschach test, and come up with at least five different interpretations for what it could be.

Apply: unleashing the imagination

When you have a problem or issue to be resolved, ask yourself 'what if?' questions. Use your imagination to come up with wild and crazy ideas. Sometimes the best solutions can be prompted by the most improbable ideas, as your mind opens up to a new range of possibilities.

Rescue strategy summary

\ Stand up to pressure.

\ Recognise that you have the power to stay in control of the impact of external circumstances.

\ Prepare a platform to unleash your imagination.

Rescuer profile 4: openness

This receptive initiator releases creative thinking. Openness enables the individual to make sense of diverse and often opposing ideas. Openness sees value in everyone and considers every option or idea. Some of the most profound ideas openness accepts don't come from the 'experts', although they should be listened to as well. Through not staying limited to preferred thinking styles but instead accessing all possible approaches, openness creates vast opportunities. The preferred rescue strategy adopted by openness is to access all parts of the brain. Openness saves us from insulation murderers such as biased media, homogeneity and lack of diversity, whose weapon of choice is *bludgeoning bias*.

Restricting your exposure to information sources can definitely be a problem when it comes to innovation, and can lead to unhealthy insulation. But although we have already identified the media as a clear creativity murder suspect, we need to apply our second creative thinking strategy here—we need to be prepared to accept ambiguity. The media itself is inherently neither positive nor negative. Depending on how it is used, it can in fact be either a murderer or a resuscitator. Like fire, which when controlled can contribute positively to our lives, but when not controlled can be incredibly destructive, the media has the potential to both harm and help.

Of course not all TV shows are dumbing us down. Some shows, for example, require the viewer to make sense of multi-threading, ambiguous themes that encourage creativity to develop.[29] (Multi-threading is a term used in computer science to refer to the ability of computers to process multiple sources of input at once and should not be confused with multi-tasking, which usually shuts creativity down.) Some of the complex plots of breakthrough mini-series, which often have numerous characters engaged in different storylines and facing different problems, can make it challenging to piece together the narrative. Shows such as *24*, *Heroes* and *Fringe* took us across different time zones and into parallel universes; one episode of *Heroes* followed more than 20 main characters in three time zones, making it a real creative stretch to be able to make sense of it all, let alone find solutions! Also, while TV comedy was traditionally based on a 30-second set-up line before the punchline, in shows such as *The Simpsons* the jokes work on a number of different levels, with new subtleties of humour becoming apparent only after a few viewings.

There is a difference between intelligent shows and shows that force the watcher to be intelligent. When the intellectual activity takes place only on the other side of the screen, there is no need for the viewer to be creative. It is no more challenging for your mind to watch intelligent shows than it is challenging for the body to watch football on TV—unless you respond to it and act on it. But when the watcher is forced to fill in the details and call on demanding cognitive brain power, creative thinking has the opportunity to thrive.[30]

When you play chess or Monopoly there is no ambiguity in the rules or the progression from beginner to advanced. In fact, in most games if the rules were ambiguous there would be a fatal flaw in the game. In many video games, however, the rules are rarely established upfront and become apparent only as you play deeper. Many people think video games are only good for developing hand/eye coordination, but the ultimate key to success in video games lies in deciphering the rules and probing the complex physics of a world as a scientist might. Scientific methods need to be applied in assessing probability risk, pattern recognition, participatory thinking and analysis. Reality shows also use a device that's important in video games: again, the rules are not established. Through probing the system's rules for weak spots and opportunities, the viewer is encouraged to think through different options to different potential outcomes. When solving puzzles, detecting patterns or unpacking a complex narrative system, the brain is exercised.[31]

Beyond the media, there are plenty of other opportunities to open up to creative thinking. It is important to know how to access all areas of the brain, to break out of the single-track thinking imposed by insulation, and to be open to opportunities other than those to which the brain is naturally predisposed.

It has been known for some time now that each hemisphere of the human brain has different dominant roles. According to the 'split brain theory',[32] which was originally popularised more than 35 years ago, the two hemispheres of the brain have two distinctly different functions. While the left brain is dominant for speech and language, ultimately also focusing on logical and detailed tasks, the right brain is responsible for visual and motor tasks. The researchers discovered this specialisation when they severed the *corpus callosum* (the thick cord of neurons connecting the two distinct halves of the brain) of patients seeking relief from epilepsy. The concept has more recently become so common that people are being labelled 'left-brain' thinkers and 'right-brain' thinkers according to which hemisphere is thought to be dominant.

However, neuroscience has not emphatically demarcated functions to either the left or the right. The brain is so holistic and so complicated that it is difficult to trim it down to such a simplistic principle. To help keep the concept straightforward and practical, then, we will merely discuss the brain as having a binary function; to go any further than this would be to make the discussion too complex to serve our purpose. So to keep it simple: some people look at problems purely practically and factually, ignoring imagination and emotion, while others view them from a more imaginative and reflective perspective based on feelings, rejecting logic. (Different areas of the brain specialise in emotion, but they are deeper, and not specifically on the right side.) To address this problem simplistically we have referred to this as 'left-brain dominance' and 'right-brain dominance', although this idea is now a little outdated.

Interestingly, animals do not have the same hemispheric specialisation but have been found to have the same capacities in roughly equal amounts in both sides on the brain. (Dolphins never sleep because they are able to rest one side of the brain while using the other, alternating between the two sides of the brain!) This originally indicated that the lateralisation in humans was an evolutionary development, but more recent research has found that lateralisation is a way for the brain to find more space for development. This is demonstrated by the fact that when you drop some functions on one side of the brain and allow the other side of the brain to develop a specialisation, the ability to utilise more functions is enabled.[33]

These functions are not so location specific that you can have only one ability or the other. The two hemispheres of the brain are connected by several neuron bridges, known as commissures (the largest of which is the *corpus collosum*). This bridge, along with other, smaller neuron bridges, enables us to synthesise information from both sources, so we are not completely right or left brained. The more we learn to use these bridges the more flexible our mind becomes and the more capable it is of coping with a wide range of tasks.

It has also been shown that because the brain has significant plasticity, although there may be an initial dominance, each hemisphere can be retrained to learn the skills of the other hemisphere. It was found, for example, that someone who had had a stroke that affected the left brain, and had lost the use of speech as a result, learned to speak again with specific training.[34]

Creative people can, to some degree, master conscious awareness. They can make conscious choices about which brain process they are using, train themselves to direct an issue to be looked at by one and/or another part of the brain, and arrive at both logical and intuitive solutions as a result. Accessing both sides of the brain is about knowing first what your natural brain dominance is and knowing how and when to switch. It's also about knowing how often you switch compared with the average person. Unconsciously becoming stuck in one hemisphere or the other for very long periods of time can be a symptom of bipolar disorder.

But for many people it is also possible to control the switch rate. Mathematicians need to stay on one side of the brain longer and remain focused, so they switch less, but artists, musicians and dancers learn to switch more quickly.[35] Buddhist monks are able to maintain a very slow switch rate through meditation and deliberately remain in the left side of the brain for long periods of time.[36] Neuroscientist Jack Pettigrew believes that brain switching speed could determine what we'll be good at in life. As you might have already noticed, like most that are worthwhile, this skill often takes long practice, but it is also possible that we can train ourselves to control switching.

The final antidote to the impact of potentially murderous Insulation is to ensure diversity within groups. A diverse group of independent individuals is likely to make certain types of decisions and predictions better than individuals or even experts. Diversity ensures that groups are not drawn towards extremes, but rather are able to take in all perspectives and come to a balanced conclusion. 'The absence of debate and minority opinions is dangerous in a team,' believes James Surowiecki. 'Diversity of opinion is the single best guarantee that the group will reap benefits from face to face discussion.'[37]

As noted in chapter 2, when forming a new software venture at HP, Peter Karolczak began by gaining multiple perspectives, ensuring divergent expertise. Leaders with the ability to select diverse teams have been found to obtain the most creative groups in a scientific environment.[38] While many people continue to build like-minded, homo-geneous teams, it is important to find structures to support heterogeneous diverse teams that allow for a range of individuals and ideas.

Rescue strategy 4: access all parts of the brain

You know your children are growing up when they stop asking you where they came from and refuse to tell you where they're going!

P. J. O'Rourke

Having a teenager has its moments. It seems to be a stage in life when kids become incredibly inventive and accomplished at not telling (or at least stretching) the truth. One common trick is for them to say they are sleeping over at a friend's place, while they are actually up to mischief elsewhere. With each parent assuming that the other is watching over the children, the kids themselves manage to slip under the radar undetected. When asked, 'What did you get up to last night?' there are only two real responses teenagers can make: (1) they can tell the truth, or (2) they can lie. When they are telling the truth they are accessing the more factual side of their mind, recalling real events recorded inside their brain. When they are lying, they are actually telling stories. They are making up an event that didn't happen (or changing the facts), which takes a lot more concentration and imagination. What has been discovered is that storytelling and recalling facts access different parts of the brain, and this offers a clue as to how we can start to revive creative thinking.

A handy secret for parents is that we can now discover when teenagers are telling stories (or, to avoid the euphemism, lying). The TV program *Lie to Me* popularised psychologist Paul Ekman's research into body language. The underlying assumption is that when a person is lying they are accessing the right side of their brain (imagination), and their eyes will look upward and to the left to access the relevant part of the brain. Fortunately, carefully checking the eyes of your potentially deceitful teenager the morning after a night out can also help to assess the possible lack of sleep and/or consumption of harmful substances, so it's in any case a useful exercise.

Dr Jason's research reminds us also that we can utilise spontaneous processes by giving the brain time to 'incubate' and thereby access both emotional and cognitive solutions that may have been previously unavailable to conscious awareness. This can enable us to fully utilise the brain's capabilities and learn and train creative thinking.[39]

Understand: the power of accessing all parts of the brain

Accessing all parts of the brain enables effective integration of the following, apparently opposing functions:

- predominantly left-brain functions: logical, sequential, analytical, methodical, focused on details
- predominantly right-brain functions: holistic, synthetic, artistic, emotional, focused on the big picture.

Although most of us are born with the ability to utilise all parts of the brain, and our natural development encourages this process, life experience can stifle the ability. The more we use one part of the brain to solve a problem, the more we tend to use that area again. But it is possible to regain a balance by deliberately exercising the non-dominant parts of your brain.

The term 'dialectical bootstrapping'[40] has been used to describe how we can learn to tap into more perspectives that are already inside our heads. This concept involves the unique idea that each of us has a diverse board of directors in our heads, but that we can only run a good board meeting if we learn to listen to each perspective and incorporate it in our decision making.

We have discussed how in order to be creative you need to be able to balance left-brain functions with right-brain functions, so the outcome of creative thinking that successfully accesses and synthesises both sides of the brain is much deeper and more enriched. The process becomes:

- not just function but design
- not just argument but story

ɣ not just focus but symphony

ɣ not just logic but empathy

ɣ not just seriousness but play

ɣ not just accumulation but meaning.[41]

Unlock: accessing all parts of the brain

Raise your right hand. Did you know your left brain is controlling this function? Now tap your left foot. This is being controlled by your right brain. Those who predominantly use their left brain will be trying to analyse this information. They will be analysing the details and asking, 'Is it true? Will it work? How can I prove it/quantify it?' The right hemisphere of the brain processes information 'holistically, as a big picture'. Those who predominantly access their right brain will find it easier to accept the imaginative approach.

We must learn to accept and utilise all approaches: to understand the world not only as a set of logical propositions but also as patterns of experience. We all have natural pre-dispositions and preferences — for example, which hand we use to do things. The more we use this hand, the more comfortable we feel using it, but the opposite is also true: the less we use the hand, the less comfortable we feel using it. If you are asked to catch something with one hand, which hand would it be? As we grow, we develop certain muscle coordination and preferences. The same is true with the ways we think, but to be truly creative we must break these patterns and open up to new ways of thinking.

In our seminars, when we ask people to produce mind maps to illustrate a problem, it's amazing how often their responses are heavily weighted to one hemisphere, usually the left-brain approach. When we explain the importance of being open to looking at both sides for solutions, a whole new set of ideas emerges.

So before you next tuck your teenager into bed for a good night of sleep (hoping they won't sneak out later), if you'd like to develop their skills at using all parts of the brain, ask them to try cleaning their teeth with their non-dominant hand!

Practise: to access all parts of the brain

By looking at a problem from different angles (dialectical boot-strapping), it is possible to create diversity in thinking. Try using the following method of devising your own mental board of advisers to consult when facing a problem or planning to come up with something new[42]:

ϟ Assume that your first solutions are off the mark or incomplete.

ϟ Think about a few reasons why that could be so. (Which assumptions and considerations could have been wrong?)

ϟ What do these new considerations imply?

ϟ Based on this new perspective, develop a second, alternative set of solutions.

Mind mapping seeks to use the whole brain to solve a problem or understand an issue. Instead of the usual approaches, which force the mind to think in a logical way, mind mapping incites more creative solutions by 'cooperating' with brain structure and physiology through thinking in radial forms—much like the pattern of thoughts as they move across the neurons in the brain—and stimulating both hemispheres equally.

To practise, use colour pens and develop your own symbols, icons and visual vocabulary for your mind maps. Making a list is a *left*-brain task; the use of colour, visuals and radiating forms are *right*-brain tasks.

ϟ Write down a work-related issue you would like to address, and list possible solutions from the mind map. Identify which of these are left- and right-brain focused. If you were heavily dominated by one side of the brain, try now to find solutions using the other side of your brain.

ϟ Record a task you had to complete recently at work, and write down how you approached it to determine what your natural orientation is. Now look at how you could use the other side of your brain more by using associated skills.

ϟ Record a question that needs to be answered from the issues that you identified:

166

- Make a list on the left side of how this task could be approached logically.
- Make a list on the right side of imaginative and more emotional responses.

As a warm-up, practise drawing a symmetrical picture with your left and your right hand at the same time. Next, try to draw a face in profile with your dominant hand, and then draw a mirror image of that face with the other hand.

To improve left-brain performance, try:

✱ mathematical puzzles
✱ word definition exercises
✱ magic squares.

To improve right-brain performance, try:

✱ creative writing
✱ letter and word puzzles
✱ spatial awareness games.

Apply: accessing all parts of the brain

At the top of a piece of paper write down a task you need to complete. Divide the page into two columns, and list how you could approach the task from a logical, 'left-brain' perspective in the left column and a more imaginative and feeling-based, 'right-brain' perspective in the right column.

Rescue strategy summary

✱ Be open and receptive to different opinions and ideas.
✱ Ensure there is receptivity to apparently opposing logical and more feelings-based perspectives.

CRIME SCENE DO NOT CROS

Stage 3: motivation — the passion to drive transformation

The third stage of the regenerative rescue process treats apathy and ensures there is inspiration for continued growth. This stage focuses on **passion**, which is not content with conservative and standard ways of thinking, but rather continues to push the boundaries with new ideas and concepts born from a deeper commitment.

Rescuer profile 5: passion

This zealous motivator understands the importance of the labour of love. Passion recognises that the most successful people often are not the most talented but the ones who are impelled by innate curiosity. Passion is not satisfied with accepting or conforming to the way things are, but instead is prepared to break apart the old in order to make way for creative new connections. Its healing power and intrinsic motivation helps to restore self-belief and confidence and drive towards outstanding outcomes. Passion's preferred resuscitation

strategy is to reconstruct common concepts. It offers rescue from apathy murderers such as lack of motivation, lack of initiative and lack of drive, whose weapon of choice is *lacerating lethargy*.

Vikki Howorth is someone who exemplifies the creativity that can come from a focused passion. She is a woman on a mission. After building a successful PR business with her husband Mike, she now has the opportunity and financial independence to devote her time and energy to making a difference in others' lives. She uses her experience to increase awareness of global poverty issues, and she has a targeted strategy. She is a supporter of the 'Micah Challenge',[43] which has established specific steps for helping to ensure politicians remain accountable for working towards the UN's 'Millennium Development Goals'. These are eight international development objectives that all 193 United Nations member states and at least 23 international organisations have agreed to achieve by the year 2015. In these goals, governments have promised to reduce poverty in specific ways—for example, by reducing the child mortality rates, eradicating extreme poverty, fighting global disease epidemics such as AIDS, and developing global partnerships for development. It is an ambitious venture, but one that is so goal oriented and practical that it really could make a difference.

What strikes you when you meet Vikki is her exuberance and enthusiasm for the task at hand, and her perseverance in following through to get the job done. Determined not to give up and to continue to be a 'voice for the voiceless', she is proud of the fact that she has been labelled 'the loudest nagger' on behalf of the poor by her local federal government member. She travels to Canberra to lobby politicians, bringing clever artistic expressions of community commitment to the Millennium Development Goals. In partnership with a creative team from her Christian community, who are just as passionate as she is, Vikki has previously been involved in such projects as presenting larger-than-life-sized pictures of politicians with notes from children urging them to continue to support the Millennium Development Goals. To address the global midwife crisis, she presented a 'Special Delivery' to our foreign affairs minister—a jacket adorned with cards of 'hope'—that read 'our hopes are pinned on you'. And she persuaded politicians to sit on a giant toilet on the Parliament lawn to draw attention to global sanitation issues. Along with Mike and her family, she has also spent time on the ground in the countries she supports. Through her church she works with Compassion Australia, also committed to following through on the Millennium Development Goals. A highlight of their fundraising activities is a fundraising walk, which raises up to $50 000 at a time from sponsorship of just a small number of walkers. The walk confronts participants with challenges faced in developing countries—for example, they are asked to carry buckets of water to represent the distance many people in the world need to walk to get access to drinking water.

When you have a passion, you have a purpose and often become incredibly driven and creative. You have the desire to keep persevering and to follow through. When you have this sort of desire to do something, you devote time and energy to it. You don't simply accept things the way they are; you put in the effort to look at them from a different perspective. Changing the world takes passion; changing a small area in your life takes this sort of passion and commitment too.

Benjamin Bloom, a professor of education at the University of Chicago, found that all the high achievers in his research study had been inspired by keen teachers and supported by devoted parents. And they had all developed a high level of expertise generated from the intense passion that leads to commitment, rather than from having any particular innate skill or talent. Later research building on Bloom's pioneering work, as compiled in *The Cambridge Handbook of Expertise and Expert Performance*, also revealed that high achievers are made, not born. This is an illustration of how passion can also create the conditions for the growth of creativity in others.

Harvard professor Teresa Amabile focuses on motivation in her studies of successful creative thinking because, as she believes, 'The desire to do something because you find it deeply satisfying and personally challenging inspires the highest levels of creativity, whether it's in the arts, sciences, or business'.[44]

Malcolm Gladwell, a writer who has helped to humanise and popularise economics over the past few years, has cleverly calculated the number of hours that any individual needs to put in to become an 'expert' in a specific area—10 000 hours, which adds up to about 10 years in most cases.[45] That's a huge amount of time, and yet he brings up example after example to illustrate how this has consistently been the case with high achievers.

So who would put in these sorts of hours if they didn't have passion? Yet even with all this practice, there is still a big difference between those who become 'technical experts' in a field and those who move beyond what others have done before them. Gladwell points out that Mozart wrote his first completely original masterpieces after the age of 40—after having built up 10 000 hours of compositional practice (there's that magic number). Mozart's passion enabled him not only to produce technically accomplished music, but to utilise his creativity to write music that would engage and inspire others. But don't mistake our point here. We are not suggesting that you need to put in 10 000 hours of practice to be creative—we are saying passion facilitates creativity. All of these highly creative individuals already had a passion that supercharged their subsequent creative output.[46]

Think of people who have inspired others through their passion and commitment: Alexander Fleming was not the first physician to notice the mould formed on an exposed culture while studying deadly bacteria. A less gifted physician would have ignored this seemingly irrelevant occurrence, but Fleming found it 'interesting', wondered if the process had scientific potential and after further investigation discovered penicillin, which would save millions of lives.

Organisations that have thought simple monetary incentives could motivate creativity or trigger passion have been disappointed. In a study performed in the US, moderate incentives were offered for better performance on creativity tasks; in a similar experiment in India massive incentives (up to several months' wages) were offered. It turned out that creative performance was actually lower under increased monetary incentives. What, then, does incentivise people to be creative? One of three key factors appears to be autonomy, which stimulates a personal passion and pride.[47]

Like Henning's discovery of phosphorus, if you don't take initiative and just 'get going' with the creative process you will never get anywhere. Similarly, if you don't have the drive and perseverance to push the creative process through to a practical outcome, you won't actually achieve much. Intrinsic motivation is critical here, as unless the motivation is intrinsic the creative passion will not survive. When Arthur Schawlow, winner of a Nobel Prize in physics in 1981, was asked what he thought made the difference between highly creative and less creative scientists he replied, 'The labor of love aspect is important. The most successful scientists often are not the most talented. But they are the ones who are impelled by curiosity. They've got to know what the answer is'.[48]

Rescue strategy 5: reconstruct common concepts

In 1997, when Philippe Kahn's wife Sonia was in labour, he puzzled over how he could send photos of the event quickly and easily to his friends. Not satisfied with the usual solution of taking a photo, loading it onto the computer and emailing it through, Kahn was motivated to find a better solution. Thinking on the spot, he wrote a computer program on his laptop, connected his camera to his phone (after his friends had delivered the necessary electronic supplies) and sent through the photos instantly. It must have been a long labour, or quick thinking and action on Kahn's part! We're not sure how much of Sonia's labour Kahn was emotionally present for, but his camera phone idea has had significant impact worldwide. By reassessing the accepted separation between two different electronic devices and combining them in an original way, Kahn had hit on a winner. His intrinsic motivation and passion had driven him towards invention. You can now see people everywhere pulling out their camera phones to take spontaneous photos and immediately upload them onto Facebook or send them to their friends.

All through the ages people have been limited by current beliefs and capabilities, but being creative is all about suspending belief and imagining what else might be possible. By reconstructing common concepts it is possible to come up with something creative and new. This empowers us to start to construct new ideas and turn them into practical solutions, but it actually involves a process of destruction first!

'Reconstructing common concepts' can often involve a disruptive hypothesis — an intentionally unreasonable approach that can change established ways of thinking and turn in a completely different direction. According to Luke Williams,[49] there are three simple steps that need to be followed:

\ Define the situation.
\ Search for clichés.
\ Twist those clichés around.

Like 'punctuated equilibrium', in which the tediously slow process of evolution is interrupted by a sudden change, a disruptive hypothesis is designed to stir things up a bit and promote accelerated change. For example, says Williams, instead of making a reasonable prediction such as, 'if I charge the battery, the phone will work', you make an unreasonable provocation such as, 'What if a cell phone didn't need a battery at all?'

The creative act is first and foremost an act of destruction.

Pablo Picasso

Understand: the power of reconstruction

It is easy to become overly attached to common concepts and connections, but it is important to look beyond the accepted boundaries to create new possibilities. It can help to ask the question, 'If [this issue] was not a limitation, what would the solution look like?' It is important to start with what is needed, not what is possible.

To achieve extraordinary results you may need to dismantle familiar concepts and make completely new connections. When we ask ourselves, 'What made that happen?', we are learning to look for causes or underlying factors, the building blocks behind every situation, not just the situation itself. Creativity is about continually separating and connecting: creative ideas often come from joining two apparently irrelevant ideas together. It is finding the hidden link between two situations that might seem unrelated. Right-brain thinking, for example, is able to synthesise rather than simply analyse, to see the relationship between unrelated fields, to detect broad patterns, to cross boundaries, to see the big picture.

Reconstructing common concepts is also about finding relationships. Research at MIT shows that many deadlocks in engineering issues have been broken by non-engineers.[50] This is because perspective is sometimes more important than IQ. The ability to make large leaps in thought is important. Boundary crossers reject the limitations of an either/or approach and accept ambiguity. These individuals usually have a broad (as opposed to a narrow-minded) approach to life.

173

A large part of self-understanding is searching for appropriate personal metaphors to help us make sense of our lives. Metaphors are bridges that help us see the gaps and connections between relationships. Only one cognitive ability has been found to distinguish star performers from others: the ability to recognise patterns and see the 'big picture'.[51] Seeing the big picture allows leaders to spot trends from an oversupply of information.

Unlock: the potential of reconstruction

Many new inventions come about from people making unlikely connections between two objects or ideas that might not previously have been linked in any way. Compaq and Dell offer one example. As they saw other, non-related companies such as Sony and Kodak moving into their territory, these two IT companies realised that they could not continue simply to sell black boxes (computers). They were selling a commodity. So they started advertising that they were selling 'business solutions' through computers. Each presented a combination of computers, cameras and other electronic devices.

Here are some other examples of successful new connections:

- 3M Post-it notes/sticky yellow tabs—stick paper (glue + paper)
- windsurfing and kite surfing (surfboard + wind)
- wheelchairs (chair + wheels)
- PDA /phone/camera etc. (diary + phone + camera etc.).

It helps to practise by taking individual unconnected elements that have been pulled from other areas and finding ways to connect them. The *Washington Post*[52] ran a competition asking entrants to take any word from the dictionary, alter it by adding, subtracting or changing one letter, and supply a new definition. Try it yourself. Winning entries included:

- *Intaxication* (n): the euphoria at getting a tax refund, which lasts until you realise it was your money to start with.
- *Bozone* (n): the substance surrounding stupid people that stops bright ideas from penetrating.

〉 *Cashtration* (n): the act of buying a house, which renders the subject financially impotent for an indefinite period.

Reconstructing common concepts must involve more than clever wordplay or simply joining two ideas together with a hyphen, however. At best, hyphenation means multiplication, not addition. Profitable hyphenation requires combining themes in such a way that extra value is created—that is, the value created must be greater than the sum of the parts combined.[53]

Inventors are visionaries who have seen beyond the obvious to new possibilities. Here's just one example. Over the years there have been many horrific train crashes around the world. A European Commission review revealed that the main cause of fatalities in end-on collisions was a phenomenon called 'overriding', in which one carriage rides up on top of another, crushing the people beneath. For decades engineers tried to solve this problem by building stronger carriages, but then in 1994 Professor Smith came up with a completely different solution. When he saw a crushed plastic drink bottle he noticed that between its ribs were built-in weak spots that could dissipate the energy. From this insight a new crash science developed, with train coaches designed to include unoccupied, crushable end zones that would dissipate the collision energy, thus saving many lives.[54]

Without the ability to look at old ideas from a fresh perspective, advances would not be possible.

Practise: the techniques of reconstruction

It's surprising what you can discover for yourself when you make new connections on issues that seem to have limited solutions. Adhering to conventional, commonly accepted ways of thinking will often lead to ordinary results. To achieve *extraordinary* results you may need to disassemble familiar concepts and make completely new connections.

Creative ideas reconstruct reality as we know it. Just like dreams, where diverse elements from your day-to-day thoughts and experiences are accessed from memory and then unconsciously combined into new versions, creative ideas are formed out of a colourful patchwork of experiences. To become creative you need to learn how to consciously dream! Here are some exercises that will help you to practise:

Exercise 1

Choose a workplace issue on which maximum results are not being achieved. Try pulling the issue apart to identify the different elements involved. Find relevant examples from different successful projects and reconstruct a new approach based on making new connections. Try to connect unrelated areas in mind maps to make new connections and create new possibilities.

Exercise 2

Many inventions start with seemingly incompatible connections (for instance, as introduced earlier: wheelchair = wheel + chair, windsurfer = wind + surfboard). Collect eight everyday objects (such as sunglasses, calculator, mobile phone and paper) and place them in a bag. Pull two items out of the bag and come up with a new invention that effectively utilises both items.

Exercise 3

Record a dream you have had recently. Identify the different elements and reflect on how the dream was assembled.

Apply: reconstructing common concepts

Think of a project where optimum results are not being achieved:

- Try pulling apart the issues and identifying all the various elements involved.
- Pose a disruptive hypothesis that unsettles established ways of thinking.
- Find relevant positive examples from different successful projects.
- Reconstruct a new approach based on making new connections.

Remember, the key to reconstructing common concepts is that the value created must be more than that of the sum of the parts combined.

Rescue strategy summary

\ Focus on ensuring engagement (and driving away apathy).

\ Find ways to connect with individual passions.

\ Encourage people to come up with fresh ways of thinking rather than sticking with old, conservative habits.

RIME SCENE DO NOT CROSS

Stage 4: transformation — the flexibility and positivity to make real changes

The final stage of the rescue process ensures there is long-term change and provides real hope for the future. It involves the **flexibility** to deal with new ideas and challenges as they arise, and **positivity** — the ability to sustain development through optimism.

Rescuer profile 6: flexibility

This divergent explorer is not constrained by what it thinks ought to be done. Flexibility has an innate elasticity that ensures it is able to find new, original ways of doing things. Rather than sticking within the confines of known experience, Flexibility stretches the mind and ensures it is prepared to explore numerous options. This intrepid adventurer implements a process that can lead to real change and, ultimately, transformation. Its preferred resuscitation strategy is exploring different

FLEXIBILITY

Flex A. Bility

RESCUER

paths. Flexibility rescues from narrow-minded murderers such as expertise, prejudice and groupthink, whose favoured weapon is *intractable intolerance*. Flexibility is a key quality that children possess and appear to lose later in life.

In a recent competition, a 12-year-old girl came up with a brilliant idea. She envisaged a 'Google Image Search', in which users could draw what they were looking for rather typing in key words. This was just ahead of the announcement from Google that they had developed this very concept. A seven-year-old boy imagined robot toys that could play games with him—an idea already in prototype stage.[55]

These astonishing responses were two among many from children who were asked the question: 'What would you like your computer or the internet to do that it can't do right now?'[56] They were actually envisioning ideas that were already in development or had been explored by adults, and thus showed remarkable foresight. The reason children are so good at coming up with advanced ideas is that they have incredible flexibility in the way they think, a fresh perspective and a wonderful innocence unhampered by expectations and perceived limitations. They are able to think divergently, which counteracts the sort of narrow-mindedness that smothers creative thinking in adults. Yet we often assume that only experts, after a long period of training and learning, can come up with new ideas.

Traditionally the education system and society in general have rewarded and deferred to knowledgeable experts. People able to negotiate these systems successfully have been blessed with high test results and grades, promoted to high positions and paid according to their knowledge and expertise. Now, with a greater amount of information more widely available, it is becoming apparent that it is not possible for one person to be the single expert, so learning and leadership models will have to adapt. Leaders today don't need the most information; they need to be able to spot and encourage the smartest ideas. Traditional experts' focus is very narrow, which means they can build up a great deal of knowledge about a specific subject or area, but this can kill creativity, so the leader of the future will need to be a broad thinker who is open to new thinking and ideas.

Experience has many plus points, but the one minus point is the loss of innocence. Creative innocence happens to people who don't know how something ought to be done. They are able to find an original way to do it. To know too much is to be constrained by the concepts and directions already established in a field of work, making innovation impossible.

Edward de Bono[57]

Only the innocent mind, the mind that is open, that is willing to become vulnerable and take risks, that can feel and think as a child, that is unpressured and uncluttered—only this mind can be truly creative. De Bono calls this open mind and attitude 'creative innocence'.

This idea of creative innocence is now recognised as so important that some organisations actively engage children in the ideas generation process. For example:

ᚴ Toyota once put together a 'board' of children to advise the company on product development.

ᚴ Hasbro has done the same with toys.

ᚴ Xerox's Palo Alto Research Center once asked some school kids to attend a series of brainstorming sessions on the future of technology.[58]

The development of knowledge may depend on maintaining an influx of the naïve and the ignorant.

James G. Marsh[59]

Although it is almost universally assumed that accumulated experience is needed to excel in an area, and in many situations (for example, biology, history or novel writing) this will be the case, there are a few notable exceptions to this rule. Psychologist at UC-Davis Dean Simonton[60] has shown that physicists tend to make their first major discovery while still in their late twenties. Another field that peaks even before this time, he suggests, is poetry. He believe these people benefit, at least in part, from their willingness to embrace novelty and surprise. Because they haven't become 'encultured', or weighted down with too much conventional wisdom, they're more willing to rebel against the status quo. After a few years in the academy, however, Simonton says, creators start to repeat themselves.[61]

Consider, for example, James Watson, who co-wrote one of the most important scientific papers of all time (on the structure of DNA) in 1953 at the tender age of 25; Isaac Newton, who began inventing calculus at age 23; Albert Einstein, who had published several of his most important papers by age 26; and Werner Heisenberg, who came up with the concept of quantum mechanics in his mid twenties. Archimedes, Marie Curie, Galileo and Robert Oppenheimer are a few other examples of young achievers who made major scientific contributions in their twenties.[62]

With recent reductions in major grants for young scientists, the freshest new ideas may not now be accessed adequately. In a disturbing trend in the US, whereas most grants from the National Institute of Health went to young scientists in 2008, today more grants are going to 70-year-old researchers than to researchers under the age of 30! Some have explained this as a growing conservatism and fear of risk taking in the organisation. A graph plotting creativity across a person's life span will usually show an inverted 'U' curve. The concern now is that by the time most people have the opportunity to get the funding and recognition they deserve, they will most likely have passed their creative peak.

Rescue strategy 6: explore different paths

The InterContinental Hotel in Bali had a major issue to deal with. They were promising their top-paying guests a stress-free and relaxing holiday experience coordinated by their efficient and professional staff team, but the guests' first holiday impression was most often established at Denpasar's uninspiring airport before they had even reached the hotel. The airport's inefficient immigration and customs process was adding to the exhaustion of often long-haul travel, and many people were starting their holidays upset and dissatisfied.

After looking at the complexity of the arrival process and noting the impact on their VIP guests, the hotel introduced a number of measures to reduce the perceived cycle time for guests and to increase the guests' impressions that they were being well looked after. At first it had seemed impossible to reduce the number of steps the guests needed to complete (or hoops they had to jump through), but creative minds were at work. The hotel offered a luxury check-in lounge at the airport. The arrival lounge meant that the guests relaxed in comfortable sofas with cool drinks and warm towels while the hotel staff completed the customs and immigration procedures for them, saving them from having to queue for hours. They then offered hotel check-in for these VIP guests: the front desk completed the formal check-in process to ensure there were no further hold-ups when they reached the hotel. As a result of these measures, many travellers were prepared to pay more money for the comfort and security provided. While the process did not change from the customs and immigration perspective, what mattered was that the guests experienced a dramatic reduction in processing hurdles (from 12 steps to three). Through 'exploring different paths' and looking for new possibilities, Bali's InterContinental Hotel managed to find a way to maintain an exclusive guest experience and high income at a time when other hotels were dropping their rates (owing to an Asia-wide economic crisis). When most people think of improvement, they are happy if they can cut one step out of a complex process or make improvements that amount to a few percentage points, but in this case a radical change was introduced with phenomenal outcomes.

On workplace issues it is essential to be able to find more efficient paths. An example is improving customer total cycle time. Total cycle time is made up of the sum of all the times of each process between the external customer's request for a product or service and the delivery or availability of that product or service to the customer. A process's cycle time is the sum of all sequential work-steps in the process. Some steps occur in parallel, so only the longer work-step is added to the total. Idle or wait time also counts in total cycle time.

The biggest obstacle to achieving effective innovation is slow development times.[63] Fast-changing consumer demands, global outsourcing and open-source software make speed to market paramount today. Yet companies often can't organise themselves to move faster, says George Stalk Jr, a senior vice-president with BCG who has studied time-based competition for 25 years. Fast cycle times require taking bets even when huge payoffs aren't a certainty. 'Some organizations are nearly immobilized by the notion that [they] can't do anything unless it moves the needle,' says Stalk. In addition, he says, speed requires coordination from the hub: 'Fast innovators organize the corporate center to drive growth. They don't wait for [it] to come up through the business units.'

Process redesign is a great example of how exploring different paths can open up more creative approaches.

Understand: the power of exploring different paths

As already discussed, our brains establish neural networks from early in life and we quickly slip into set patterns of thinking based on our ongoing experiences. It is all too easy to settle into a groove. It is important to develop systems as ways of understanding and organising information effectively, but these systems can in the end become limiting and can stifle the creative development process. Deliberately moving off those set tracks and exploring new pathways, even establishing completely new processes and pathways, can be a start to coming up with creative new ways of doing things and dealing with difficult issues.

In a typical creativity challenge designed to test divergent and convergent thinking, college students were asked to think of all the things that could interfere with their graduating from college. They were then instructed to choose one of those items and to come up with as many solutions for the problem as possible. A large number of students could quickly list every imaginable way things could go wrong, but many were unable to demonstrate flexibility in finding creative solutions. And those who could not come up with a range of possible solutions, the challenge revealed, were more easily subject to despondency and despair.[64]

Whether working with personal or business-related issues, it is important to recognise your typical problem-solving style, and to think of alternative ways of solving problems that normally you would not consider. You can do this by taking unusual routes that you may not have explored before. This process can be uncomfortable, it may mean breaking some old habits, but it can also be a positive and liberating experience.

Let's start with a simple exercise in which people are asked to join four dots (positioned at the four points of a square) with three straight lines. They are required to start and finish at the same spot, without picking up their pen and without going back. Many have trouble doing this because success requires that the three lines continue outside the boundaries of the box. When your mind sees a box (or in this case four dots that visually suggest a box), it tends to stay inside the box. It takes a special effort to think outside of the box, or outside of the system. Every system, just because it is a system, is a limitation. A creative mind must look first for solutions outside of the system, for new paths. Getting out of the system (changing the system of reference) is more innovative than staying within the system.

When asked to connect the four dots with two straight parallel lines most people say it's impossible. But that's true only for the person who is trapped inside a certain style of geometrical thinking. When we look at life, we think of it operating on a flat, two-dimensional surface where two parallel lines will go on being parallel for ever, but if these dots were pasted onto the face of the Earth and the parallel lines run longitudinally, they would actually meet at the poles. Our belief that parallel lines never cross originates with our school geometry lessons. But Euclidean geometry, the study of flat surfaces, is only one type of geometry. Non-Euclidian geometry is the study of curved spaces. Meridians (vertical lines) cross the equator (a horizontal line) at 90 degrees. Euclid said that two lines are parallel if an opposing line crosses both of them at 90 degrees. So, outside of the box of Euclidean geometry, parallel lines both can be parallel and can cross—there's an ambiguity you may need to accept to be creative.

Now, for the really creative. Can the four dots be joined by one straight line? They can be connected with a single stroke—if you use a wide enough paintbrush!

Unlock: different paths

To illustrate the way standard channels can limit thinking and how we can start to overcome that limitation, we turn an Edward de Bono exercise[65] into an animated demonstration. In this version of the exercise, letters drop down into the screen one at a time. The first letter to appear is A. This is followed by T to give the word 'AT'. The next letter to appear is R, which is simply added to give 'RAT'. When the letter E drops down, you are starting to get the hang of it, so you add it onto the end of your word to make the new word 'RATE'. The next letter is G, which can be added to give you 'GRATE'. So far the new information has been easily added on to the existing structure, but the next letter to appear disrupts the system—it doesn't slip into the familiar channel. The letter is T, and there is no simple way this can be added on ... so a reshuffling needs to occur. The new word that can be formed from these letters is 'TARGET', but it can be formed only if you are prepared to disrupt/reshuffle the letters and start again from scratch.

In this simple example we can see how the time sequence related to the arrival of the information sets up structures. These structures have to be disrupted or restructured in order to form new concepts and ideas in a different way, and this process is a useful definition of creativity. Without creativity we cannot move forward in such a system. We need creative thinking in order to break free from the temporary structures that have been set up by a particular sequence of experiences. Creativity is not simply a way to make things better; without creativity we are unable to make full use of information and experiences already available to us. It is locked up in old structures. Too often we take the first or quickest way out, but it is not always the best way. By looking at problems creatively we can find more efficient ways to move ahead.

Exploring different paths can improve the bottom line and the overall experience up to 300 per cent. Consider these case studies:

- P&G initiated the *Global Data Synchronization* program exclusively in China, and invited major retailers such as Carrefour to join a program that would help connect retailers and P&G using high-technology tools. The program made it possible for retailers to get in-time information about products, inventory and the latest sales trends. The new process enabled P&G to increase the availability of products on the shelves and cut inventory by up to 30 per cent, which of course meant greater efficiency, effectiveness and ultimately profitability.[66] (See the more detailed case study and rescue plan in chapter 9.)

- When Southwest Airlines executives benchmarked their turnaround time against other airlines, they found they were already one of the leaders, so they looked outside the airline industry for the most efficient turnaround professionals in the world, and found them in Formula One motor racing. Adopting the turnaround processes used during pit stops, Southwest Airlines reduced refuel time from 40 minutes to 12 minutes.[67 68]

- With the arrival of the new boss, Sergio Marchionne, and his innovative ideas, Fiat was able to speed up time to market from four years to eighteen months. When he took over, Sergio was quoted as saying, 'When you walked around the factory floor you could feel the waste. It wasn't just the mess, it was the way people moved and worked'.[69]

- Research on supermarkets showed that repositioning check-out staff could reduce annual labour hours by 12 500 hours, which has meant up to $2.5 million savings of wages for the supermarkets that have adopted this strategy.[70]

- Aldi quickly moved into the supermarket arena as a viable competitor in a tightly held field, coming up against giants Coles and Woolworth's, by keeping prices much lower and providing a much faster checkout experience. They did this through the following simple process[71]:

- fewer products = less storage + handling + smaller shop size
- own brand = special multi-barcoding = faster checkout
- faster checkout = fewer staff + happy customers.

While many people spend too much time trying to understand how to make an existing process work better, innovators are more likely to challenge the assumptions behind the process.[72]

Nothing beats the example of the bank that faced appalling queuing times of up to five hours. The bank called us in to help redesign their processes, and we used the 'explore different paths' exercise to see how they could deal with the problem. Through the process they discovered that people who didn't even have an account at that bank were coming in to cash checks for $5 amounts just to get out of the 45-degree heat and enjoy the nice airconditioning! They came up with the solution of positioning an employee at the front door simply to ask people what their purpose was at the bank. People cashing checks were redirected to another bank, while the bank's target market, those wanting to open an account or conduct other banking transactions, were welcomed in.

Many companies would like to double their revenue, and thinking only inside the box they assume this means doubling their growth profit. But are there other ways to increase growth beyond simply generating more sales? The InterContinental Hotel in Bali, and other case studies discussed here, were able to change the process, often without altering the systems outside their control (making a creative breakthrough). In hindsight, although it doesn't always sound very glamorous, each of these creative breakthroughs gave the company concerned a great advantage in their market. When a passenger arrives at an airport it may not be possible to land the plane directly outside the hotel guest's room and cut through all the bureaucratic red tape, *but* through clever thinking it is possible to change the customer's perception and experience. Nowadays, thanks to those who reconstructed common concepts and explored different paths, we think nothing of checking in online and accessing our room door using our smart phones, making the whole experience quicker, easier and cheaper!

Practise: the technique of exploring different paths

You can practise using this tool by exploring solutions to one of the issues you have identified in the last section. Look at the mind map you created in the last step, and identify pathways that are overused, 'congested traffic spots' or double-up of labour. See if you can find alternative, more efficient pathways that will achieve the solutions sooner. If you're stuck in a rut, creating a worn path along the same track, you may need to explore different possibilities and try different routes.

In order to 'follow different paths' and come up with simpler and more efficient solutions in process redesign, for example, it is necessary to:

\ Map the process.
\ Identify who is responsible for each step.
\ List the areas where things can go wrong.
\ Look at ways of reducing these danger spots.
\ Reduce the errors by reducing the number of steps.

Remember that every step is another opportunity for error. To practise, start with a regular daily activity, and try doing it completely differently:

\ Take a different route to work, and see what you notice along the way.
\ Try cooking something completely new, or substituting different ingredients in a favourite recipe.
\ Change your 'getting ready in the morning' routine.

Apply: exploring different paths

Think of a problem that has to be solved. Identify the usual solution, then think about the path others in your situation might take. Come up with several different possible ways the problem could have been solved.

> ### Rescue strategy summary
>
> \ Be open to the idea that there can be more than one way of approaching situations.
>
> \ Use divergent thinking that comes from a place of creative innocence.
>
> \ Be prepared to explore different options and take different paths to improve efficiency and effectiveness.

Rescuer profile 7: positivity

This optimistic opportunist profile represents both the attitude and the approach needed to survive and thrive through any challenge. By providing the underlying reason for action and the ongoing stimulus, positivity supports and maintains the transformation process. With optimistic thought and language strategies, true positivity is not a mere state of mind but a belief or value system that focuses action. It counteracts the negativity that can follow failure, and ensures success over the long term. Positivity's preferred resuscitation strategy is to embrace optimism. It helps rescue from pessimism murder suspects such as negativity, lack of hope and lack of trust, whose chosen weapon is *noxious negativity*.

POSITIVITY

Posy T. Vitty

RESCUER

The way positivity works can be seen in the way young kids approach sports. When children are learning tennis they can miss-hit balls and then recover instantly and try again and again, as many times as once every 10 seconds — that's an amazing 360 times in an hour! Tennis, golf and many other ball sports are often won, not by simply having good shots, but through the ability to manage mistakes effectively. The champions are those who can recover quickly and keep going after failure.

Failure can make anyone feel at least temporarily helpless. It's like a hefty punch in the stomach. The pain usually strikes hard and then goes away, but for some the hurt lasts. For these people the pain can be crippling over the long term, and can build into a grudge or an entrenched feeling of helplessness. Those not able to bounce back easily from failure can find it difficult to maintain enthusiasm for what they do. The key difference in recovery lies in the way the failure is explained. People who don't recover easily think, 'It's my fault [or my problem]. It's going to last forever. It's going to undermine everything I do.' Those who do recover easily are able to say, 'It was just circumstances. This feeling of failure will pass soon. There is so much more to be positive about in life.'

When pessimism strikes, the ability to think positively and impartially about a situation can be destroyed. Under a gas attack in World War I, the brain could be starved of life-saving oxygen, rendering the victim unable to think clearly. When starved of life-saving optimism, the mind can also be severely depleted. Positivity, on the other hand, is the great resuscitator, providing life-saving oxygen for any situation. This is not a mindless positive outlook that ignores the reality of a situation. In fact, researchers have found that painting too rosy a picture of what you expect to achieve, if too far beyond the bounds of reality, will actually harm your chances of success.[73] Neither is positivity a constantly happy state; rather, it is the sort of oxygen cleansing that takes away the fogginess and brings a clarity of mind and purpose.

Optimistic people have been found to be more productive in all areas of their lives, staying healthier and living longer. When individuals are optimistic they work with more focus, achieve more, encourage those around them, see problems as opportunities, find themselves in less conflict and are more enthusiastic in the work environment.[74] The optimist and the pessimist will both encounter problems in life, but the optimist is better able to weather all circumstances. Remember, this is not purely about the power of positive thinking; it's about how we react to events, especially failure. The way we respond to adverse events can easily turn into habitual behaviours and have consequences in other areas of our lives. These responses can mean the difference between giving up and persevering to achieve.

The words we choose to use to describe an event can also influence our perceptions, and consequently our behaviour. Whenever we articulate what we see, our language interacts with our direct experience, and our reality arises from this interaction.[75] The most important conversation we have each day is with ourselves. Self-talk shapes our self–image, and our self–image is responsible for our success, or conversely our self-destruction. Without a positive self–image, individuals will simply 'plod along' and teams can only 'do okay'. With a positive self-image, a whole new world is possible. The subliminal process of self-talk or learned optimism can be used as a powerful aid to learning and a therapeutic tool in treating disorders, banishing fears and phobias, and resuscitating creativity.

Optimism animates the creative thinking process, ensuring that any bright sparks or ideas are not quickly extinguished and that there is enough life-saving oxygen for the flame to be fanned and the fire to burn bright.

Rescue strategy 7: embrace optimism

In 1870, in his novel *20,000 Leagues under the Sea*, Jules Verne imagined a nuclear submarine. But it was more than just a vague futuristic idea. The *Nautilus* had a cylindrical hull 70 metres long and eight metres wide. The double hull had tapered ends, 'like a cigar'. The four-bladed propeller was six metres in diameter with a pitch of 7.5 metres. There was an ordinary rudder fixed to the stern and two diving planes fastened to the sides at the centre of flotation. On the surface the *Nautilus* remained 90 per cent underwater so its platform was 0.8 metres above the water. Verne demonstrated remarkable foresight of how science and technology would develop. He also predicted elements of the coming environmental problems and, through the Captain Nemo character, implicitly criticised the exploitation of colonised peoples. Instead of focusing on what *could not* be done at the time, Verne believed in what *might* be done in the future. Optimism always focuses on future possibilities rather than present limitations or past failures. Albert Einstein once said that, 'Imagination is a preview of life's coming attractions'. If we can learn to stretch our minds, we can not only see new possibilities but also often make them a reality.

By now we hope you can see that the people who can solve the problems of hours-long queues at banks and airports, or who can connect four dots in a square with a single straight line, share a special overriding quality. Those who say, 'We can't do this' finish the challenge at that point, as they have taken themselves out of the game. Their 'learned helplessness' ensures they just can't proceed to a better solution. Those who believe they can find solutions often do.

Understand: optimism

Shell Petroleum's advertisement (see chapter 2) demonstrates the final all-encompassing strategy in the creative thinking process (actually more an essential attitude than a strategy): the importance of belief, of remaining optimistic in the light of apparent challenges.

The final piece of the puzzle reminds us of the need to conti-nue to persevere—to accept mistakes and failures as temporary setbacks. Optimists use setbacks as learning experiences, picking themselves up and trying again with renewed determination. An optimist will perceive a bad situation as a challenge, and try harder. It is only through 'embracing optimism' that we can appreciate the value of trial and error in the creative process, and remain motivated enough to see the creative development process through to its conclusion. Pessimists tend to believe that bad events will last a long time, will undermine everything they do and are their own fault. Pessimism can transform setbacks into disasters. Judiciously employed, mild pessimism has its uses but if left to run rampant in our minds it can be paralysing. Optimism, on the other hand, is empowering.[76]

Unlock: the power of optimism

Success comes in 'cans'. As Edward de Bono says, 'We need not only to look at measuring certainty but also possibility'.[77] By recognising what we can learn from failure, and the importance of remaining optimistic through setbacks, we can embrace and utilise the power of optimism.

What can we learn from failure? Try the following exercise to discover some solutions:

⟍ Take an apparently impossible solution from your mind map, and look at how it could be achieved. Follow one path on the mind map and look at how the issue could be resolved.

We can gain inspiration for persevering and remaining optimistic from others who have taken up the challenge. How hard is it for you to 'step out'? What holds you back and why? Think of disabled athletes who have persevered to overcome physical challenges to achieve their goals. What inspiration can you take from their stories? There are many stories and case studies of individuals who have imagined the future to make a creative breakthrough or connection, and have gone on to become famous. Consider how you can start to create your own possibilities.

Practise: embracing optimism

⟍ Try positive affirmations instead of putdowns.

⟍ Practise saying 'not yet' instead of 'no' or 'I can't'.

⟍ Take up a new hobby or sport, and don't give up until you have mastered it.

⟍ Keep a diary of the positive things that happen each day. Take a few minutes to reflect on and write up your experiences each night.

Apply: embracing optimism

⟍ Write a statement that expresses the way you feel about a problem you're having trouble solving at work or at home.

⟍ Now rephrase that statement so that it is positive (achievable, manageable, solution oriented).

Rescue strategy summary

\ Model and teach positive self-talk and language.

\ Practise positive, optimistic thinking to build resilience and boost optimism.

\ Reword or rework limiting language and experiences into positive outcomes.

Once you have developed all these skills, you will find it is possible to descend into the abyss and rescue creative thinking—one step at a time. And you will discover it can be revived in every area of the organisation.

Where can creativity be revived?

Casing out the potential rescue locations

While the personal app that identifies criminal hotspots (introduced at the start of chapter 3) is a relatively recent invention, the idea of mapping the locations where crime most frequently takes place is not new. The influence of statistical analysis on criminology began with Quetelet's observations in 1842 that some parts of France produced more crime than others. In Minneapolis more recently, a comprehensive analysis of 323 000 calls to the police found that a small number of hotspots (3 per cent of the city) produced 50 per cent of police call-outs.[1]

If rescuers can be dispatched to all areas of the organisation, but particularly to those that have been identified as 'hotspots', and if the resuscitation devices are on hand at all times, the creativity crime rate should be dramatically reduced. Conversely, potential hotspots for creativity development need to be elevated and more widely recognised in the organisation. Creativity should be free to move around all places in an organisation through non-siloed collaboration.

The common association between creativity and artistic originality often leads to confusion about the appropriate place for creativity in the organisation. Most people assume that although creativity killers hang out in more tightly structured areas of the organisation, such as the accounting department, creativity should not be introduced here. In fact, about 80 per cent of managers say they don't want creativity to be introduced into the accounting department of their organisation.[2] When we told a good friend, an air traffic controller, that we were writing a book on creative thinking, he promptly responded, 'But who on earth would buy a book on that!' To him there was no place for creativity in a role that involved factual precision. He may not have recognised what many people fail to see: that creativity can make a significant difference in any organisation, and in any area of the organisation. Even for air traffic controllers, roster procedures can be improved, work techniques enhanced, management processes adapted. This same friend had not long before lamented about how the management approach never changed, and how intolerant and archaic it was. It is in just such areas that creative thinking can make a major difference.

Building innovation hothouses — revisiting the boss's office and the coffee shop

If there are hotspots where criminals hang, there are also hothouses where creativity often lives. Funnily enough, as many people recognise, it commonly flourishes around the water-cooler, in the hallways or in the cafeteria, rather than formally established 'work' places in the organisation. Perhaps that explains why they are hothouses for creativity — because they are where people meet and talk informally, relaxed and out of earshot of overbearing characters such as Control, Pressure and Fear, who probably think that these places are not worth patrolling.

Clever workspace designers should look at creating environments that foster creativity. Factors that should be taken into account when designing workspaces include[3]:

- creating spaces for informal discussion (for example, large, casual meeting spaces and coffee rooms)
- contriving spatial closeness between departments to foster contacts between them
- avoiding large, impersonal offices that might discourage informal discussion.

Positive social environments that encourage creativity can also be provided through:

- common lunch breaks, which provide good opportunities for communication between employees in different organisational areas
- schedules that allow and encourage interaction.

Smart leaders will recognise that the work environment can inhibit creativity and will ensure individuals maintain a creative development focus. Management guru Jim Collins consciously spends only 50 per cent of his time on administration tasks. To ensure he stays focused and creative he turns down many speaking opportunities, consulting jobs and even the temptation to expand his company. He is so adamant about this key point that he logs everything he does, including his sleep. He knows that at those times when he is overworked with administration, his creative thinking and ability to focus on developing and researching new ideas suffers.[4]

Organisations of the future will need to work harder to engage increased dimensionality and foster greater creative thinking. The design and innovation consultancy IDEO, in Chicago, exemplifies the way work environments will need to evolve to support creative development. In this office an open studio is surrounded by project rooms, demonstrating the principle that open thinking and experimentation combined can lead to positive practical results. The open design encourages collaboration between individuals. The studio is seen as a space where employees from different disciplines, such as engineers, designers, business strategists and programmers, can also collaborate effectively. The IDEO building includes a central cafe and forum area combined, along with a dedicated prototyping workshop. The open rooftop community garden provides a communal focus and stimulates the imagination.[5]

In the past companies valued tight top-down controls. Now, though, it is most important to mobilise resources for innovation and entrepreneurship. As a result, argues Harvard professor of management Christopher Bartlett, there needs to be a shift to empowering people right through to the lower levels of the organisation, because the freshest ideas will often come from the brightest young minds. 'There is a shift to a much more empowered organization,'[6] he says, 'in which you have to shift the power away down to people who have access and who understand technology, to those closest to the customer and able to develop the ideas.'[7]

In an article in the *Sydney Morning Herald*, Steve Ballmer, CEO of MSN, is reported to have told business leaders of the company's strategy to 'systematise innovation',[8] but Alan Noble, a senior Australian engineer with Google, challenged this approach to innovation. 'What Ballmer presented was pretty much a top-down driven response, almost reactive in that he said "we need to figure out how to innovate better",' said Noble. 'If it's so central to your culture there's nothing to systematize. It's there, it's like the air you breathe—you innovate to survive ... it's just what you do.'

The article goes on to outline some of the unusual strategies Google has used to ensure innovation becomes a part of the system. These have included allocating 20 per cent of their engineers' time to design (Google's web-based email service came from ideas explored during this time), and decentralising their research facilities (about 40 of these have been established internationally, which saves on red tape and fosters more rapid generation of ideas). These strategies provide more independence and agility, and ensure that fresh ideas are coming through from all levels.

Another striking advertisement from Shell that reveals how it can work in practice states:

Do you see solutions in unlikely places? Shell engineer Jaap van Ballegooijen watched his son drink a milkshake, using a bendy straw upside-down to reach the bits of froth in the corners of the glass. Hey presto, the snake well drill was born. Inspired thinking, innovation and even leaps of imagination are part of our daily lives at Shell.[9]

It is not so much that we lose our creativity as we become adults; rather, it seems that we lose our creative confidence and as a result need to work harder to regain it. In the adult world, the right environments and opportunities are not being built for creativity to flourish. We must reverse this in order to ensure we can all cope with the demands of the future.

Potential rescue site 1: the boss's office

IBM's survey[10] identifies the qualities that characterise creative leaders (qualities that tie in closely with our seven strategies). The survey results indicate that creative leaders:

⟨ expect to make more business model changes to realise their strategies (strategy 1: cultivate curiosity)

⟨ are comfortable with ambiguity (strategy 2: accept ambiguity)

⟨ invent new business models based on entirely different assumptions (strategy 3: unleash the imagination)

⟨ score much higher on innovation (strategy 4: access both sides of the brain)

⟨ invite disruptive innovation (strategy 5: reconstruct current concepts)

⟨ consider previously unheard of ways to change the enterprise (strategy 6: explore different paths)

⟨ are creative and visionary enough to make decisions that alter the status quo (strategy 7: embrace optimism).

Furthermore, since the top-performing organisations are 54 per cent more likely to respond swiftly with new ideas to address the deep changes affecting their organisations, CEOs must learn to make clever decisions fast, and this involves disciplined creative thinking.

Potential rescue site 2: the boardroom

Healthy boardroom dynamics are critical for open dialogue and therefore for boardroom success. One of the most significant points that governance experts agree on is the need for open and challenging discourse with the CEO. Constructive critical dialogue is the single best indicator of board effectiveness. Trust and confidence are built on open relationships in which people can ask questions and offer different, perhaps challenging viewpoints. Ensuring diversity and a heterogeneous mix is also important. It's not enough simply to have different backgrounds represented; variations in perception must also be encouraged.[11] The boardroom must be open to ambiguities. This means including paradoxical pairings such as creativity and criticality, cohesion and cognitive conflict, trust and distrust, independence and involvement, engagement and closeness but also non-executive distance. Managing these ambiguities involves an approach that accepts tension and is open to creative thinking.

Potential rescue site 3: accounts/finance

It might not be a surprise that the accounting department was ranked very highly (by both our seminar and online survey participants) as a likely location for the murder of creativity. Only 6 per cent of survey respondents indicated it is a place where creativity can be revived. Recently we stood before 60 Financial Controllers of the (InterContinental Hotels Group) IHG to challenge them on this topic. We asked them to respond to these accusations, and we were impressed by their articulate answers. The Financial Controller we were working most closely with explained:

At IHG we view the Finance team as 'trusted & valued business partners'. We moved away from simply being the number crunchers a number of years ago. Today we attempt to support IHG's strategy and ensure it is supported by the right resources. Other departments value the input from Finance in decision making and planning. So I don't believe the Finance department is a big killer of creativity. Do they need to ensure decisions are commercial? Yes. Do they need to ensure there is an appropriate balance amongst various stakeholders (owners, employees, customers) when making decisions? Yes. Do they need to ensure certain compliance and governance is in place? Definitely. As long as Finance can logically support their views then I don't believe they are killing creativity. At our recent Australasia Finance and Business Support Meeting we recognised individuals who have performed exceptionally throughout the year. For the first time we had an award category for 'Best Innovation'. We can't have the attitude that 'this is how it has always been done'. Interestingly, I think we have been innovative in our region because we have had to be to remain competitive. Due to the connotations around the term 'creative accounting' we certainly tend to speak more to 'innovation' at IHG as opposed to being 'creative'. Being creative in the finance field is more associated with doing the wrong thing, cutting corners, unethical behaviour etc. Innovation, on the other hand, is perceived differently and is aimed at changing or implementing processes to improve either efficiency or effectiveness. Innovation can be thinking outside the box, utilising your 'savvy' to come up with new solutions to issues we face.

200

The accounting department itself is not the only suspected murder loacation here, of course. There is also the accusation that the Finance focus can actively kill creativity elsewhere. Social psychologist Sam Keen believes that this focus has a stranglehold on too many areas of a company and raises an imaginative, perhaps even inspiring proposition worth considering:

It would be interesting to see what would happen within corporations if, for one hundred days, it was forbidden to talk about profits, losses, stockholders, competition, or market share. Some workers might wonder out loud if what they were doing with fifty or sixty hours a week truly reflected how they wished to spend their fleeting years. Others might wonder whether the product being promoted was ecologically viable, or if their contribution to a global economy was likely to benefit those on the planet who needed it most, or whether we might choose to measure the success of our society by gross national happiness [as they do in Bhutan], rather than by gross national product.[12]

Potential rescue site 4: executive offices

According to the Centers for Disease Control and Prevention (CDC), hospital-acquired infections in the US account for an estimated 1.7 million infections and 99 000 associated deaths each year. A 2003 CDC study reported that 52 per cent of US doctors did not wash their hands between patients.[13]

Knowing that doctors tended to be reluctant to take direction from others, Connie Jastremski, chief nursing officer for Bassett Healthcare Network, knew she had a major challenge on her hands when she was called in to help deal with the hygiene problem. The creative idea of having all clinicians wear a badge reading 'Ask me if I washed my hands' was introduced, but it was not readily accepted. Jastremski recalls how in the beginning the badges were actually thrown at her, but eventually she was able to change the culture — with remarkable success.

Health executives are usually subject to the pressures of government regulatory requirements, so it is often difficult to generate creativity and innovation in this context. The Bassett Healthcare Network introduced a 'paid sabbatical days' system that places a big emphasis on ensuring leaders have the time and space to explore creative ideas.[14]

In all organisations, the executive offices will need to acknowledge, embrace and actively promote creative development. They will also, in turn, need to be supported to ensure that they have the time and the space to be innovative themselves.

Potential rescue site 5: research and development

To build a truly creative environment in the R&D department, the R&D team will need to have the opportunity to follow through on innovative ideas and see them to completion. More than just artistic achievements or products and ideas that are 'similar but slightly different', real innovation is both novel and useful. Innovation cannot be occasional or erratic; rather, it needs to be systematic and purposeful.[15]

For creativity to thrive in R&D over the long term a culture of innovation needs to be created. Such a culture can be represented as four quadrants of a system formed by the two axes 'Introversion (internal care) — Extroversion (external organisational awareness)' and 'Flexibility (adaptability) — Control (top-down management orientation and bureaucracy)'.[16] This system is striking in that although the concepts at the extremes of the axes appear incompatible, both extremes can provide the openness needed for transformational change and the readiness to take risks. Both can help to create a culture of *adhocracy* (as opposed to bureaucracy) in R&D if similar values are inculcated and if creative thinking is actively promoted as they reflect the need for both diversion and conversion. Adherence to strict rules and hierarchical systems are clearly detrimental to the establishment of an *adhocracy* culture, so it is important to ensure R&D is not limited by these.[17]

In order to involve people at all levels of the organisation in the R&D process, Toyota was clever enough to give everyone in the organisation a 'quality control' role. This immediately empowered people to make suggestions to head office about what could be done better, generating more ideas by involving everyone in the creative process. By moving this element of R&D to the factory floor, they effectively upskilled shopfloor employees to active contributors on a higher level.

R&D must learn to persuade finance, CEOs, boards and executive offices to contribute new ideas, helping all to understand that R&D is a valuable central (but not exclusive) place for creativity to be cultivated. There can be a reluctance to invest in R&D, as it is not possible to 'plan' creative outcomes. Many a company, particularly in the pharmaceutical sector, has been burned from poor results in R&D. But stable funding provides more freedom for innovation and ultimately produces better results.[18] Pressures from the Fear Family must never be allowed to shut down ideas in this department and must be dealt with swiftly.

Potential rescue site 6: sales and marketing

After the bustling New York City metropolis, the town of Kingfield in Maine offers a stark contrast. It has one main street, one petrol station, one post office — probably just one of everything that might be considered vital to a small community. Everyone knows each other here, and has done for generations, which explains why the crime rate is low. When we fly in from the city we notice that everything is crisp and clean, from the fresh air to the pure snow, and there is no evidence of pollution. We've always been fascinated by the chutzpah of companies that can successfully market and sell something that is already plentiful, and the town of Kingfield demonstrates in practice exactly what 'selling snow to Eskimos' really means.

Many brands of bottled water in the US boast that their water offers the pure taste of 'Maine spring water' in a bottle. The water from Maine is so good that people are happy to pay for it all over the country. So the irony is not lost on us when our friend, an outdoor enthusiast who moved to Maine to enjoy pure country living and have this wonderful Maine water on tap, points out that the lady in front of us at the supermarket checkout is purchasing a large case of bottled water. Yes, you guessed it, *Maine spring water*! A four-year scientific study recently made public by the National Resources Defense

Council found that bottled water sold in the United States is not necessarily cleaner or safer than most tap water, and we'd imagine nowhere could this be more true than in Kingfield, Maine. Yet some clever sales and marketing person had managed to sell Maine spring water to the people of Maine.

When you come to think of it, the very idea of selling water in a bottle is an incredible S&M coup. Thirty years ago bottling water barely existed as a business in the United States. By 2006 Americans were spending as much as $15 billion a year on spring water, more than they spent on iPods or movie tickets.[19] Perhaps, like ordinary run-of-the-mill water, creativity has had poor branding for many years. Perhaps an association with dope-smoking artists engaged in not much more than cloud watching and navel gazing has meant that Creativity has not been given the serious attention it deserves. Until recently it has been difficult to convince companies to invest money on creative thinking skills because of the perception that it will involve no more than an irrelevant feel-good workshop or a fun day out. Now, however, there is a recognition that creative thinking is an investment in the future. Perhaps S&M should be utilised internally to help create a more positive and innovative culture.

Bottled water isn't safer or healthier than tap water; in fact, in some cases bottled water has been found to have more bacteria. Anyone who chooses to buy water instead of a soft drink from a vending machine is undoubtedly making a healthier choice, but it's still not a necessary choice. In most developed countries you could bring a bottle of water from home. In developing countries any source of clean water is so incredibly appreciated we forget that we have that option so readily available and free of charge. There are many who have to travel miles every day to collect clean water in a bucket to carry back home. And that water is not necessarily safe or clean. If an innovative S&M team can sell bottled water in Maine, perhaps they could think about solving global water access problems.

Creativity has the opportunity to thrive in the S&M department. Whatever starts in S&M can and should bring hope to all. They can certainly start by using their skills and a persuasive and integrated process to sell the need for creativity within the organisation.

Potential rescue site 7: the coffee shop

Why was Starbucks such a huge success when it started? And why have many other independent and chain coffee shops imitated the Starbucks model? Because they came up with the revolutionary idea of setting up coffee shops as if they were open living rooms. They recreated a home environment, designing a place where you could sit, relax, read, surf the net and wind down through long conversations with friends in comfortable, casual settings.

Many people felt it was the end of an era when we started watching video movies at home instead of going to the cinema. Now there has been a revival of interest in movie-going. In the same way, there has been a revival in the communal coffee culture. Lloyds of London was originally named after a coffee house. Influential scientists Robert Hooke and Edmond Halley solved significant scientific problems together over a freshly brewed pot of coffee.[20] This culture is now being brought back into the organisation. In the new office building of One Raffles Quay, Singapore, where the Barclays Bank offices are located, a luxury coffee shop area has been designed for employees and their guests to connect over coffee. Electronic Arts (EA) in Singapore has gone one step further by adding a games room that encourages people to play together, including a basketball net and EA video games.

Of course, the coffee shop will fail to provide the environment for open thinking if it is seen as just another location for continuing work. We have developed the erroneous belief that the more work we create, the more productive we are being, and yet sometimes it is only when we switch off that our mind is really free to be creative. Yes, coffee shops may be a nice place to continue working while enjoying a change of scene, but they should also be a place where it's possible to connect with other people and completely switch off in the middle of a busy day. Every day we should set up 'Purposeful Opportunities' (De Bono's POs) to give our minds the chance to wander freely, and the coffee shop just might be the ideal place for this.

Potential rescue site 8: the lecture room

When you spend four hours a day walking through dangerous guerrilla territory and rugged terrain just to go to school, you need to be serious about learning. We spent some time teaching about learning and development on a large island in the middle of the Philippines, and during our time there we interviewed impoverished school children who did just this. We have never seen students who were more alert and enthusiastic or with a greater thirst for learning. Despite the challenges, or perhaps precisely because of them, there was an appreciation you seldom see in children from more affluent areas. In stark contrast to the indifferent, unenthusiastic or even hostile attitude of many of the children we had worked with previously, these children valued the opportunity to learn and to better their lives through education.

After up to 14 years of schooling our children receive a relative ranking and mark that is supposed to reflect their level of intelligence and capability. By the time they hit the workplace many will see learning and development as a 'tick and flick' process which will be dictated by HR and/or training. Some may value this as part of their personal growth and development; others can become cynical about the usefulness and purpose of it. By the time we come along to run workshops for organisations, sometimes we find that 80 per cent of our effort needs to go into developing an appreciation of the learning process. We are constantly battling against the problem that many people feel it's simply not worth taking time out for personal or group development. Participants sit in a workshop worrying about the work that will be piling up in their Inbox. Worse still, some continue to check their email and field calls during the day on their tiny mobile offices.

Where organisations continuously transform themselves through wisely facilitated learning opportunities, individuals benefit and the organisation flourishes. The organisations that learn and adapt the fastest will best survive in changing times. On the other hand, organisations that are trapped by established mental patterns and fail to learn flexibility will inexorably flounder.[21]

206

An inventor is someone who hasn't taken his education too seriously.[22] While failing exams is an indication that you are not up to standard in the education system and can mean it's the end of the road for you, inventors must learn to fail over and over again and believe that what they're doing is still valuable and worthwhile. In the education system it may take only one failure after a series of successes to be cast out of the system, but for an inventor it takes only one success after a series of failures to achieve a positive outcome. Failing intelligently—learning from setbacks, and growing through them—is the single most important survival skill; it will motivate people to learn and propagate creative thinking for life.

Potential rescue site 9: the playground

Google is undoubtedly high on the list of 'best places to work'. Apart from the allocated hours employees can devote to creative thinking pursuits, Google also offers great benefits, such as free meals and doctors. The Silicon Valley Google office is not just a great place to work, it's also a great place to play![23] With a swimming spa, on-campus beach volleyball courts, foosball, video games, pool tables, table tennis and roller hockey twice a week in the parking lot, one wonders when the employees find time to get their 'serious' work done. It's not surprising that Google receives 1300 resumés a day.[24]

Free play creates a mental state in which it is possible to feel safe to explore ideas without restrictions. Parents who try to maximise their children's education opportunities by shuffling them between countless after-school activities and planning rigorous study schedules may actually be in danger of shutting down the innovative, creative part of their brains as the exhausted children struggle to get through their day. Free play, as we have mentioned, is one of the conduits needed to divert brain resources from dealing with the primitive survival functions so they can access creative thinking. If creative thinking is not accessed regularly, strong pathways in the brain cannot be established, and the ability to think creatively can actually wither away.

Some may complain that there is no space in their workplace for play. But play can be a state of mind or an attitude. A creative mind doesn't distinguish between reality and imagination, so mental exercise is a powerful way to play no matter where you are, and it undoubtedly keeps the morale up.

Behavioural scientist Jack Stuster spent time in Antarctica to research how to keep isolated teams motivated. His research findings would be applied to isolated teams in a variety of environments, including on space stations. Stuster discovered that the physical environment makes a huge difference to team morale in these situations, right down to specific details such as the colour of walls. As he says, 'Researchers have discovered that the less meaningful the work is the more important aesthetics should be. The paradox is that people can endure and perform under amazing circumstances *But* a good environment enhances the chances of success'.[25]

You may not be able to change many of the specifics of your work environment, but you can at least ensure that your own workspace and those you may have influence over are conducive to creative thinking and have a positive impact on morale. It might not be a world-saving project, and not everyone can build a playground to make work more fun, but we can all be responsible in some way for helping to build a playful, creative environment. And we can start to appreciate how a playful state of mind can seriously contribute to genuine development.

Bringing the bedroom to the boardroom

It's a common fear that more crime takes place at night than in daylight because the criminal has more cover—although British Home Office statistics show that most criminals need light to see what they are doing! It might be discomforting to know that 60 per cent of burglaries in the UK happen when the home is occupied, often while people are asleep.[26]

Creativity killers are all around us and can strike anywhere, at any time, but the resuscitators are on hand too. This emergency rescue crew is always on call to come to the place they are most needed. In fact, one of the busiest times for creative revival is at night while people are sleeping. Sleep is an important opportunity for the brain to rejuvenate and recover from the day's activities, and perhaps not surprisingly, it is also when the most profound creative development can take place.

It has been clearly established that sleep deprivation can be detrimental for performance and judgement. For example, when lab rats are kept awake for hours by providing them with stimulating activities and toys, it has been found that small groups of neurons begin flipping over into a sleep-like state, eventually impairing their judgement and performance.[27] Lack of sleep has also been linked to aggression and disordered sexual behaviour as well as depression.[28] Professional athletes are often advised to take a short nap before competing to ensure they are in peak condition. Chronic sleep loss can lead to a 30 to 40 per cent reduction in glucose metabolism, 11 per cent reduction in the time it takes to reach a state of exhaustion, and lapses in attention and reactivity. Extra sleep improves split-second timing, reaction time and alertness.[29] Other benefits of a good night's sleep range from weight loss to improved heart health.

We know intuitively that 'down time' stimulates creativity. When we suggest to someone that they 'sleep on it' to help them arrive at a solution, we are allowing their divergent thinking to work and giving their imagination room to breathe. It increases the total space in the brain that is open to new ideas. 'Free thinking' time allows the mind to wander into new territories and stumble on new ideas; the brain can slip into alpha brainwave activity, during which the mind is not specifically focused. As Csikszentmihalyi, reveals, 'The content of the conscious line of thought is taken up by the subconscious, and there, out of reach of the censorship of awareness, the abstract scientific problem has a chance to reveal itself for what it is.'[30] Unfortunately these days, as most people's time is strictly scheduled and structured, there is very little time for 'free thinking'.

The mind uses sleep as an opportunity to reboot and problem-solve, says Harvard psychologist Deirdre Barrett. In one experiment, Barrett had college students focus on a homework problem each night before they went to sleep. At the end of a week, about half the students said they had dreamt about the problem and about a quarter had 'a dream that contained the answer'. According to Barrett, in the same way that our brain works to solve problems when we are awake, the mind also works at resolving issues when we are dreaming.[31]

When people are asked to name a place they'd most like to be, they don't say 'in the middle of a busy, crowded city' or 'in a high-rise office'; they most often name a calm, peaceful place of natural beauty—a pristine beach or a mountain retreat. By escaping to such a place, whether literally or simply in our mind, we can induce the calm state that will foster creative thinking. By mentally switching over into a 'psychologically distant' state, we separate ourselves from the pressures and stresses of the 'here and now' and open up to creativity. According to the Construal Level Theory (CLT) of psychological distance,[32] it is possible to create that same sense of psychological distance by simply thinking differently about a particular problem, taking another person's perspective, or imagining that the question is unreal or unlikely. A team at Indiana University has found a clear link between the ability to increase psychological distance and creativity. They have demonstrated that there are a number of simple, practical things we can do to increase creativity, including travelling to faraway places (either physically or in the mind), thinking about the distant future, communicating with people who are dissimilar to us and considering unlikely alternatives to reality. Travelling and living abroad have been found to be linked with creativity.[33] It has even been suggested that our modern cosmopolitan communities, which enable contact with a wide variety of cultural elements (such as people, music and food), give us opportunities to think more abstractly.[34]

If at this stage in your life you can only dream about that exotic travel, then take a look around you. Next time you go to your local Chinese or Thai restaurant you might take the time to talk to the staff to find out how they cook and what makes their lives different. All cities have their culturally rich areas: in certain parts of Los Angeles it is possible to imagine you are in Mexico, London or India, and in most major cities in the world you can go to Chinatown, where you can feel like you've just stepped into downtown Shanghai. All cities have their areas of diversity, and rather than be threatened by this we have learned to embrace the experience, especially countries that pride themselves on multicultural diversity. Perhaps rather than focusing on the negative impact of the city (the pressures, the stresses), you can use the opportunities the city creates to find that psychological distance you need to be creative.

Of course, travelling to another country alone does not guarantee you will be more open to new ideas. You will find many Australian tourists travelling to Bali on their home airline (Qantas), eating Australian food (steak, peas and mash), drinking Aussie beers at Aussie-style pubs while watching Aussie football on TV, and staying at hermetically sealed Westernised hotels. These tourists somehow manage to completely bypass the local culture.

The lesson here is that open-mindedness is a state of mind rather than a location. Whether you live in an impoverished area of a city, a plush beachside suburb in the 'insular peninsula' region of North Sydney or an exotic tropical island, it is possible to learn to be open to new ideas and ways of thinking. So now you have a justifiable excuse to nap or daydream during work hours. But if you can't afford to be caught sleeping on the job, and the boss won't go with the idea that you are being creative, then at least try to change the environment you are in so that it supports creative thinking. Bring the bedroom to the office floor, and sleep on it.

And they lived happily ever after ... or did they?

Putting creativity on trial for the final twist in the plot

Just a few months before the revolutionary events in Egypt our family wandered through Cairo's Tahrir Square as carefree tourists. We attracted the usual attention and interest with our blond hair and the corresponding expectation of easy foreign money, and were frequently pressed to buy copy watches and fake artefacts, but nothing out of the ordinary for a typical travel experience, and we generally felt pretty safe. Not long after that, a tidal wave of reform swept through the Middle East. Images of Tahrir Square under siege were beamed around the world, and what had so recently been a peaceful open market became a barricaded battleground. After a brief period of euphoria, the same darkness that had dwelt in the country before the revolution crept back in under the new powers.

At the height of the uprising, which had successfully ended Mubarak's 30-year reign of power, blonde veteran CBS reporter Lara Logan was on location in the thick of the celebrations at Tahrir Square. With history in the making and the world watching, she reported that she felt safe. Shortly afterwards, though, the mood around her turned hostile, and a 200-strong mob turned on Lara and brutally attacked and sexually assaulted her.[1]

The crowd mentality is dangerous. Social psychologist Sam Keen[2] believes that mob killers universally use a language of prejudice and stereotypes to tap into the crowd's most visceral emotions. And another, more insidious thing happens: the diffusion of responsibility enables the abdication of individual sense of values. Sound like any workplace you have been in? Underneath the mask of the enemy, says Joseph Campbell,[3] we ultimately recognise ourselves, but it is when a mob can whip a crowd into such an emotional frenzy that personal contact is lost that the situation can become dangerous.

Before you prepare to attack the creativity killers in your working or living environment, and before you rally around similarly incensed fellow workers or citizens, bear in mind that these potential killers are only suspects (and all of them also live in each one of us to varying degrees). We know from the investigation of the crime scene that the issue is real, but the factors involved can be incredibly complex. Each individual should soberly assess their personal situation to determine creativity's killer for them, without going on a witch hunt and externalising the blame.

Can the killers be redeemed ... and are the rescuers squeaky clean?

As much as we have described the suspect creativity killer profiles in black and white, setting them up as evil serial killers, we admit to employing creative licence to make our points. Inherently 'good' people or systems can be capable of doing destructive things, and apparently 'bad' people and systems are equally capable of being constructive. This ambiguity is at the core of creativity. If you are now able to accept this level of ambiguity, then well done — you have already learned one essential lesson. The creativity killers cannot be reduced to simple villains, and they will not be reported on the front page of the newspapers with a big 'wanted' sign and a reward for any information about their whereabouts or leading to their arrest.

It often comes down to the specific environment and mindset that is created, and the ability of good teaching and leadership to bring out the positive behaviours and traits. Some individuals or systems that display characteristics of control, bureaucracy or fear, for example, incorporate these traits in careful moderation for specific purposes. Often those who suppress creative thinking are unaware of the effect of their actions and will be willing to change. Consider some possible positive flipsides to our 'most wanted' list:

Ʌ *Control.* You don't see an emergency response team
leader in the midst of an emergency asking if the team
would like to spend some time brainstorming ideas.
There are times when you simply need to take action
swiftly and expertly, and these are times when control
is needed.

Ʌ *Fear.* This is one of the most adaptive responses we have.
Fear keeps us alive. It is only when this physiological
response is wrongly applied (or manipulated) that it
becomes harmful.

Ʌ *Pressure.* Pressure can be positive, when it is experienced
as 'eustress'. It has been shown to enable people to rise
to an occasion and even to focus, particularly for short-
term events.

Ʌ *Insulation.* All of us have a selective filter that enables us
to sort through incoming information so we can focus
on what is valuable. If we were to take in every piece of
information we are exposed to, we'd go crazy! So this can
be an important quality.

Ʌ *Apathy.* People who would like to find ways to be more
efficient may be able to channel this drive in a positive
way. Working long hours doesn't necessarily lead to greater
success or productivity. We have already seen that the best
creative ideas can come when the brain is in a relaxed
state (such as sleep or deep relaxation), so be careful not
to mistake the need to rest and have some down time
with apathy.

Ʌ *Pessimism.* People can harness the power of negative
thoughts to increase their self-esteem and make significant progress towards personal goals.[4] As described earlier,
defensive pessimism recognises the adaptive value of
thinking through worst-case scenarios and springboarding
from anxiety to motivate and carry out effective actions.

As with many things in life, a level of balance is required, as well
as a need to view things perceptively, to know where the balance
point is, because swinging to either extreme will most likely
be counterproductive. Sometimes the 'murderer' attributes

are everyday qualities that can be used either positively or negatively. But remember that one of the key determinations in this book is that over the long term heightened states of fear, pessimism and pressure will sap brain bandwidth and drain the energy needed for creative thinking.

On the other side, the rescuers may not always be as squeaky clean as we have made them out to be. Consider how, for example, blind positivity can actually be as dangerous as fatalistic pessimism, in that blind optimists are unable to spot dangers easily. Optimists and idealists have wrought havoc over the centuries through ignorance of the truths of human nature and human society, and naive hopes of what can be changed.[5] In a similar way, too much freedom can lead to anarchy, too much independence can be counterproductive for collaborative innovation, and too much flexibility can mean there is no structure for disciplined growth. As in many areas in life, we need to set boundaries and clear guidelines for constructive creative development.

The yin and yang of creativity

What about creativity herself? Perhaps she is not the innocent victim we have portrayed her to be. She may have personality challenges of her own ...

While we were thinking over this final chapter Kallen needed help with an assignment about famous artists — and we were struck by the flipside of creative genius. Kallen chose to focus on Van Gogh's self-portrait after he had cut off his own ear, a not-so-positive self-reflection from a tormented creative individual. (There are, of course, a multitude of other examples.) This simple assignment, more than anything else, illustrated for us the struggles that can accompany creative genius. While we might admire what exceptionally creative people have achieved, it is important to recognise that many creative geniuses are in fact tortured souls. Their emotional sensitivity and passion are often so consuming that their lives are deeply dysfunctional and shaped by constant, relentless struggle. For some, indeed, there appears to be a fine line between creative genius and madness.

It is not difficult to see that many creative geniuses carry with them elements of madness and are characterised by qualities or behaviours that strike others as odd. Consider the following examples[6]:

- Albert Einstein picked up cigarette butts off the street to collect tobacco for his pipe.
- Howard Hughes spent entire days in a self-created germ-free zone in the middle of his Beverly Hills hotel suite.
- The composer Robert Schumann believed that Beethoven directed his musical compositions.
- Salvador Dalí liked to keep exotic pets.
- Michael Jackson showed an unhealthy obsession with plastic surgery.
- Steve Jobs was known to be obsessive in a number of ways, including diet.

Historically, geniuses were often persecuted, although in enlightened times these nonconformists have had the opportunity to make great contributions to science and society.[7]

Creativity and eccentricity may, in fact, be closely biologically related. Some have argued that there is evidence that both are the result of genetic variations that increase cognitive disinhibition—the brain's failure to filter out extraneous information.[8] When unfiltered information reaches conscious awareness in the brains of people who are highly intelligent, and they can process this information without being overwhelmed, it can lead to exceptional insights. Certain other cognitive traits, such as the ability to make unusual or bizarre associations, are shared by schizophrenics and healthy, highly creative people, who score well on divergent thinking tests just as mentally ill people can. Interestingly, both groups share a lower density of D2 receptors in the thalamus than the average population. However, correlation should not be confused with causation. 'Thinking outside the box might be facilitated by having a somewhat less intact box,' suggests Dr Fredrik Ullén of the Karolinska Institute, Stockholm, about these new findings.[9] The point at which 'the box' becomes unable to sustain healthy functioning is a fascinating idea.

Since we have given all the creativity killers personality characteristics in this book, let's go way out on a limb to contemplate for a minute the idea that creativity herself might also have unique behaviour traits.[10] If we were to describe creativity as a personality type, perhaps we could say there are two distinct sides to her personality—a fast-paced, active explorer, and a slower-paced, deeply reflective artist. Bipolar disorder (otherwise known as manic depression) has a similar manic, charged state, in which there can be exciting flashes of perception, and a depressed slower state, in which there can be deep emotional insights. In bipolar disorder the manic state opens up creative thinking by allowing the individual to believe there are no boundaries. Like the active creative state, the manic state is physically alert and able to respond quickly (perhaps sometimes irrationally) through a range of changes (for example, emotional, perceptual, behavioural). The depressed state, conversely, can also induce creative insights through enabling the individual to access his or her deeper emotional side. (Unfortunately, in clinical depression lows can have both artistically impressive and destructive force.) Creativity can express herself in either of these two ways. Perhaps by learning to access our creative thinking ability we are opening ourselves up to both the explorer and artist, accessing deeper skills and emotions than we might otherwise encounter.[11]

Of course this is not to say that creativity equals crazy, and you certainly don't need to be crazy to be creative. Remember, 30 per cent of us meet the criteria for a major psychological disorder at some stage in our lives, so many of us cross the boundaries of what is 'normal' at some time. Perhaps at times creativity will appear in unusual ways, but creativity in itself is neither a positive nor a negative quality. It is simply what it is. The point is we need to use creativity in a constructive way, making the most of both the reflective and active sides of her personality in balance.

Think about the importance of being truly open to our innermost feelings and emotions. Reflect on how, by facing these emotions, responding to them and dealing with them, we may in fact be able to connect with the deeper feelings that bring passion and meaning into our lives, possibly even enabling a sense of connection and purpose. Surely that is a form of liberation that is worth pursuing despite the potential challenges?

Playing with fire and other disruptive innovations

When driving in remote areas of Australia it can be a very strange sight to see firefighters with flamethrowers rather than water hoses. Why are these emergency workers setting fire to the bushland instead of putting out fires, as you would expect them to do? The reason is they know a secret they learned from Australian Aboriginals, something the Indigenous people have known for many thousands of years. The Australian bushland needs to be regularly regenerated. Back-burning helps to protect inhabited areas by reducing fuel build-up in a controlled way, but burning the bush also encourages its regeneration over the long term. After the fire the native trees and bushes sprout fresh shoots and buds and grow back even thicker and hardier than they were before. The practice of back-burning has to be evaluated in the context of the full life cycle of the bush. Without this bush burning, the natural habitat would not thrive.

Bringing creativity into your life or into your organisation can be like the preventative actions of Australian firefighters. A deliberately lit bushfire may be an act of arson (causing havoc and leaving a path of destruction) or a proactive rescue process (controlled back-burning, leading to long-term protection and, ultimately, new life). Back-burning is also a preventative measure, as without deliberate, carefully executed controlled burning eventually a wild fire will ravage the environment mercilessly.

Back-burning can be compared to what is known in behavioural economics as 'disruptive innovation'—that is, intervening by means of a radical, apparently destructive act in pursuit of a higher purpose. Such a scorched earth process may be needed to get to the heart of an organisational problem and to break down poor foundations before it is possible to rebuild constructively. But some organisations may not be prepared to take this step. Sometimes the transformation required for real innovation is just too much of a challenge.[12] And sometimes people are not ready for the fuzzy grey ambiguities of creativity itself. The practice of questioning current beliefs, systems and processes can be painful and harsh, the pursuit of the murder suspects can be relentless, but it may be a necessary evil to reach a positive outcome over the long term.

Even if we agree that new creative ideas will produce better results and are needed to move forward, how many people would willingly trigger such a disruptive process, either in their own lives and or in their organisations? What leader can really afford to introduce a major innovation revolution by moving the company through a 'back-burning' stage? Who would be prepared to raze a company to enable it to grow stronger and hardier from the ground up? Who would begin such a massive renovation, knowing that the benefits would not be felt until the next generation, when the CEO's immediate pressure is to make this year's budget? Think of most politicians. They are reluctant to do anything likely to be unpopular in the short term, even if it means the country would benefit in the longer term, because they won't risk losing elections.[13]

As an interesting reflective exercise, let's turn the tables on the main premise of this book and think about this whole whodunit scenario in reverse. Let's imagine for a moment that creativity is the murder suspect and stands accused of threatening or killing other values that can be vital to survival—perhaps stability or continuity or longevity. Then we might be asking the questions, 'Who killed the system that provides stability?' or 'Who challenged the status quo?'

Geoffrey West believes the average company lasts for only 40 years because leaders do not recognise the need to go through this back-burning and regeneration process, or do not want to risk going through it while the business is profitably growing. To survive the inevitable growth and decline cycle, West says, companies have no choice but to 'die' in a sense. But if they manage this inevitability cleverly, they will prepare for it by initiating completely new life cycles from the virtual death of the initial enterprise. Although it can be a major jolt to the system, as a defibrillator machine literally shocks the heart back to life, it will reset the clock and enable productive life to begin all over again.[14] Just as this needs to happen on the macro and organisational level, it can and should also happen on a micro individual level.

In the 1800s, when New York's streets were crammed with horse-drawn carriages, the city was threatened with an overwhelming horse manure problem. The city almost didn't survive the ecological disaster, but out of the mire there was a positive result. The crisis led to the need to reset the clock through a massive new technological innovation — through the mass production of the new machine known as the 'automobile'. The innovation was introduced just in the nick of time, but as a result anyone involved in the horse-and-buggy industry would have lost their income, if they hadn't kept abreast of these changes.[15]

Innovate or die — the commercial and social consequences of regeneration

If you weren't around to see the transition of New York from the age of horse-drawn carriages to automobiles, or if you missed the shift to relatively clean electric power in the home after the burning of depleted fossil fuels such as coal had poisoned the lungs of generations, you may still be lucky enough to witness a new regeneration phase for human civilisation. Our insatiable appetite for more things 'quicker, better and cheaper' is demanding ever more innovative thinking.

So what form will the next creative reset take? The current critical issue of global warming provides a big 'creative reset' opportunity. It now appears to be a clear case of 'do or die', lest we end up in an apocalyptic 'Mad Max' type world. In other areas, we are now witnessing the emergence of smaller, more nimble organisations that can compete with the larger, more established companies on a number of fronts. Think of how the creative kid with a laptop working out of his garage is currently simultaneously respected and feared by the once dominant corporate executive.

Consider another area of rapid change: book publishing. If you are reading this book in printed form you should cherish it — it may be the last of a dying breed. But it is more likely that you will be reading it in ebook format. As we were in the process of writing this book, bookshops and publishers were experiencing the collapse of the industry on which they relied, one that has been in the process of being reborn online (although, as often happens when facing the possibility of physical death, denial has been a prevalent emotional response). A turning point in this regeneration revolution was Amazon's announcement in 2011 that sales of ebooks had overtaken sales of print books and that they were taking on authors themselves, writing publishers out of the deal.[16] The same year saw the big bookshop chains disappear from the local malls across the country.

Why have these organisations missed the innovative shift and therefore died from uncontrolled burning? According to Tim Harford:

> *Disruptive innovations are disruptive precisely because the new technology doesn't appeal to the traditional customers: The problem for a market leader in the old technology is not necessarily that it lacks the capacity to innovate, but that it lacks the will. When a disruptive technology appears, it may confound an existing player because the technology itself is so radically different. A sufficiently disruptive innovation bypasses almost everybody who matters at a company: In short, everyone who counts in a company will lose status if the disruptive innovation catches on inside that company — and whether consciously or unconsciously, they will often make sure that it doesn't. As a result, the company may find itself in serious trouble. It may even die.[17]*

Lonely Planet is an example of a publisher that adapted to the digital age and the changing needs of travellers; it did so through new digital audio tours and a 'pick and mix' function that allows customers to download and print chapters of books.[18] Indigo, Canada's largest bookseller, promotes books as a 'lifestyle', not a product, selling giftware, children's toys, video games, music, gourmet food and even flowers along with their books. It is an example of a contemporary independent bookseller leveraging on people's affection for books and desire to give beautiful gifts. The Apple Newton crashed and burned, but out of the ashes rose the iPad, along with the Kindle and other, similar portable electronic reading devices.

Many organisations in the entertainment industry, struggling to survive following the rapid technological changes, are using creative thinking to generate clever solutions. Before the pirating of music and TV shows became a major issue, for example, successful clothing brands were often copied. In the markets of Bali, for a number of years surf wear companies struggled to compete against the fake knock-offs being sold on every street corner. At only a few dollars per item, these copies were hugely attractive to tourists wanting to snap up a quick bargain at a fraction of the regular cost. Then the owner of one of the largest surf brands came up with an ingenious way to deal with the problem. He found out who the biggest culprits were in the knock-off market, and he offered them the chance to own the licence and represent the real brand in Bali. In return, they were to ensure the fake brands were no longer an issue. While the big brand owners had not been able to control what was happening in the local markets and on the streets of Kuta, the locals did have this power. The immediate success of this arrangement was astonishing.

What we are witnessing today is not just an interesting natural growth-and-death cycle, but a regeneration model in which the stakes are higher than they have ever been before. Creative thinking will need to be applied to solve the world's problems. Not just to sell more products, feather more nests, build more insanely wealthy personal incomes and support the limited capitalist cycle. Driven by people power, those who have learned they can take the future into their own hands will do so. With open accessibility, this innovation revolution will be wider reaching and more pervasive than anything previously experienced. And it will be a test of how willing we are to recognise the needs identified through this new empowering process and respond to them creatively.

Change is inevitable, so scale the slopes constructively

Change is inevitable. There will always be new mountains to climb. We will always need to innovate to conquer these mountains as they continue to loom larger and larger. Innovation is neither good nor evil — it just is. It will happen whether we are actively involved in the process or not, so it's up to us to decide if we are going to be a positive part of the process, or if we are going to become its hapless victims.

Organisations will need to recognise the impact this innovation will have on their future. If creativity doesn't come from the organisation it will come from the people, and if the organisation can't change it will become obsolete. 'Disruptive innovation' will emerge with or without an organisation's assistance or approval. The customer will innovate with or without help. People started downloading TV shows not necessarily because they enjoyed doing things illegally, but simply because they didn't want to be dictated to on what to watch and when to watch it. After all, a teenage kid illegally downloading the latest TV show from The Pirate Bay through uTorrent would probably rather download it from ABC TV virus free and in HD quality. Even if they have to put up with legitimate advertisements, it would be better than having to put up with the banner ads for porn sites that accompany uTorrent pages. Heaven forbid if they accidently click on the wrong 'upload' button!

As Patricia B. Seybold sees it, 'Customers have taken control. Their rampant comparison shopping is eroding your margins. Their renegade behaviour is challenging your business models and endangering your intellectual property. Their demanding expectations for customized products, wonderful experiences and high service levels are draining your resources. Customers' insistence on open access is exposing your industry's policies and challenging your inflexible business processes.'[19]

Because innovation emerges out of the structural tension between the way things are and the way we imagine they could be, the gap between what people can do today and what they want to be able to do is driving change beyond what anyone may have anticipated. Rather than waiting for Mother Nature's inevitable environmental reset, proactive steps will need to be taken to deal with global climate change. Rather than creating the products or services for the customer, organisations will have to learn to allow the customer to identify and drive innovation.

Even simple changes are now being found to make a significant difference. Consider the 'trayless cafeteria', as implemented in some universities in the US. By simply ceasing to use trays, less food is wasted, less water and energy is used in cleaning, less trash and waste water is produced, and less food is consumed—all positive benefits. Before the introduction of the scheme in the University of Nebraska's dining halls it was observed that students threw away 1300 pounds of solid food, 800 pounds of liquid and 90 pounds of paper in just five hours. Studies have shown that trayless dining programs reduce food waste by 25 to 30 per cent per person.[20]

In the now struggling retail clothes industry, retailers must now contend with unscrupulous shoppers who try on their clothes to check the fit and then verify the best prices online on their smart phones. Some stores deal with this by charging a fitting fee—as much $50 for ski boots, or $300 for a wedding dress! While many companies might find themselves burned by this reactive charging, stores like Myer have started a proactive 'back-burning' process, responding to the 'disruptive innovations' by setting up their own online stores offshore (in Hong Kong) to get their foot in the door of the exponentially growing online market.

Rather than assuming that the organisation has 'experts' who are smarter than its customers, which is no longer always the case, argues Seybold, smart organisations will be open to and value the customer's or client's input. Traditionally, the organisation was set up as the specialist, and products were designed to anticipate what the customer might want. The marketing team would then work to sell that product by creating an active need. Today, however, by starting with the customer's input, products are more user friendly and relevant and largely sell themselves. Some see this as one of the major differences between Microsoft and Apple: Microsoft innovated around their products, while Apple innovated around their customers.

For example, Apple beat the usual imposed limitations of the dimensionality curve by making it possible for anyone to design a new application for their iPhone or iPad. This effectively increased their workforce by more than 100 000 people, without any of the associated costs or commitments! It represented a complete turnaround from how Apple and Microsoft had once been differentiated. Microsoft had first built an open system in which their product could be used with any hardware, while Apple had remained restricted, but now Apple has turned the tables with this opportunity for open access. What this may be demonstrating is that the organisations that are able to open up their offerings become freer to be more creative, and these are the organisations that will ultimately win out.

Maybe the time has come to reset the clock and let creativity find new and better ways to grow. Just as there are a few ways to get down a mountain safely, ensuring you don't free-fall off the precipices or slide out of control down the steep slopes, we have provided you with a few approaches to get through the changes the future will bring. Like the skilled off-piste snowboarder, you can exercise your brain and practise your personal skills to learn to react quickly and expertly to any hidden obstacles. And like the abseiler who descends the cliff by a series of manageable planned pitches, you can take the time to address specific challenges slowly and carefully, one step at a time, remaining open to new creative possibilities, as you introduce practical innovations to your team and your organisation.

Why the Mexico rubbish dump dwellers might just save the planet

If ever there was a place to abandon hope for civilisation, it would be found on the outskirts of one of the largest and most polluted cities in the world, in one of the poorest areas on earth. We still have a clear image in our heads of two nine-year-old children flying homemade kites, running as fast as they can. Their kites soar four metres above our heads before suddenly plummeting onto a stinking pile of garbage. But this was not just an isolated rubbish pile. This mound was a small part of a huge mountain of rubbish that stretched as far as the eye could see, at least a mile or two in each direction. The constantly smouldering rubbish mountain is home to a whole community of people who fossick for scraps of food and collect recyclable materials to sell. Hundreds of people live here in houses knocked together out of discarded bits of tin and wood—people who have moved from the country looking for work, people who have fallen on hard times. And this is just one of four such rubbish mountain communities that ring Mexico City, between them housing literally thousands of impoverished people. (To see a video interview with the children go to <www.whokilledcreativity.com>.)

For the first time in history more people now live in cities than in rural areas. As we race into the future the pace of urbanisation will continue to increase. Billions more people will move into cities over this century, and as they do these fringe communities will continue to grow and evolve. The changes are too large and too fast to allow planners and policymakers to respond adequately.[21] The down side of urbanisation is not inescapable, and it's going to be a race between sigmoidal growth that could lead to an unavoidable reset and possible death and new growth from creative intervention and deliberate regeneration (back-burning).

As much as the Mexico City rubbish dump might sound like an exceptionally depressing place, we found a vibrant community of purposeful people with winning smiles and positive attitudes. The houses were positioned along tidy streets carved through the piles of garbage and swept meticulously daily to give some semblance of order in chaos. Small 'gardens' (struggling plant cuttings in rusty old tins, old painted salsa jars and tyres) epitomised the spirit of hope and creative playfulness of the community. Although the children worked hard each day collecting the recyclables to contribute to the family income, they also had time to play — and to create. They made their kites out of discarded plastic and sticks, they constructed original playthings from toys wealthy children had discarded, putting together bits and pieces that other children would have found useless. Having nothing, and possibly because they had nothing, they were original and inventive. Rather than watching ready-made stories on TV and playing with ready-made toys, they worked from a clean slate, using their imagination to create what they did not have.

We reflected on the irony of the situation. We couldn't have found ourselves further from the affluent Sydney Northern Beaches community we had come from, where children complained of being bored and having nothing to do and yet had access to any number of pre-packaged gadgets, toys and amusements. It was a long way too from our paradise in Bali, where powerful external forces had led to the death of a

227

pristine beach, the loss of creative innocence and the demise of the creative spirit in the village community. We had found the epitome of original creative thinking in the most unlikely of places. And we realised that day how important it was to discover and learn from the mindset that enabled those with no means to build something from nothing and to keep hoping for a better future.

Our cities and civilisations don't need to die, and we need not let creativity expire. As we race towards the future we need to stimulate a cross-pollination of ideas from the top floor of the CEO's office down to the rubbish dump and back again. It might seem crazy, but the smart application of creativity can ensure it will continue to be reborn into more inspiring places with better connections for positive ongoing growth.

Like the mythical phoenix firebird rising from the ashes, as often as creativity is destroyed, it rises again in the most unlikely of places, even in the smouldering wreckage of our civilisation. Each of us has the ability to make something better out of what we have been given. Whether it's the kids who made the kites to fly over the rubbish dump that is their home, the school teacher who inspires his or her students to explore new ideas, office workers creating their own pockets of creativity in an otherwise uninspiring workplace, or a leader who can transform the whole company, we each have our own unique skills to bring and something special to give.

By opening ourselves up in this way, we diminish the power of the creativity killers and revitalise the creative process, helping to make the world a better place. We hope you are inspired to open yourself up to this process and find a way to make your own positive contribution.

9

The rescue plan in action

Solving the mystery

On the last day of her final school exams, Zoe crossed the school quad feeling absolutely shattered. Despite having put her best efforts into studying, she felt she had failed the exams she had spent 13 years building up to and preparing for. She had valiantly tackled the five three-hour exams she had sat over three days, but had finally broken down when the overwhelming anxiety and nausea had become too much. She cried through the last two exams and her face was red and puffy as a result, but she didn't care what anyone thought. She was too exhausted to care about anything anymore.

When Zoe was halfway across the playground she was stopped in her tracks by an all too familiar booming voice behind her. 'Young lady, where is your proper school uniform!' It was the school principal, who irregularly ventured out of his lair just to prey on unsuspecting students who had dared to express a modicum of independence, or so it seemed. After being berated and reduced to tears once more, she left the school that day for the last time, incredibly relieved she would never have to go back.

Somehow the school system had depleted Zoe's confidence over time, reducing her to a mere shadow of her former pre-school self. After she had struggled through school for all those years, the system seemed to have failed her. A creative and obviously intelligent child, she had been placed in the top 5 per cent of children of her age in verbal reasoning, but having visual dyslexia meant it was difficult for her to 'get it right' and to feel she was capable of 'achieving'. We reminded Zoe that her dad had failed school but gone on to be successful in life in so many ways (including gaining high distinctions at university). She too had the capacity to thrive, but with her confidence so low it was difficult to convince her of this. As she faced her future, Zoe had to pick up the pieces and start to believe in herself again, and in her ability to make a valuable contribution to society. We had to convince her to think creatively and to find ways to reignite her passion and imagination. But it was of course a hard lesson to learn and a hard way to learn it.

In the week following that fateful last day of school, a new child was born. With her newfound freedom, a huge cloud was lifted from Zoe's mind and she began to imagine what her life could become. She started to make dramatic changes. That week she designed a music video clip for a friend, planned for travel in Europe, organised her eighteenth birthday, prepared for a university interview, and shopped for and cooked up a creative feast. She set herself goals with practical action plans that included finding ways to get a job, looking for volunteer work possibilities, reading books and completing a photography course ... among many other ideas. She felt like she had achieved more in that one week than she had in the whole previous year, and she felt incredibly engaged and empowered in the process. The world had suddenly opened up for her!

School children and working adults spend more of their waking hours at school or work than anywhere else. Ensuring there is a positive environment for growth is both an ethical and an economic imperative. If those who lead organisations support the individuals and teams in them better, continually checking there is a continuing process of regeneration built on solid, positive principles for growth, we can create much higher levels of engagement and creative confidence. Which means everybody wins.[1]

In this final section of the book we summarise graphically all that has been discussed so far to help you put all the pieces together. Here you can see at a glance the connections and relations between the killers and rescuers of creative thinking. We trust this will help equip you to meet the personal and organisational challenges you face and to be proactive.

Disarming the killers

For every killer there is also a rescuer, and for every means of destruction there is a corresponding strategy for positive growth. Table 9.1 will help you to see the full picture in context, matching a solution to every potential creativity problem you, your team or organisation may face.

Table 9.1: the Creative Thinking Life Cycle Model™— death and regeneration

	THE DEATH OF CREATIVE THINKING: the stages of degeneration		RESCUING CREATIVE THINKING: the stages of regeneration	
	Murder process	Murder weapon	Rescue process	Rescue strategy
Stage 1	**Oppression** ➤ *The use of CONTROL and FEAR to limit open thinking*		**Liberation** *The FREEDOM and COURAGE to step out and think freely*	
	Control	Crushing coercion	Freedom	1 Cultivate curiosity.
	Fear	Drowning dead	Courage	2 Accept ambiguity.
Stage 2	**Restriction** ➤ *The use of PRESSURE and INSULATION to restrict ideas*		**Initiation** *The INDEPENDENCE and OPENNESS to let go and grow*	
	Pressure	Strangling stress	Independence	3 Unleash the imagination.
	Insulation	Bludgeoning bias	Openness	4 Access both sides of brain.
Stage 3	**Degeneration** ➤ *Inhibition of growth driven by APATHY*		**Motivation** *The PASSION to drive transformation*	
	Apathy	Lacerating lethargy	Passion	5 Reconstruct common concepts.
Stage 4	**Destruction** ➤ *Destructive NARROW-MINDEDNESS and PESSIMISM*		**Transformation** *The FLEXBILITY and POSITIVITY to make real changes*	
	Narrow-mindedness	Intractable intolerance	Flexibility	6 Explore different paths.
	Pessimism	Noxious negativity	Positivity	7 Embrace optimism.

Where can you see the potential pitfalls and blockages may be in creative thinking for yourself, your team and your organisation?

Coming the full circle: the complete Creative Thinking Life Cycle Model™

At every point where creativity can be stifled, there is an opportunity to rescue it instead. We trust you are now better equipped to understand the choices you face at each stage and to choose the paths that will inspire creative growth. Figure 9.1 offers a visual representation of this growth path. Can you see where there might be opportunities to change your or your organisation's path?

Figure 9.1: the Creative Thinking Life Cycle Model™—the pathway to growth

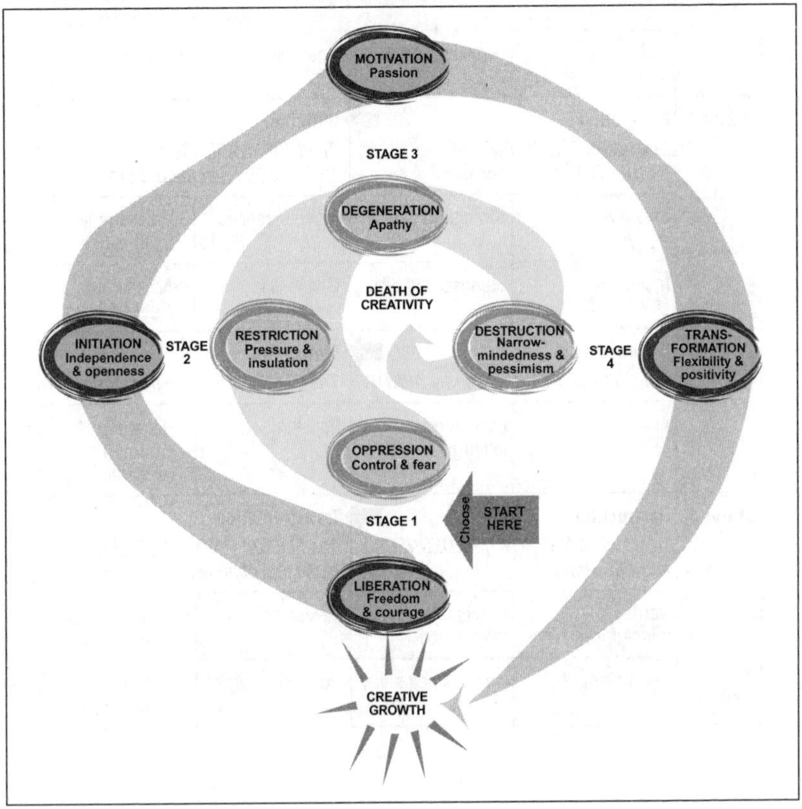

Implementing the seven creative thinking strategies — a case study

One of the world's most successful and innovative companies, Procter and Gamble (P&G), was established in April 1837 with the merger of the candle-making business of William Procter and the soap-making business of James Gamble. They set up a shop in Cincinnati, Ohio, which they nicknamed 'Porkopolis' because their candles and soaps were made from the leftover fat of pigs.

P&G has defied the typical growth and death cycle of the average company by surviving for almost 200 years. In 2006 it was voted one of the most creative and innovative companies in the world. P&G is known as an industry leader focused on innovation, knowledge sharing, improved efficiencies, cost reduction and first mover advantage—that is, getting new ideas from conception to the shelf quickly. The company is the most successful foreign marketer in China, measured by market share.

If we map P&G's journey through our seven creative thinking strategies we can see how the model works in action. This model, combined with practical exercises from our seminar, has helped many clients to work through their own challenges, move to a new level of innovative capability and generate outstanding new ideas. P&G's decision to move into this market was the result of a mix of solid research, gut instinct and some luck, all supported by an optimist but also realistic mindset and a culture willing to consider good new ideas. From its early days of soap and candles, P&G has never stood still. Creative thinking and clever innovation have seen it evolve into one of the world's most admired companies.

Consider how the strategies work in practice in the P&G case study shown in table 9.2 (overleaf)[2 3].

Table 9.2: implementing the seven creative thinking strategies—the P&G case study[4]: cracking China

STAGE 1: LIBERATION Step out and think freely	
KEY CONSIDERATIONS	**P&G ACTIONS**
Control **Will the systems ultimately stifle or support new ideas and transformation?** **Has a democratic environment been established?** **Is there enough freedom for ideas to flourish?**	**Opened up market opportunities** • Prior to 1984 it was almost impossible for an overseas company to get access to China because of strict controls, but when new channels were opened in 1984 P&G saw new possibilities. • China had a large rural population that remained poor by Western standards and a labour force accustomed to the 'iron rice-bowl' of state ownership. • Two to three years before they actually started selling, they 'introduced' themselves to the political authorities and the public and had a team on the ground to get a feel for what it would be like to operate in China.
Freedom *Strategy 1:* cultivate curiosity **Decide on the best questions to ask to best define the needs and to open up the opportunities.**	**Used questions to determine real needs and options** • For P&G the first question was how to crack the consumer market in large developing countries such as India and China. • From asking questions to determining real needs, P&G went from wanting to launch laundry detergent to realising that launching shampoo would be a better choice. No-one was interested in expensive washing powder brands in China! • In 1988 P&G used market surveys to discover that the shampoo market in China was almost non-existent, even in urban areas. Consumers recognised only a handful of local brands, while in rural areas some people still bought shampoo by scooping it out of vats at state-owned retailers. Many men still washed their hair with soap. *'Over several years one can only imagine how the process happened of asking 5 questions, and then asking 5 more until one thinks it starts getting silly—and then ask some more. Trust the process—these questions can be a "spark" that leads you to different ways of tackling the issue.'*[5]

Fear	Addressed directly the challenge of bringing a premium product to a low-income market
Are there any unknown elements that need to be addressed?	• In a model called Serving the World's Poor: Innovation at the Base of the Economic Pyramid, Anderson identifies 'Four As':
Is there a safe environment to support possible failure?	**Awareness**: In P&G's case it needed to be aware of three ambiguities.
Have the boundaries been clearly defined?	**Affordability**: Can low-income consumers be served profitably? How do you sell to this market fairly?
	Access: How can low-income consumers access usually expensive products?
	Availability: How can it be assured that low-income consumers will be able to access these products regularly as needed?
Courage *Strategy 2*: accept ambiguity Identify potential conflicts, challenges and ambiguities, and decide how these can be understood and integrated where appropriate or adequately dealt with.	**Considered both cost and product protection perspectives and found ways to incorporate both** • How do you change the product and make it inexpensive without making it cheap? How do you make it affordable without losing profitability and reputation? • To avoid cannibalisation while stretching a brand, P&G decided to focus on product equity — how to sell more without discounting the price.

235

Table 9.2 (cont'd): implementing the seven creative thinking strategies — the P&G case study[4]: cracking China

STAGE 2: INITIATION Let go and grow	
Pressure **Have realistic expectations been set?** **Are individuals feeling relaxed and ready?**	**Gave the confidence to explore all possibilities with the chosen approach** • A considerable amount of time, energy and money was invested into this project, so the P&G team would definitely have felt the pressure to come up with a successful solution. • Although the P&G team on the ground started to worry that selling premium shampoo was going to be a challenge, the senior leadership team gave them the confidence to stick with it and explore all possible solutions. • Through setting realistic expectations while still providing a creative challenge, the senior leadership ensured that the pressure did not become crippling but instead opened up the way for independent exploration and discovery. • The team on the ground gained confidence through this valued support.
Independence *Strategy 3:* unleash the imagination Brainstorm ideas freely, without prejudice or judgement.	**Explored all possible ways to make the shampoo idea work** P&G would have explored ideas freely at this point, e.g. through mind mapping to follow different branches of thought such as: • relook at product/cost > where to produce it • pricing > materials • quality > change the formula?
Insulation **Are information sources unbiased?** **Is there diversity?** **Is there an openness to different ideas?**	**Opened up to 'emotional' as well as 'cognitive' perspectives** • P&G's focus in the early stages was on the more 'left-brain', logical approach. They would have initially examined such bottom-line business imperatives as products, quality, advertising and production. • P&G would need to engage the emotional approach as well as the cognitive approach to appreciate the real impact the introduction of their product might have.

Openness
 	
Strategy 4: access all parts of the brain
 	
Address both sides of an argument and consider all perspectives openly.
	Considered the 'people' impact as well as the business imperatives
	
	• What needed to be added to the business considerations was:
	
	   – how the consumer might feel about the change: many were washing their hair with soap, so how important was it to them to have healthy hair?
	
	   – how they wanted to look: they were proud of the way they presented themselves, and with higher incomes and more media exposure to higher beauty standards were they now ready to spend on these items?
	
	   – P&G needed to consider consumer needs and the potential social impact.

STAGE 3: MOTIVATION Drive transformation	
Apathy Is full engagement evident? Have any blockages to motivation or possible growth been identified? Is there any cynicism or sarcasm to deal with? ➡	**Pushed through the challenge of competing against standard bulk shampoo sales** • At a stage when it would be easy to give up, it was important for P&G to push through the challenges. • They realised the standard accepted was to sell a lower quality product in bulk, which shampoo users in China were used to doing. At the time the only shampoo product available was a jelly-like substance that was sold in large containers — people could take these containers back for refills.
Passion *Strategy 5*: reconstruct common concepts **Take the different perspectives and reconstruct ideas to come up with possible new solutions.** **Keep persevering until you are satisfied all solutions have been considered.**	**Introduced the new 'reconstructed concept' of high-quality shampoo in small inexpensive sachets** • Rather than accepting the standard construct (bulk sales of cheap shampoo products) and apparent resistance to change, P&G pushed through to come up with a breakthrough revolutionary concept, believing it was possible to produce a win/win solution for all. • At this stage P&G introduced the concept of single-use sachets (rather than multiple-use 750 ml bottles).

Table 9.2 (cont'd): implementing the seven creative thinking strategies — the P&G case study[4]: cracking China

STAGE 4: MOTIVATION Make real changes	
Narrow-mindedness <u>Which pathways are being followed — the 'conservative', familiar paths or breakthrough new ideas?</u> Is there a willingness to embrace ideas that might not fit the 'expert' opinions or might not feel safe or comfortable?	**Realised it would be important to localise products** • Conventional wisdom had said to ignore this group because 'there isn't any money there to earn' and 'the poor are not brand conscious', but P&G refused to be confined by the accepted wisdom and found a positive solution. • When it came to implementation, rather than simply transferring accepted and tried concepts directly from Western countries, P&G realised it would need to localise its products.
Flexibility *Strategy 6:* explore different paths Consider all the different paths that may need to be taken to reach full implementation, and then choose the best of these.	**Presented their breakthrough new idea in a way that the chinese people could relate to** • Analysts attribute P&G's success in China to its localisation strategies. The company customised product packaging, product formulas and advertising campaigns to cater to the Chinese market. • The P&G researchers were not content to settle for the standard approaches that had been successful in their home countries, but instead realised that they would need to have the flexibility to consider how the product would be accepted and sell in a completely different cultural context. • After experimenting with different ways of localising the new product, the P&G team came up with some successful solutions that ensured the local needs were met.

Pessimism	Refused to focus on the negatives and built positive foundations
Is there a focus on making the solution work and ensuring the process is successful, or on potential failure? **Is there a trust that a collaborative win/win solution can be reached in the end?**	• Production of commercial shampoo sachets began in 1988 (cost 14c per sachet to buy), and they became the global model for Asia. Sachets are now used in all developing countries. • P&G realised in their research that people are marching up the income ladder (the bottom of the pyramid is shrinking). In the next few decades, the very-low-income market is expected to shrink by 24 per cent, while the medium-low market will change little and the wealthy will grow by 80 per cent. • Unlike the other companies in the region, P&G also considered local cultural needs and built long-term relationships.
Positivity *Strategy 7:* embrace optimism **Ensure the chosen solution has a strong values base and supports a clear vision.** **Find ways to make the chosen solution work in practice.** **If there is a problem with implementation, don't give up — try and try again!**	Built for the long term • P&G approached China 'not as a market to be invaded, but as an opportunity to build new partnerships and develop local capabilities'. In recognition of this commitment, the Chinese government granted the company unusual concessions.

239

Now have a go at applying this approach to a specific project or problem you, your team or your organisation are facing. Use this template in table 9.3 to guide you through the different stages and ensure you can apply our seven strategies.

Table 9.3: implementing the seven creative thinking strategies — a template

The problem/project challenge: _____

STAGE 1: LIBERATION Step out and think freely			
Considerations:	**Your approach:**	**Actions:**	**Your actions:**
Control Will the systems ultimately stifle or support new ideas and transformation? Has a democratic environment been established? Is there enough freedom for ideas to flourish?		<u>**Freedom**</u> *Strategy 1: cultivate curiosity* Decide on the best questions to ask to best define the needs and to open up the opportunities. Ask as many questions as you can.	
Fear Are there any unknown elements that need to be addressed? Is there a safe environment to support possible failure? Have the boundaries been clearly defined?		<u>**Courage**</u> *Strategy 2: accept ambiguity* Identify potential conflicts, challenges and ambiguities, and decide how these can be understood and integrated where appropriate or adequately dealt with. Look for and be comfortable with 'paradoxical pairings'.	

STAGE 2: INITIATION Let go and grow			
Considerations:	Your approach:	Actions:	Your actions:
Pressure		**Independence**	
Have realistic expectations been set?		*Strategy 3: unleash the imagination*	
Are individuals feeling relaxed and ready?		Brainstorm ideas freely, without prejudice or judgement.	
Insulation		**Openness**	
Are information sources unbiased?		*Strategy 4: access all parts of the brain.*	
Is there diversity?			
Is there an openness to different ideas?		Address both sides of an argument and consider all perspectives openly.	

STAGE 3: MOTIVATION Drive transformation			
Considerations:	Your approach:	Actions:	Your actions:
Apathy		**Passion**	
Is full engagement evident?		*Strategy 5: reconstruct common concepts*	
Have any blockages to motivation or possible growth been identified?		Take the different perspectives and reconstruct ideas to come up with possible new solutions.	
Is there any cynicism or sarcasm to deal with?		Combine themes in such a way that extra value is created. (The value created must be greater than the sum of the parts combined.)	

Table 9.3 (cont'd): implementing the seven creative thinking strategies — a template

STAGE 4: MOTIVATION Make real changes			
Considerations:	Your approach:	Actions:	Your actions:
Narrow-mindedness **Which pathways are being followed — the 'conservative', familiar paths or breakthrough new ideas?** **Is there a willingness to embrace ideas that may not fit the 'expert' opinions or may not feel safe or comfortable?**		**Flexibility** ⬆ *Strategy 6: explore different paths* Consider all the different paths that may need to be taken to reach full implementation, and then choose the best of these.	
Pessimism **Is there a focus on making the solution work and ensuring the process is successful, or on potential failure?** **Is there a trust that a collaborative win/win solution can be reached in the end?**		**Positivity** ⬆ *Strategy 7: Embrace optimism* Ensure the chosen solution has a strong values base and supports a clear vision. Find ways to make the chosen solution work in practice. If there is a problem with implementation, don't give up — try and try again!	

Endnotes

Introduction

1   <http://en.wikipedia.org/
     wiki/CSI:_Crime_Scene_
     Investigation>

2   Research conducted in 1989
     by Deborah J. Mitchell, of the
     Wharton School; Jay Russo, of
     Cornell; and Nancy Pennington,
     of the University of Colorado
     <http://hbr.org/2007/09/
     performing-a-project-premortem/
     ar/1University of Colorado>.

Chapter 1

1   <www.smh.com.au/national/
     education/academic-paints-a-
     picture-of-arts-as-a-priority-in-
     classrooms-20110112-19oba.
     html>

2   IBM 2010 Global CEO Study:
     IBM biennial Global CEO
     Study series, 4th edn, 'Creativity'
     <www-03.ibm.com/press/us/
     en/pressrelease/31670.wss>.

3   Austin Carr (2010). 'The Most
     Important Leadership Quality
     for CEOs? Creativity' <www.
     fastcompany.com/1648943/
     Creativity-the-most-important-
     leadership-quality-for-ceos-
     study?partner=homepage_
     newsletter>.

4   Teresa M. Amabile (1998). 'How
     to Kill Creativity'. *Harvard
     Business Review* <http://hbr.org/
     product/how-to-kill-creativity/
     an/98501-PDF-ENG>.

5   Geoffrey West (2011). 'Why Cities
     Keep Growing, Corporations
     and People Always Die, and Life
     Gets Faster', interviewed by John
     Brockman <http://edge.org/
     conversation/geoffrey-west>.

6   George Land & Beth Jarman
     (2000). *Breakpoint and Beyond.*
     Champaign, IL: HarperBusiness
     (ISBN: 0962660523).

7   Michael F. Shaughnessy (2011).
     'An Interview with Jonathan
     Plucker: Creativity, the Creative
     Person and the Creative Mind'
     <www.creativity.or.kr/bbs/
     board.php?bo_table=2011_
     01&wr_id=3>.

8   Kyung Hee Kim (College of
     William and Mary), Po Bronson
     & Ashley Merryman (2010).
     'The Creativity Crisis'. *Newsweek*
     <www.thedailybeast.com/
     newsweek/2010/07/10/the-
     creativity-crisis.html>.

9   Tom Wujec (2010). 'The Marsh-
     mallow Challenge'. TED talks
     <http://marshmallowchallenge.
     com/Welcome.html>.

10   Andrew & Gaia Grant (2009).
     Hands Up (video):

     Part 1: 'How creative are
     you?' <www.youtube.com/
     watch?v=MhBIiNl3edk>.

     Part 2: 'Creativity secrets from
     the kids' <www.youtube.com/
     watch?v=77LYUTLH6hQ>.

     Part 3: 'Creativity secrets from
     the experts (the teachers'
     response)' <www.youtube.com/
     watch?v=AX6VgVQ3CMs>.

     Watch the video *Hands Up* at
     <www.whokilledcreativity.
     com>, Parts 1, 2 and 3 on
     youtube.com.

Chapter 2

1   Richards Laura (2006). 'Jack
     the Ripper's face "revealed"'

<http://news.bbc.co.uk/2/hi/uk_news/6164544.stm>.

2   Thomas R. Insel & Philip S. Wang (2010). 'Rethinking Mental Illness and Mental Health vs Mental Disorders'. *Journal of the American Medical Association* 303(19): 1978–9.

3   In the first 2010 issue of *Nature*, editor Philip Campbell suggested that the next 10-year period is likely to be the 'decade for psychiatric disorders' <www.nature.com/nature/journal/v463/n7277/full/463009a.html>.

4   Martha Stout (2010). *The Sociopath Next Door* —*The Mask of Sanity*, Sextante (ISBN: 857542551X) <www.cassiopaea.com/cassiopaea/psychopath.htm>.

5   Janet Potter (2011). 'Mad, Mad World: Jon Ronson's The Psychopath Test' <www.themillions.com/2011/05/mad-mad-world-jon-ronsons-the-psychopath-test.html>.

6   Jon Ronson (2011). *The Psychopath Test*. Riverhead (ISBN: 1594488010).

7   Omega Foundation. 'Stun Weapons and Their Effects'. Draft paper to the International Meeting of Experts on Security Equipment and the Prevention of Torture, London, 25–26 October 2002.

8   Brian Martin, with contributions from Truda Gray, Hannah Lendon & Steve Wright (2007). *Justice Ignited*. Lanham, MD: Rowman & Littlefield (ISBN: 0742540855).

9   Vicky Ward (2010). *The Devil's Casino*. John Wiley & Sons (ISBN: 0470540869).

10 Michael Lewis (2008). 'The End'. *Portfolio* <www.portfolio.com/news-markets/national-news/portfolio/2008/11/11/The-End-of-Wall-Streets-Boom>.

11 Oriana Bandiera (2001). *Private States and the Enforcement of Property Rights: Theory and Evidence on the Origins of the Sicilian Mafia*. London School of Economics and CEPR, <http://econ.lse.ac.uk/staff/bandiera/mafia1101.pdf>.

12 Tony Tysome (2007). 'Creativity Campaign to Attack Red Tape'. *Times Higher Education* <www.timeshighereducation.co.uk/story.asp?storyCode=207402&sectioncode=26>.

13 Malcolm Wallis (1989). *Bureaucracy*. London: Macmillan (ISBN: 0333440684).

14 Scott Belsky (2011). *Making Ideas Happen*. Portfolio (ISBN: 1591844118).

15 David Osborne & Ted Gaebler (1992). *Reinventing Government*. New York: Plume (ISBN: 0452269423).

16 Michael Balle (1999). 'Making Bureaucracy Work'. *Journal of Management in Medicine* 13: 190–200.

17 Belinda Jane Board & Katarina Fritzon (2005). 'Disordered personalities at work'. *Psychology Crime and Law* 11: 17. doi:10.1080/10683160310001634304.

18 According to leading leadership academic Manfred F.R. Kets de Vries, it seems almost inevitable these days there will be personality disorders in a senior management team. See Manfred F.R. Kets de Vries (2003). 'The Dark Side of Leadership'.

Business Strategy Review 14(3), Autumn, p. 26.

19 Antoine Bechara, associate professor of neurology at the University of Iowa, said the best stock market investors might plausibly be called 'functional psychopaths'. Baba Shiv, of Stanford Graduate School of Business, said many company chiefs and top lawyers may also exhibit psychopathic traits. See 'Emotions Can Negatively Impact Investment Decisions' (2005), <www.gsb.stanford.edu/news/research/finance_shiv_invesmtdecisions.shtml>.

20 Robert Hare & Paul Babiak (2006). *Snakes in Suits: When Psychopaths Go to Work*. New York: HarperCollins.

21 Catherine Mattice & Brian Spitzberg (2007). *Bullies in Business: Self-Reports of Tactics and Motives*. San Diego State University.

22 Hare & Babiak (2006).

23 Steven Morris (September 2011). 'One in 25 business leaders may be a psychopath, study finds'. *Guardian* <www.guardian.co.uk/science/2011/sep/01/psychopath-workplace-jobs-study>.

24 Alan Deutschman (July 2005). 'Is Your Boss a Psychopath?' Fast Company <www.fastcompany.com/magazine/96/open_boss.html>.

25 Rayner & Keashly (2004). <http://en.wikipedia.org/wiki/Workplace_bullying>.

26 Josh Bornstein (30 August 2011). 'Time to outlaw toxic bullies in the workplace'. *Australian Financial Review* <http://afr.com/p/national/work_space/time_to_outlaw_toxic_bullies_Xfa9LfQaUlVv3KjHHzGTrI>.

27 Nearly half of all American workers (49 per cent) report having been affected by workplace bullying, either as a target or as a witness of abusive behaviour against a co-worker. See 'Workplace Bullying Survey' (2010) <www.workplacebullying.org/wbiresearch/2010-wbi-national-survey>.

28 Roffey Park Management (2003). Survey of 372 managers in the UK in 2003 <www.roffeypark.com/SiteCollectionDocuments/Research%20Reports/manag2003.pdf>.

29 Virginia Matthews (January 2003). 'Kill or be killed'. *Guardian* <www.guardian.co.uk/money/2003/jan/27/careers.jobsadvice1>.

30 Matt Ridley (1998). *The Origins of Virtue*. London: Penguin (ISBN: 0670874493).

31 Jim Collins (2001). *Good to Great*. London: Random House Business (ISBN: 0712676090).

32 Veronica Alfonso (2009). 'Pessimists' and Optimists' Reactions to Interruptions on a Creativity Task' <http://dspace.sunyconnect.suny.edu/handle/1951/44812>.

33 Inauguration of President Franklin Delano Roosevelt, 1933. Joint Congressional Committee on Inaugural Ceremonies.

34 More than 50 per cent of respondents in our 'Who Killed Creativity' survey listed 'fear' as the biggest killer of creativity—more than every other category combined. Tirian (2011).

35 Psychologists Kahneman & Tversky (1979), cited in Peter

L. Bernstein (1998), *Against the Gods: The Remarkable Story of Risk*. New York: John Wiley & Sons.

36 Roffey Park Management Agenda <www.roffeypark.com/SiteCollectionDocuments/Research%20Reports/manag2003.pdf>.

37 Edward de Bono (2007). *Tactics*. London: Profile Business (ISBN: 1861975376).

38 'The Invention of Scotchgard'. About.com. Retrieved 21 August 2006.

39 'Prudential sells Egg to Citigroup' (January 2007). <www.finextra.com/news/fullstory.aspx?newsitemid=16435>.

40 Jamer Hunt (2001). 'Among Six Types of Failure, Only a Few Help You Innovate' Fast Company <www.fastcodesign.com/1664360/lets-be-clear-failure-isnt-always-good>.

41 Roger L. Martin (2009). *The Design of Business*. Boston, MA: Harvard Business School Press (ISBN: 1422177807).

42 Nassim Taleb (2001). *Fooled by Randomness*. New York: John Wiley & Sons (ISBN: 0471511447).

43 Tim Harford (2011). *Adapt: Why Success Always Starts with Failure*. New York: Farrar, Straus and Giroux.

44 Taleb (2001).

45 Interview with Roger Schank (2007), 'The Business of Innovation. Innovators & Iconoclasts, CNBC <http://innovation.cnbc.com/en/programmes/innovators_iconoclasts>.

46 *Hands Up*, Part 3: 'Creativity secrets from the experts (The teachers' response)'. (2009). Tirian <www.youtube.com/watch?v=AX6VgVQ3CMs>.

47 Interview with Roger Schank (2007).

48 Virginia Matthews (January 2003), 'Kill or be killed', *Guardian*.

49 Alain Gratton (1988). 'Effects of electrical stimulation of brain reward sites on release of dopamine in rat: An in vivo electrochemical study'. University of Colorado Health Sciences.

50 Peter M. Milner (March 1991). *Canadian Journal of Psychology/Revue canadienne de psychologie* 45(1): 1–36.

51 A male psychiatric patient and a female epileptic had brain electrodes implanted 'for therapeutic purposes', and when stimulation occurred in areas of the limbic system, both reported experiencing sexual pleasure. The wired-up guy, in fact, gave the rats a run for their money, hitting the button some 1500 times an hour! 'Not surprisingly, he also begged for a few more jolts just before the apparatus was put away' <www.funtrivia.com/askft/Question49662.html>.

52 Paul R. Abramson & Steven D. Pinkerton (1995). *With Pleasure*. New York: Oxford University Press (ISBN: 6610441995).

53 The 2010 MetLife Study of the American Dream (2010). <www.metlife.com/assets/cao/gbms/studies/10062017_AmDrm_web_version.pdf>.

54 Carol Morello (January 2010). 'Results of polls on job satisfaction are at odds'. Conference Board report, *Washington Post* <www.washingtonpost.com/wp-dyn/content/article/2010/01/05/AR2010010503977.html>.

55 Andrew Mowatt, John Corrigan & Doug Long (2010). *The Success Zone*. Global Publishing Group.

56 Damon Young (2008). *Distraction*. Carlton, Vic.: Melbourne University Publishing (ISBN: 0522853749).

57 B.S. McEwen (2007). 'Physiology and neurobiology of stress and adaptation: Central role of the brain'. *Physiological Review* 87(3): 873–904. doi:10.1152/physrev.00041.2006. PMID 17615391.

58 E. Dias-Ferreira, J.C. Sousa, I. Melo, P. Morgado, A.R. Mesquita, J.J. Cerqueira, R.M. Costa & N. Sousa (2009). 'Chronic Stress Causes Frontostriatal Reorganization and Affects Decision-Making'. *Science* 325(5940): 621–5. doi:10.1126/science.1171203. PMID 19644122.

59 Matthias B. Schmidt & Lars Schwabe (September 2011). 'Splintered by stress: The good and bad of psychological pressure'. *Scientific American*.

60 NIOSH (1999). *Stress at Work*. U.S. National Institute for Occupational Safety and Health, DHHS (NIOSH) Publication no. 99-101.

61 Northwestern National Life Insurance Company (1991). *Employee Burnout: America's Newest Epidemic*. Minneapolis, MN: Northwestern National Life Insurance Company.

62 Princeton Survey Research Associates (1997). *Labor Day Survey: State of Workers*. Princeton, NJ: Princeton Survey Research Associates.

63 R.Z. Goetzel, D.R. Anderson, R.W. Whitmer, R.J. Ozminkowski, R.L. Dunn & J. Wasserman (1998). 'The relationship between modifiable health risks and health care expenditure: An analysis of the multi-employer HERO health risk and cost database'. *Journal of Occupational and Environmental Medicine* 40: 843–54.

64 NIOSH (1999).

65 N. Turner, J. Barling & A. Zacharatos (2002). 'Positive psychology at work'. In C.R. Snyder & S.J. Lopez (eds), *Handbook of Positive Psychology* (pp. 715–28). New York: Oxford University Press.

66 J. Jonge, P. Landsbergis & N. Vegchel (2005). 'Occupational Stress in (inter)action: The Interplay Between Job Demands and Job Resources'. *Journal of Organizational Behavior* 26(5): 535–60. doi:10.1002/job.327.

67 Daniel Sieberg (2011). *The Digital Diet*. New York: Three Rivers Press (ISBN: 0307887383).

68 Will Knight (2005). '"Info-mania" dents IQ more than marijuana'. *New Scientist* <www.newscientist.com/article/dn7298-infomania-dents-iq-more-than-marijuana.html>.

69 Dan Ariely (2010). *Predictably Irrational*. New York: Harper Perennial (ISBN: 0061353248).

70 Matt Richtel (2008). 'Lost in E-Mail, Tech Firms Face Self-Made Beast'. *New York Times* <www.nytimes.com/2008/06/14/

technology/14email.html? pagewanted=all>.

71 Joe Robinson (February 2010). 'Tame the E-mail Beast' <www.entrepreneur.com/magazine/entrepreneur/2010/march/204980.html>, <http://news.bbc.co.uk/2/hi/uk_news/4471607.stm>.

72 '"Infomania" worse than marijuana' (April 2005) <http://news.bbc.co.uk/2/hi/uk_news/4471607.stm>.

73 Martin Lindstrom <www.fastcompany.com/article/work-smart-stop-multi-tasking-and-do-one-thing-at-a-time.MORE>, <www.entrepreneur.com/magazine/entrepreneur/2010/march/204980.html>.

74 Charlie Gilkey <www.productiveflourishing.com/multithreading-the-complexity-of-modern-experience>.

75 Martin Lindstrom (July 2008). 'The Cure for ADD-vertising', Fast Company <www.fastcompany.com/1753945/the-cure-for-add-vertising?partner=homepage_newsletter>.

76 Randy K. Chiu. 'Relationship among Role Conflicts, Role Satisfactions and Life Satisfaction: Evidence from Hong Kong'. *Social Behavior and Personality* <http://findarticles.com/p/articles/mi_qa3852/is_199801/ai_n8803995>.

77 R.E. Kopelman, J.H. Greenhaus & T.F. Connolly (1983). 'A model of work, family, and interrole conflict: A construct validation study'. *Organizational Behavior and Human Performance* 32: 198–215.

78 W.D. Hicks & R.J. Klimoski (1981). 'The impact of flextime on employee attitudes'. *Academy of Management Journal* 24: 333–41.

79 D.A. Zatz (1995). 'Job involvement and interrole conflict'. Doctoral dissertation, Columbia University.

80 Derrick Hand & Janet Fife-Yeomans (2008) [2004]. *The Coroner: Investigating Sudden Death.* Sydney, NSW: Allen & Unwin (ISBN 9780733322211).

81 Stuart Grassian, 'Psychiatric effects of solitary confinement (redacted, non-institution and non-inmate specific version of a declaration submitted in September 1993 in Madrid v. Gomez, 889F. Supp.1146. California, USA. Retrieved 18 June 2008.

82 Sam Vaknin & Lidija Rangelovska (ed.) (2006). *Malignant Self Love— Narcissism Revisited.* Czech Republic: Narcissus Publications (ISBN: 8023833847).

83 David Hasselhoff (2006). *Making Waves—The Autobiography.* London: Hodder & Stoughton (ISBN: 0340909315).

84 PsycINFO Database Record. William W. Maddux & Adam D. Galinsky. *Journal of Personality and Social Psychology* 96(5), May 2009, 1047–61. ©2009 APA, all rights reserved.

85 West (2011).

86 Baggage with Jerry Springer <www.youtube.com/watch?v=kOB9CYpfhOI>.

87 <www.fastcompany.com/1742398/the-twitter-news-cycle-elizabeth-taylor-overtakes-crises-in-japan-libya?partner=homepage_newsletter>

88 Po Bronson & Ashley Merryman (2010). 'The Creativity Crisis'.

Newsweek <www.thedailybeast.com/newsweek/2010/07/10/the-creativity-crisis.html>.

89 Jessica Irvine (2011). 'There's no time like the present to let yourself go'. *Sydney Morning Herald* <www.smh.com.au/national/health/theres-no-time-like-the-present-to-let-yourself-go-20110916-1kdwr.html#ixzz1Y9Xqma5C>.

90 Morgan Spurlock (dir.). *The Greatest Movie Ever Sold* (2011).

91 Ralph Nader (September 2007). 'Fighting Back Against the Commercialization of Everything Wrapping the World with Advertising' <http://moderate.wordpress.com/2007/09/03/ralph-nader-wrapping-the-world-with-advertising>.

92 Alex Riley (2011). 'Secrets of the Superbrands' <www.psfk.com/2011/05/secrets-of-the-superbrands-how-apple-products-affect-your-brain.htm>.

93 Jane Bunce (May 2011). 'Cult of Apple: Why the must-have brand triggers brain reaction "similar to religious devotion"'. *Mail Online* <www.dailymail.co.uk/sciencetech/article-1389256/Apple-brand-triggers-brain-reaction-similar-religious-devotion.html#ixzz1bSMIsZG5>.

94 Clive Thompson (October 2003). 'There's a Sucker Born in Every Medial Prefrontal Cortex. *New York Times* <www.nytimes.com/2003/10/26/magazine/26BRAINS.html?pagewanted=1>.

95 James Surowiecki (2005). *The Wisdom of Crowds*. London: Abacus (ISBN: 0349116059).

96 James Surowiecki (2005).

97 Jeff Mauzy & Richard A. Harriman (2003). *Creativity, Inc.* Boston, MA: Harvard Business School Press (ISBN: 1578512077).

98 Chuck Frey (September 2002). 'Are we too busy to think creatively?' <www.innovationtools.com/Weblog/innovationblog-detail.asp?ArticleID=21>.

99 West (2011).

100 Lewis (2008).

101 Malcolm Gladwell (2008). *Outliers*. New York: Little, Brown and Co. (ISBN: 0316036692).

102 Corporate Leadership Council, cited in Karalyn Brown (2010), 'Engaging People'. Australian Institute of Management <www.aim.com.au/DisplayStory.asp?ID=746>.

103 'Overcoming Apathy in the Workplace Smart Manager' <www.smartmanager.com.au/web/au/smartmanager/en/pages/125_apathy.html>.

104 'Net abuse hits small city firms'. News.scotsman.com, Edinburgh. Retrieved 7 August 2009.

105 Nicholas Carr (2010). *The Shallows: What the Internet Is Doing to Our Brains*. New York: W.W. Norton (ISBN: 978-0393072228).

106 Ken Robinson & Lou Aronica (2009). *Element: How Finding Your Passion Changes Everything*. Tantor Media (ISBN: 1400140609).

107 Online readers have criticised Robinson's research as weak and unsubstantiated.

108 Mihaly Csikszentmihalyi (2002). *Flow*. London: Rider (ISBN: 0712657592).

109 Taleb (2001).

110 Lewis (2008).

111 Taleb (2001).

112 Daniel H. Pink (2003). 'How to Make Your Own Luck'. Fast Company <www.fastcompany.com/magazine/72/realitycheck.html>.

113 Gladwell (2008).

114 *Classic Albums: The Making of The Dark Side of the Moon*, Eagle Rock Entertainment, 2003.

115 <www.motorsportsetc.com/info/f1_innov.htm>

116 Duncan Scott (2009). 'The Edge of the World: How the Rule of Three Can Save F1' <http://bleacherreport.com/articles/117975-the-edge-of-the-world-how-the-rule-of-three-can-save-f1>.

117 Hare & Babiak (2006).

118 Edward de Bono (1993). *Serious Creativity*. New York: HarperBusiness (ISBN: 0887306357).

119 Stephen L. Macknik & Susana Martinez-Conde (2010). *Sleights of Mind: What the Neuroscience of Magic Reveals about Our Everyday Deceptions* <www.scientificamerican.com/article.cfm?id=mind-over-magic>.

120 Rob Minkodd (dir.), *The Forbidden Kingdom* (2008).

121 James Cameron (dir.), *Avatar* (2009).

122 K. Anders Ericsson, Michael J. Prietula & Edward T. Cokely (2007). 'The Making of an Expert'. *Harvard Business Review* <http://hbr.org/2007/07/the-making-of-an-expert/ar/1>.

123 Ericsson, Prietula & Cokely (2007).

124 Shunryu Suzuki-roshi (1988). *Zen Mind, Beginner's Mind*. Audio Literature (ISBN: 0944993079).

125 De Bono (1993).

126 Surowiecki (2005).

127 Surowiecki (2005).

128 Richard Watson (4 October 2004). 'A Beginner's Mind'. Fast Company <www.fastcompany.com/resources/innovation/watson/100404.html>.

129 Jennifer S. Mueller (2011). 'Why People Desire But Reject Creative Ideas'. University of Pennsylvania <http://digitalcommons.ilr.cornell.edu/cgi/viewcontent.cgi?article=1457&context=articles>.

130 <http://think-such.blogspot.com/2010/08/blocks-prejudice.html>

131 Surowiecki (2005).

132 Jonathan B. Tucker (2006). *War of Nerves: Chemical Warfare from World War I to Al-Queda*. New York: Pantheon (ISBN 0375422293).

133 Martin E. Seligman (2006). *Learned Optimism: How to Change Your Mind and Your Life*. New York: Vintage (ISBN: 1400078393).

134 Julie K. Norem (2001). *The Positive Power of Negative Thinking*. Cambridge, MA: Basic Books (ISBN: 0465051391).

135 Carolin Showers & Cherie Ruben (1990). 'Distinguishing defensive pessimism from depression: Negative expectations and positive coping mechanisms'.

Cognitive Therapy and Research 14(4): 385–99 <www.springerlink.com/content/v26002p7w2731g33/Carolin Showers and Cherie Ruben>.

136 Richard Wiseman, University of Hertfordshire <www.richardwiseman.com/contact.html>.

137 See chapter 8 for more on the manic/depressive states that can contribute to creativity.

138 J.R. Minkel (October 2006). 'Happiness: Good for Creativity, Bad for Single-Minded Focus'. *Scientific American* <www.scientificamerican.com/article.cfm?id=happiness-good-for-creativity>.

139 'Pessimism and depression' (2008). Trusted.MD Network <http://trusted.md/blog/completecounseling/2008/07/17/pessimism_and_depression#ixzz1XbEV3iaC>.

140 Shawn Achor (2010). *The Happiness Advantage*. Random House Audio (ISBN: 0307749347).

141 Shell TV advertisement on how the Snake Oil Drill was discovered <www.shell.com/home/Plain PageServlet?FC=/aboutshell-en/html/iwgen/shell_real/shell_solutions/films/app_transcript_film.html>.

142 Seligman (2006).

143 Ayatullah Ja'far Subhani, 'Being Pessimistic About Others' <www.alhassanain.com/english/articles/articles/ethics_and_supplication/ethics_articles/being_pessimistic_about_others/001.html>.

144 Carl Panzram (1891–1930).

145 Pete Earley (1993). *The Hot House*. New York: Bantam Books (ISBN: 0553560239).

Chapter 3

1 'The crime hotspot map where Britain's most hardened criminals live' (2010). <www.dailymail.co.uk/news/article-1258197/The-crime-hotspot-map-Britains-hardened-criminals-live.html#ixzz1Y5DKZwsE>.

2 Palmetto Security <www.palmettoalarm.com/crime-statistics.html>.

3 Who Killed Creativity Survey (2011). Tirian <www.whokilledcreativity.com/survey>.

4 Malcolm Gladwell (2007). *The Tipping Point*. Playaway Audio (ISBN: 1602525951).

5 Gladwell (2007).

6 Catherine Fox, 'Workers by design' <www.afrboss.com.au/magarticle.asp?doc_id=22153&rgid=2&listed_months=0>.

7 Robin Speculand (2009). *Beyond Strategy*. John Wiley & Sons (ISBN: 0470824980).

8 IBM 2010 Global CEO Study.

9 Who Killed Creativity Survey (2011).

10 James C. Collins & Jerry I. Porras (1998). *Built to Last*. London: Century Business (ISBN: 0712679618).

11 Adam Galinsky (2009). Losing Touch Power diminishes perception and perspective. Study from the Kellogg School of Management <http://insight.kellogg.northwestern.edu/

index.php/Kellogg/article/losing_touch>.

12 Sam Keen (2010). *In the Absence of God*. New York: Harmony (ISBN: 0307462293).

13 Justin Lin (dir.), *The Fast & Furious 5* (2011).

14 Jessica Kennedy (2011). 'Marketing needs to "pull up its socks" to help sales' <www.bandt.com.au/content/articles/marketing-needs-to--pull-up-its-socks--to-help-sal.aspx>.

15 'Bridging the Divide: Process, Technology, and the Marketing/Sales Interface', *Market Viewpoint* 15(4), October 2004, Aberdeen Group, Boston.

16 Tom Fishburn (January 2011). 'Blamstorming' <http://tomfishburne.com/2011/01/blamestorming.html>.

17 'A different game: Information is transforming traditional businesses' (February 2010). *Economist* <www.economist.com/node/15557465>.

18 Stefan Stern (March 2006). 'Wake up and smell the coffee on your corporate culture'. *Financial Times* <www.ft.com/intl/cms/s/1/7ecca3c4-dba7-11db-9233-000b5df10621.html#axzz1badX4FNW>.

19 Edgar H. Schein (2004). *Organizational Culture and Leadership*, New York: John Wiley & Sons.

20 Roger von Oech (1990). *A Whack on the Side of the Head*. New York: Warner Books (ISBN: 0880794798).

21 Harford (2011).

22 M. Pedler, J. Burgogyne & T. Boydell (1997). *The Learning Company: A Strategy for Sustainable Development*, 2nd edn. London: McGraw-Hill.

23 P.M. Senge (1990). *The Fifth Discipline*. London: Century Business.

24 Howard P. Chudacoff (2008). *Children at Play*. New York: New York University Press (ISBN: 0814716652).

25 Laura Sergeant Richardson (2009). 'Frog Design: The Four Secrets of Playtime That Foster Creative Kids' <www.fastcodesign.com/1662826/frog-design-the-four-secrets-of-playtime-that-foster-creative-kids>.

26 Melinda Wenner (28 January 2009). 'The Serious Need for Play'. *Scientific American*.

27 Stuart Brown (2008). 'Play is more than fun'. TED talks <www.ted.com/talks/stuart_brown_says_play_is_more_than_fun_it_s_vital.html>.

28 Bruce Charlton, cited in Jennifer Viegas (2006), 'Serious Study: Immaturity Levels Rising', Discovery News <http://dsc.discovery.com/news/2006/06/23/immature_hum.html?category=human>.

29 Virtual Team Performance Facilitation: Grovewell <www.grovewell.com/virtual-team-facilitation.html>.

30 Morten T. Hansen (2009). *Collaboration*. Boston, MA: Harvard Business School Press (ISBN: 1422115151).

31 Nick Allen (2009). 'Burglar with photographic memory admits 500 crimes'. *Telegraph* <www.telegraph.co.uk/news/uknews/4358671/Burglar-with-photographic-memory-admits-500-crimes.html>.

Chapter 4

1 Sadie F. Dingfelder (January 2011). 'Rats to the rescue', by Monitor Staff, vol. 42 <www.apa.org/monitor/2011/01/rats.aspx>.

2 'Microsoft needs to .innovate: Google' (June 2007). *Sydney Morning Herald* <www.smh.com.au/news/biztech/microsoft-needs-to-let-staff-innovate-google/2007/06/01/1180205491599.html>.

3 Don Tuite (2007). 'Better, Faster, Cheaper — Pick Any Two' <http://electronicdesign.com/article/analog-and-mixed-signal/better-faster-cheaper-pick-any-two14997.aspx>.

4 Keith Cowing (2003). 'NASA Responds to the Columbia Accident Report: Farewell to Faster – Better – Cheaper' <www.spaceref.com/news/viewnews.html?id=864>.

5 Robert Greene (1998). *The 48 Laws of Power*. New York: Viking.

Chapter 5

1 M. Chipman, B.E. Hackley & T.S. Spencer (February 1980). 'Triage of mass casualties: Concepts for coping with mixed battlefield injuries'. *Military Medicine* 145(2): 99–100. PMID 6768037.

2 Norman Doidge (2007). *The Brain That Changes Itself*. New York: Viking (ISBN: 067003830X).

3 Richard Hill (2010). Creative Skills Training Council Forum (CTSC) <www.cstc-apa.com>.

4 Doidge (2007).

5 Doidge (2007).

6 Linda Geddes (March 2010). 'A slow mind may nurture more creative ideas'. *New Scientist* <www.newscientist.com/article/mg20527535.500-a-slow-mind-may-nurture-more-creative-ideas.html>.

7 Julia Hanna (14 May 2008). 'Getting Down to the Business of Creativity'. Harvard Business School <http://hbswk.hbs.edu/item/5902.html>.

8 Linda Geddes (May 2009). 'Creativity chemical favours the smart'. *New Scientist* <www.newscientist.com/article/mg20227084.300-creativity-chemical-favours-the-smart.html>.

9 Scott Berkun (2010). *The Myths of Innovation*. O'Reilly Media (ISBN: 1449389627).

10 Michael Michalko (2006). *Thinkertoys: A Handbook of Creative-Thinking Techniques*. Berkeley, CA: Ten Speed Press (ISBN: 1580087736).

11 Arne Dietrich (August 2004). Neurocognitive mechanisms underlying the experience of flow' <http://dunntastic.com/sources/Dietrich%202004%20-%20Neurocognitive%20mechanisms%20underlying%20the%20experiene%20of%20flow.pdf>.

12 Arne Dietrich (2004). 'The cognitive neuroscience of creativity'. *Psychonomic Bulletin & Review*.

13 E.B. Boyd (June 2011). 'Why "Brain Gyms" May Be the Next Big Business'. Fast Company <www.fastcompany.com/1760312/are-brain-gyms-the-next-big-business?partner=homepage_newsletter>.

14   Bronson & Merryman (2010).

15   Geddes (March 2010).

16   Geddes (March 2010).

17   Geddes (May 2009).

18   Geddes (March 2010).

19   B.L. Fredrickson (2001). 'The role of positive emotions in positive psychology: The broaden-and-build theory of positive emotions'. *American Psychologist*.

20   Richard Hill (2010). Creative Skills Training Council Forum (CTSC) <www.cstc-apa.com>.

21   Bruce S. McEwen, head of Rockefeller's Harold and Margaret Milliken Hatch Laboratory of Neuroendocrinology. *Science Daily* (11 April 2010) <www.sciencedaily.com/releases/2010/04/100410141344.htm>

Chapter 6

1   Gregory Ferenstein (May 2011). 'Beyond Hawaiian-Shirt Friday: Groupon, Hulu Inspire Employee Innovation With Radical Trust'. Fast Company <www.fastcompany.com/1754941/groupon-and-hulus-secret-weapon-workplace-democracy?partner=homepage_newsletter>.

2   Melinda Wenner (28 January 2009). 'The Serious Need for Play'. *Scientific American*.

3   Peter Drucker, cited in Christine Hogan (2003), *Practical Facilitation: A Toolkit of Techniques*. London: Kogan Page, p. 70.

4   West (2011).

5   Luke Williams (June 2011). 'Innovation Starts With Disruptive Hypotheses. Here's How To Create One'. FastCo Design <www.fastcodesign.com/1663970/innovation-starts-with-disruptive-hypotheses-heres-how-to-create-one>.

6   Jim Force (2000). 'Creative Questioning: The Art of Asking Dumb Questions'. The Banff Centre for Management. Published in *Leadership Compass*, Winter/Spring, pp. 28–9.

7   Jeffrey H. Dyer, Hal B. Gregersen & Clayton M. Christensen (December 2009). 'The Innovator's DNA'. *Harvard Business Review* <http://hbr.org/2009/12/the-innovators-dna/sb2>.

8   Dyer, Gregersen & Christensen (July 2011). *The Innovator's DNA: Mastering the Five Skills of Disruptive Innovators*. Boston, MA: Harvard Business Press.

9   Dyer, Gregersen & Christensen (December 2009).

10   Jeff Mauzy & Richard A. Harriman (2003). *Creativity, Inc.* Boston, MA: Harvard Business School Press (ISBN: 1578512077).

11   <www.airlinequality.com/Airports/Airport_forum/dps.htm>

12   Jared Diamond (1992). *The Third Chimpanzee: The Evolution and Future of the Human Animal*. New York: HarperCollins.

13   Harford (2011).

14   Nassim Taleb (2011). *The Black Swan: The Impact of the Highly Improbable*. New York: Random House.

15   Mowat, Corrigan & Long (2010).

16   Paulo Freire (2000). *Pedagogy of the Oppressed*. London: Continuum International Publishing Group.

17   Morten Huse (2007). *Boards, Governance and Value Creation: The Human Side of Corporate Governance*. Cambridge University Press, p. 219.

18   Claremont Graduate University's Mihaly Csikszentmihalyi and University of Northern Iowa's Gary G. Gute. See Bronson & Merryman (2010).

19   Jim Collins & Jerry I. Porras (2004). *Built to Last*. New York: Collins (ISBN: 0060566108).

20   Senge (1990).

21   Roger Martin (June 2007). 'How Successful Leaders Think' <http://hbr.org/2007/06/how-successful-leaders-think/ar/1>.

22   Leigh Buchanan (2008). 'Innovation: How the Creative Stay Creative' <www.inc.com/magazine/20080601/innovation-how-the-creative-stay-creative.html>.

23   'Driven to Distraction' <http://topics.nytimes.com/top/news/technology/series/driven_to_distraction/index.html>.

24   De Bono (1993).

25   Stephen A. Diamond (1 August 2010).'Evil Deeds:INCEPTION: Art, Dream and Reality' <www.psychologytoday.com/blog/evil-deeds/201008/inception-art-dream-and-reality>.

26   Dewi Susanti & Kayee Man (2007). 'Solve your Problems after a Good Night's Sleep' <http://creativity-indonesia.blogspot.com/2007/02/sleep-on-your-ideas.html>.

27   Land & Jarman (2000).

28   Tony Buzan & Barry Buzan (2003). *The Mind Map Book*. London: BBC Books (ISBN: 0563487054).

29   Steven Johnson (2005). *Everything Bad Is Good for You: How Today's Popular Culture Is Actually Making Us Smarter*. New York: Riverhead.

30   <www.productiveflourishing.com/multithreading-the-complexity-of-modern-experience>

31   Steven Johnson (April 2005). 'Watching TV Makes You Smarter'. *New York Times* <www.nytimes.com/2005/04/24/magazine/24TV.html?pagewanted=print>.

32   Michael S. Gazzaniga. 'The Split Brain Revisited' <http://cwx.prenhall.com/bookbind/pubbooks/morris4/medialib/readings/split.html>.

33   Gazzaniga, 'The Split Brain Revisited'.

34   Norman Doidge (2008). *The Brain That Changes Itself*. London: Penguin (ISBN: 014103887X).

35   Professor Jack Pettigrew (2004). 'Brain Switch', *Catalyst*, ABC TV <www.abc.net.au/catalyst/stories/s1063853.htm>.

36   <www.uq.edu.au/nuq/jack/jack.html>

37   Surowiecki (2005).

38   Thomas Heinze, Philip Shapira, Juan D. Rogers & Jacqueline M. Senker (2009). *Organizational and Institutional Influences on Creativity in Scientific Research*. Elsevier.

39   Bronson & Merryman (2010).

40   Stefan M. Herzog & Ralph Hertwig (2009). 'The Wisdom of Many in One Mind: Improving Individual Judgments With Dialectical Bootstrapping' <www.pnas.org/content/108/22/9020.full>.

41   Daniel H. Pink (2005). *A Whole New Mind*. Cyan Books (ISBN: 1904879578).

42 Herzog & Hertwig (2009).

43 Micah Challenge <www.micahchallenge.org.au>.

44 Teresa M. Amabile & Steven J. Kramer (2011). *The Progress Principle: Using Small Wins to Ignite Joy, Engagement, and Creativity at Work.* Boston, MA: Harvard Business Press.

45 Gladwell (2008).

46 Ericsson, Prietula & Cokely (July 2007).

47 Daniel Pink (2009). *Drive: The Surprising Truth about What Motivates Us,* New York: Riverhead.

48 Joachim Burbiel (2009). 'Creativity in research and development environments: A practical review'. *International Journal of Business Science and Applied Management* 4(2).

49 Luke Williams (June 2011). 'Innovation Starts With Disruptive Hypotheses'.

50 Pink (2005).

51 Daniel Goleman (1997). *Emotional Intelligence: Why It Can Matter More Than IQ.* New York: Bantam Books.

52 *Washington Post* (1998) <www.washingtonpost.com/wp-srv/style/invitational/invit980802.htm>.

53 K. Nordström & J. Ridderstrale (2002). *Funky Business.* London: Financial Times/Prentice Hall (ISBN: 0273659073).

54 Subhasish Chatterjee & John F. Carnney (January 2007). 'Passenger Train Crashworthiness Primary Collisions'. *Transportation Research Record. Journal of the Transportation Research Board* vol. 1531/1996.

55 Gregory Ferenstein (June 2011). 'Children Adorably, Accurately Predict the Future Of Computing'. Fast Company <www.fastcompany.com/pics/children-adorably-accurately-predict-future-computing?slide=1>.

56 Latitude Research completed a multi-phase innovation study, *Children's Future Requests for Computers and the Internet,* in 2010.

57 De Bono (1993).

58 Richard Watson (October 2004). 'A Beginner's Mind'. Fast Company <www.fastcompany.com/resources/innovation/watson/100404.html>.

59 Surowiecki (2005).

60 Jonah Lehrer (2010). 'Old Writers, The Frontal Cortex'. *Wired* <www.wired.com/wiredscience/2010/06/old-writers>.

61 Dean Simonton, cited in Jonah Lehrer (19 February 2010), 'Fleeting Youth, Fading Creativity in Science'. *Wall Street Journal* <http://online.wsj.com/article/SB10001424052748703444804575071573334216604.html>.

62 Lehrer (2010). 'Fleeting Youth, Fading Creativity in Science'.

63 Jena McGregor (April 2006). 'The World's Most Innovative Companies'. *Business Week* – BCG survey.

64 Mark A. Runco, cited in Bronson & Merryman (2010).

65 De Bono (1993).

66 Ding Qingfen (November 2009). 'P&G Turns to Innovation to Win More Customers in a Tough Global Economy'. *China Daily* <www.chinadaily.

com.cn/bw/2009-11/23/content_9020223.htm>.

67 Kevin Freiberg & Jackie Freiberg (1998). *Nuts! Southwest Airlines' Crazy Recipe for Business and Personal Success*. Crown Business.

68 Nirmalya Kumar (December 2006). 'Strategies to Fight Low-cost Rivals. *Harvard Business Review* <www.reservegroup.com/reference/lowcostrivals.pdf>.

69 Sergio Marchionne (December 2008). 'Fiat's Extreme Makeover'. *Harvard Business Review* <http://hbr.org/2008/12/fiats-extreme-makeover/ar/1>.

70 Tim Harford (2008). *The Logic of Life*. New York: Random House (ISBN: 1400066425).

71 Ingrid Bonn (2007). 'Case study: Aldi in Australia'. Graduate School of Management, Griffith University.

72 Dyer, Gregersen & Christensen (2009). 'The Innovator's DNA'.

73 Alla Katsnelson (September 2011). 'The Pitfalls of Positive Thinking'. *Scientific American*.

74 Seligman (2006).

75 Senge (1990).

76 Seligman (2006).

77 De Bono (1993).

Chapter 7

1 Lawrence W. Sherman (April 2002). 'Hot Spots of Crime and Criminal Careers of Places' <www.popcenter.org/library/crimeprevention/volume_04/02-Sherman.pdf>.

2 Amabile (1998).

3 Burbiel (2009).

4 Adam Bryant (May 2009). 'For This Guru, No Question Is Too Big'. *New York Times* <www.nytimes.com/2009/05/24/business/24collins.html>.

5 Carolyn T. Geer, 'Innovation 101'. *Wall Street Journal* <http://online.wsj.com/article_email/SB10001424052970204831304576595670331982774-0-1MyQjAxMTAxMDEwNjExNDYyWj.html?mod=wsj_share_email>.

6 Glenda Korporaal (16 April 2010). 'Power to your people'. *The Australian* <www.theaustralian.com.au/news/features/power-to-your-people/story-e6frgabx-1225852735945>.

7 Korporaal (16 April 2010). 'Power to your people'.

8 'Microsoft needs to let staff innovate: Google' © AAP, 1 June 2007

9 David Kiley (May 2007). 'Shell Scores with Online Video'. *Bloomberg Business Week* <www.businessweek.com/the_thread/brandnewday/archives/2007/05/shell_scores_with_online_video.html>.

10 IBM 2010 Global CEO Study.

11 Huse (2007).

12 Keen (2010).

13 'Patient Safety: Current Statistics' <www.patientsafetyfocus.com/patient-safety-current-st.html>.

14 Haydn Bush (July 2011). 'In an Era of "Doing More With Less", Executives Nurture Creativity' <www.hhnmag.com/hhnmag/HHNDaily/HHNDailyDisplay.dhtml?id=4400001030>.

15 Alan Mumford (2000). 'A learning approach to strategy' *Journal of Workplace Learning*

12(7): 265–71. M.S. Basadur (2004). 'Leading others to think innovatively together. Creative Leadership'. *Leadership Quarterly* 15: 103–21. Scott, W. Richard (1995). *Institutions and organizations*. Thousand Oaks, CA: Sage Publications.

16 Kim S. Cameron & Robert E. Quinn (2011). *Diagnosing and Changing Organizational Culture: Based on the Competing Values Framework*. New York: Jossey-Bass.

17 Cameron & Quinn (2011).

18 Joachim Burbiel (2007). 'Creativity in research and development environments: A practical review'. Fraunhofer-Institute for Technological Trend Analysis. *International Journal of Business Science and Applied Management* 4(2) <www.business-and-management.org/download.php?file=2009/4_2--35-51--Burbiel.pdf>.

19 Charles Fishman (1 July 2007). 'Message in a Bottle' <www.fastcompany.com/magazine/117/features-message-in-a-bottle.html>.

20 <http://tropicaltheartist.wordpress.com/2011/09/10/coffee-and-creativity-%E2%80%93-why>

21 Senge (1995).

22 Roger von Oech (1990). *A Whack on the Side of the Head*. New York: Warner Books (ISBN: 0880794798).

23 David L. Kurtz & Louis E. Boone (2009). *Contemporary Business*. Stamford, CT: Cengage Learning.

24 '100 Best Companies to Work For' (2007). *Fortune* <http://money.cnn.com/magazines/fortune/bestcompanies/2007/snapshots/1.html>.

25 Jack Stuster (2011). *Bold Endeavors*. Annapolis, MD: Naval Institute Press (ISBN: 1591148308).

26 'Lighting and Crime and the CfDS' <www.britastro.org/dark-skies/crime.html>.

27 Andrea Anderson (3 October 2011). 'Half Asleep. Deprived of rest, parts of the brain start to snooze'. Scientific American <www.scientificamerican.com/article.cfm?id=half-asleep-mind-sept-11>.

28 Rick Nauert (November 2006). 'Relationship Between Sleep and Crime Explored' <http://psychcentral.com/news/2006/11/24/relationship-between-sleep-and-crime-explored/431.html>.

29 Cliff Kuang. 'Infographic of the Day: Why Pro Athletes Sleep 12 Hours a Day' <www.fastcodesign.com/1663723/infographic-of-the-day-why-pro-athletes-sleep-12-hours-a-day?partner=homepage_newsletter>.

30 Mihaly Csikszentmihalyi (2002). *Flow*. London: Rider (ISBN: 0712657592).

31 Rachael Rettner (June 2010). 'Why We Dream: Real Reasons Revealed: Live Science' <www.livescience.com/8373-dream-real-reasons-revealed.html>.

32 Yaacov Trope & Nira Liberman (2010). 'Construal-Level Theory of Psychological Distance'. *Psychological Review* 117(2): 440–63. ©2010 American Psychological Association.

33 William Maddux & Adam Galinsky, 'Cultural Borders and Mental Barriers: The Relationship between Living Abroad and Creativity'. Kellogg School of Management at Northwestern University American Psychological Association via *Newswise* <www.tricitypsychology.com/blog/living-abroad-makes-people-more-creative/#ixzz1X7hAxBXS>.

34 Oren Shapira & Nira Liberman <www.scientificamerican.com/article.cfm?id=an-easy-way-to-increase-c>.

Chapter 8

1 Mark Egan (April 2011). 'CBS reporter Lara Logan recounts assault in Egypt'. Reuters <www.reuters.com/article/2011/04/28/us-media-logan-idUSTRE73R81420110428>.

2 Sam Keen (1991). *Faces of the Enemy: Reflections of the Hostile Imagination*. New York: HarperCollins.

3 Joseph Campbell (1972). *The Hero with a Thousand Faces*, Bollingen Series no. 17, 2nd edn. Princeton, NJ: Princeton University Press.

4 Julie K. Norem (2001). *The Positive Power of Negative Thinking*. Cambridge, MA: Basic Books (ISBN: 0465051391).

5 Roger Scruton (2010). *The Uses of Pessimism: And the Danger of False Hope*. Oxford, UK: Oxford University Press.

6 Shelley Carson (April 2011). 'The Unleashed Mind: Why Creative People Are Eccentric'. *Scientific American* <www.scientificamerican.com/article.cfm?id=the-unleashed-mind>.

7 Clifford A. Pickover (1999). *Strange Brains and Genius: The Secret Lives of Eccentric Scientists and Madmen*. New York: William Morrow.

8 Carson (April 2011). 'The Unleashed Mind'.

9 Aldo Rustichini (February 2010). 'Thinking Outside a Less Intact Box: Thalamic Dopamine D2 Receptor Densities Are Negatively Related to Psychometric Creativity in Healthy Individuals'. Plos One <www.plosone.org/article/info%3Adoi%2F10.1371%2Fjournal.pone.0010670>.

10 'Dopamine System in Highly Creative People Similar to That Seen in Schizophrenics, Study Finds' (18 May 2010). *Science Daily* <www.sciencedaily.com/releases/2010/05/100518064610.htm>.

11 HimaBindu K. Krishna (1998). 'Bipolar Disorder and the Creative Genius'. Serendip <http://serendip.brynmawr.edu/exchange/node/1726>.

12 Marianne English (August 2011). 'Creativity Not as Well Received as We Think'. Discovery News <http://news.discovery.com/human/creativity-110831.html>.

13 Clayton Christensen (1997). *The Innovator's Dilemma*. Boston, MA: Harvard Business School Press. L. Joseph & Clayton M. Christensen (1995). 'Disruptive Technologies: Catching the Wave'. *Harvard Business Review*, January–February.

14 West (2011). 'Why Cities Keep Growing'.

15   Steven D. Levitt & Stephen J. Dubner (2009). *Super Freakonomics: Global Cooling, Patriotic Prostitutes, and Why Suicide Bombers Should Buy Life Insurance.* New York: William Morrow.

16   David Streitfeld (October 2011). 'Amazon Signs Up Authors, Writing Publishers Out of Deal'. *New York Times* <www.nytimes.com/2011/10/17/technology/amazon-rewrites-the-rules-of-book-publishing.html?_r=1>.

17   Harford (2011).

18   Linda Morris (4 October 2011). 'Lifestyle the draw in new chapter for bookshops'. *Sydney Morning Herald* <www.smh.com.au/entertainment/books/lifestyle-the-draw-in-new-chapter-for-bookshops-20111003-1l5bj.html#ixzz1byHUu3wk>.

19   Patricia B. Seybold (2006). *Outside Innovation: How Your Customers Will Co-design Your Company's Future.* New York: HarperCollins.

20   Kim Buckley (February 2009). 'Decision on Trayless Cafeteria System Falls to Students'. *Daily Nebraskan* <www.dailynebraskan.com/news/decision-on-trayless-cafeteria-system-falls-to-students-1.1370021#.Tqkia7LYjPU>

21   In Africa and Asia, the number of people living in cities increases by an average of approximately 1 million each week. Noel McKeegan (11 June 2007).

'Over half the world now live in cities according to UN Report' <www.gizmag.com/go/7613>.

Chapter 9

1   Teresa Amabile & Steven Kramer (September 2011). 'Do Happier People Work Harder?' *New York Times* <www.nytimes.com/2011/09/04/opinion/sunday/do-happier-people-work-harder.html>.

2   Laurent Philippe (head of P&G in China) (July 2004). 'Understanding the Chinese consumer'. *McKinsey Quarterly* <www.mckinseyquarterly.com/Understanding_the_Chinese_consumer_1468>.

3   'Cracking China: In a new book, Procter & Gamble tells how it brought consumerism to an untapped market' (June 2004). *Business Library* <http://findarticles.com/p/articles/mi_m4070/is_199/ai_n6104076/?tag=mantle_skin;content>.

4   Peter Pfeiffer, Sven Massen & Ulrich Bombka. 'Serving the Low-Income Consumer: How to Tackle This Mostly Ignored Market', A.T. Kearney <www.atkearney.com/index.php/Publications/serving-the-low-income-consumer.html>.

5   More case studies are available at <www.whokilledcreativity.com>.

Bibliography

Books

ᛉ Abramson, Paul R. & Pinkerton, Steven D. (1995). *With Pleasure*. New York: Oxford University Press.

ᛉ Achor, Shawn (2010). *The Happiness Advantage*. Random House Audio.

ᛉ Ariely, Dan (2010). *Predictably Irrational*. Harper Perennial.

ᛉ Bandiera, Oriana (2001). *Private States and the Enforcement of Property Rights: Theory and Evidence on the Origins of the Sicilian Mafia*. London School of Economics and Centre for Economic Policy Research.

ᛉ Belsky, Scott (2011). *Making Ideas Happen*. Portfolio Trade.

ᛉ Bernstein, Peter L. (1998). *Against the Gods: The Remarkable Story of Risk*. New York: John Wiley & Sons.

ᛉ Carr, Nicholas (June 2010). *The Shallows: What the Internet Is Doing to Our Brains*. New York: W. W. Norton.

ᛉ Carroll, Brian James (2006). *Lead Generation for the Complex Sale*. New York: McGraw-Hill.

ᛉ Chudacoff, Howard P. (2008). *Children at Play*. New York: New York University Press.

ᛉ Collins, Jim (2001). *Good to Great*. London: Random House Business.

ᛉ Collins, James C. & Porras, Jerry I. (1998). *Built to Last*. London: Century Business.

ᛉ Csikszentmihalyi, Mihaly (2002). *Flow*. London: Rider.

ᛉ Damasio, A.R. (1994). *Descartes' Error: Emotion, Reason, and the Human Brain*. New York: Grosset/Putnam.

ᛉ De Bono, Edward (2007). *Tactics*. London: Profile Business.

ᛉ De Bono, Edward (1993). *Serious Creativity*. New York: HarperBusiness.

❧ Dyer, Jeffrey H., Gregersen, Hal B. & Christensen, Clayton M. (2011). *The Innovator's DNA: Mastering the Five Skills of Disruptive Innovators*. Boston, MA: Harvard Business Press.

❧ Earley, Pete (1993). *The Hot House*. New York: Bantam Books.

❧ Gladwell, Malcolm (2008). *Outliers*. New York: Little, Brown and Co.

❧ Gladwell, Malcolm (2007). *The Tipping Point*. Playaway Audio Books.

❧ Greene, Robert (1998). *The 48 Laws of Power*. New York: Viking.

❧ Hand, Derrick & Fife-Yeomans, Janet (2008) [2004]. *The Coroner: Investigating Sudden Death*. Sydney, NSW: Allen & Unwin.

❧ Hansen, Morten T. (2009). *Collaboration*. Boston, MA: Harvard Business School Press.

❧ Hare, Robert & Babiak, Paul (2006). *Snakes in Suits: When Psychopaths Go to Work*. New York: HarperCollins.

❧ Harford, Tim (2011). *Adapt: Why Success Always Starts with Failure*. HighBridge Audio.

❧ Hasselhoff, David (2006). *Making Waves—The Autobiography*. London: Hodder & Stoughton.

❧ Keen, Sam (2010). *In the Absence of God*. New York: Harmony.

❧ Land, George & Jarman, Beth (2000). *Breakpoint and Beyond*. Champaign, IL: HarperBusiness.

❧ Martin, Brian (with contributions from Truda Gray, Hannah Lendon and Steve Wright) (2007). *Justice Ignited*. Lanham, MD: Rowman & Littlefield.

❧ Martin, Brian & Wright, Steve. 'Countershock: Challenging Pushbutton Torture', author's prepublication version of chapter 11 in Martin (2007) <www.bmartin.cc/pubs/07ji/ji11.pdf>.

❧ Martin, Roger L. (2009). *The Design of Business*. Boston, MA: Harvard Business School Press.

⟨ Mauzy, Jeff & Harriman, Richard A. (2003). *Creativity, Inc.* Boston, MA: Harvard Business School Press.

⟨ Mowatt, Andrew, Corrigan, John & Long, Doug (2010). *The Success Zone.* Global Publishing Group.

⟨ Nordström, K. & Ridderstrale, J. (2002). *Funky Business.* London: Financial Times/Prentice Hall.

⟨ Norem, Julie K. (2001). *The Positive Power of Negative Thinking.* Cambridge, Mass.: Basic Books.

⟨ Oech, Roger von (1990). *A Whack on the Side of the Head.* New York: Warner Books.

⟨ Osborne, David & Gaebler, Ted (1992). *Reinventing Government.* New York: Plume.

⟨ Pedler, M., Burgogyne, J. & Boydell, T. (1997). *The Learning Company: A Strategy for Sustainable Development*, 2nd edn. London: McGraw-Hill.

⟨ Ridley, Matt (1998). *The Origins of Virtue.* London: Penguin.

⟨ Robinson, Ken & Aronica, Lou (2009). *Element: How Finding Your Passion Changes Everything.* Tantor Media.

⟨ Ronson, Jon (2011). *The Psychopath Test.* New York: Riverhead.

⟨ Schein, Edgar H. (2004). *Organizational Culture and Leadership.* New York: John Wiley & Sons.

⟨ Seligman, Martin E. (2006). *Learned Optimism: How to Change Your Mind and Your Life.* New York: Vintage.

⟨ Senge, P.M. (1990). *The Fifth Discipline.* London: Century Business.

⟨ Sieberg, Daniel (2011). *The Digital Diet.* New York: Three Rivers Press.

⟨ Speculand, Robin (2009). *Beyond Strategy.* New York: John Wiley & Sons.

⟨ Stout, Martha (2010). *The Sociopath Next Door —The Mask of Sanity.* Sextante <www.cassiopaea.com/cassiopaea/psychopath.htm>.

⟨ Surowiecki, James (2005). *The Wisdom of Crowds.* London: Abacus.

\ Suzuki-roshi, Shunryu (1988). *Zen Mind, Beginner's Mind.* Audio Literature.

\ Taleb, Nassim (2001). *Fooled by Randomness.* New York: John Wiley & Sons.

\ Tucker, Jonathan B. (2006). *War of Nerves: Chemical Warfare from World War I to Al-Queda.* New York: Pantheon.

\ Vaknin, Sam & Rangelovska, Lidija (eds) (2006). *Malignant Self Love—Narcissism Revisited.* Czech Republic: Narcissus Publications.

\ Wallis, Malcolm (1989). *Bureaucracy.* London: Macmillan.

\ Ward, Vicky (2010). *The Devil's Casino.* New York: John Wiley & Sons.

\ Winston, Robert (2010). *Bad Ideas?* New York: Bantam Press.

\ Young, Damon (2008). *Distraction.* Carlton, Vic.: Melbourne University Publishing.

Articles, papers

\ 'A different game: Information is transforming traditional businesses' (February 2010). *Economist* <www.economist.com/node/15557465>.

\ Allen, Nick (2009) 'Burglar with photographic memory admits 500 crimes'. *Telegraph* <www.telegraph.co.uk/news/uknews/4358671/Burglar-with-photographic-memory-admits-500-crimes.html>.

\ Amabile, Teresa M. (1998). 'How to Kill Creativity'. *Harvard Business Review* <http://hbr.org/product/how-to-kill-creativity/an/98501-PDF-ENG>.

\ Board, Belinda Jane & Fritzon, Katarina (2005). 'Disordered personalities at work'. *Psychology Crime and Law* 11: 17.

\ Bornstein, Josh (30 August 2011). 'Time to outlaw toxic bullies in the workplace'. *Australian Financial Review* <http://afr.com/p/national/work_space/time_to_outlaw_toxic_bullies_Xfa9LfQaUlVv3KjHHzGTrI>.

⟨ Aberdeen Group (October 2004). 'Bridging the Divide: Process, Technology, and the Sales/Marketing Interface'. *Market Viewpoint* 15: 4. Boston, MA: Aberdeen Group.

⟨ Brown, Karalyn (2010). 'Engaging People'. Australian Institute of Management <www.aim.com.au/DisplayStory. asp?ID=746>.

⟨ Chiu, Randy K. 'Relationship among Role Conflicts, Role Satisfactions and Life Satisfaction: Evidence from Hong Kong'. *Social Behavior and Personality* <http://findarticles. com/p/articles/mi_qa3852/is_199801/ai_n8803995>.

⟨ Dias-Ferreira, E, Sousa, J.C., Melo, I., Morgado, P., Mesquita, A.R., Cerqueira, J.J., Costa, R.M. & Sousa, N. (2009). 'Chronic Stress Causes Frontostriatal Reorganization and Affects Decision-Making'. *Science* 325(5940): 621–5.

⟨ Dingfelder, Sadie F. (January 2011). 'Rats to the rescue'. *Monitor* 42 <www.apa.org/monitor/2011/01/rats.aspx1>.

⟨ Ericsson, K. Anders, Prietula, Michael J. & Cokely, Edward T. (2007). 'The Making of an Expert'. *Harvard Business Review* <http://hbr.org/2007/07/the-making-of-an-expert/ar/1>.

⟨ Adam Galinsky (2009). 'Losing Touch Power diminishes perception and perspective'. Kellogg School of Management <http://insight.kellogg.northwestern.edu/ index.php/Kellogg/article/losing_touch>.

⟨ Geddes, Linda (March 2010). 'A slow mind may nurture more creative ideas'. *New Scientist*, <www.newscientist. com/article/mg20527535.500-a-slow-mind-may-nurture-more-creative-ideas.html>.

⟨ Geddes, Linda (May 2009). 'Creativity chemical favours the smart'. *New Scientist* <www.newscientist.com/ article/mg20227084.300-creativity-chemical-favours-the-smart.html>.

⟨ Goetzel, R.Z., Anderson, D.R., Whitmer, R.W., Ozminkowski, R.J., Dunn, R.L. & Wasserman, J. (1998). 'The relationship between modifiable health risks and health care expenditure: An analysis of the multi-employer HERO health risk and cost database'. *Journal of Occupational and Environmental Medicine* 40: 843–54.

≀ Gratton, Alain (1988). 'Effects of electrical stimulation of brain reward sites on release of dopamine in rat: An in vivo electrochemical study'. University of Colorado Health Sciences.

≀ Hicks, W.D. & Klimoski, R.J. (1981). 'The impact of flextime on employee attitudes'. *Academy of Management Journal* 24: 333–41.

≀ Insel, Thomas R. & Wang, Philip S. (2010). 'Rethinking Mental Illness & Mental Health vs Mental Disorders'. *Journal of the American Medial Association* 303(19): 1978–9.

≀ Irvine, Jessica (2011). 'There's no time like the present to let yourself go'. *Sydney Morning Herald* <www.smh.com.au/national/health/theres-no-time-like-the-present-to-let-yourself-go-20110916-1kdwr.html#ixzz1Y9Xqma5C>.

≀ Jonge, J., Landsbergis, P. & Vegchel, N. (2005). 'Occupational Stress in (inter)action: The Interplay between Job Demands and Job Resources'. *Journal of Organizational Behavior* 26(5): 535–60.

≀ Kets de Vries, Manfred, F.R. (2003). 'The Dark Side of Leadership'. *Business Strategy Review* 14(3), Autumn, p. 26.

≀ Knight, Will (22 April 2005). ' "Info-mania" dents IQ more than marijuana'. *New Scientist* <www.newscientist.com/article/dn7298-infomania-dents-iq-more-than-marijuana.html>.

≀ Kopelman, R.E., Greenhaus, J.H., & Connolly, T.F. (1983). 'A model of work, family, and interrole conflict: A construct validation study'. *Organizational Behavior and Human Performance* 32: 198–215.

≀ Loewenstein, G. & Lerner, J. (2003). 'The Role of Emotion in Decision Making', in R.J. Davidson, H.H. Goldsmith & K.R. Scherer (eds), *Handbook of Affective Sciences*. New York: Oxford University Press.

≀ Showers, Carolin & Ruben, Cherie (1990). 'Distinguishing defensive pessimism from depression: Negative expectations and positive coping mechanisms'. *Cognitive Therapy and Research* 14(4): 385–99.

✝ Macknik, Stephen L. & Martinez-Conde, Susana (2010). 'Sleights of Mind: What the Neuroscience of Magic Reveals about Our Everyday Deceptions'. *Scientific American* <www.scientificamerican.com/article. cfm?id=mind-over-magic>.

✝ Matthews, Virginia (January 2003). 'Kill or be killed'. *Guardian* <www.guardian.co.uk/money/2003/jan/27/ careers.jobsadvice1>.

✝ Mattice, Catherine & Spitzberg, Brian (2007). 'Bullies in Business: Self-Reports of Tactics and Motives'. San Diego State University.

✝ McEwen, B.S. (2007). 'Physiology and neurobiology of stress and adaptation: Central role of the brain'. *Physiological Review* 87(3): 873–904.

✝ 'Microsoft needs to let staff innovate: Google' (June 2007). *Sydney Morning Herald* <www.smh.com.au/ news/biztech/microsoft-needs-to-let-staff-innovate-google/2007/06/01/1180205491599.html>.

✝ Milner, Peter M. (1991). 'Brain-stimulation reward: A review'. *Canadian Journal of Psychology/Revue canadienne de psychologie* 45(1), March, 1–36.

✝ Minkel, J.R. (18 December 2006). 'Happiness: Good for Creativity, Bad for Single-Minded Focus'. *Scientific American* <www.scientificamerican.com/article.cfm?id=happiness-good-for-creativity>.

✝ Morello, Carol (January 2010). 'Results of polls on job satisfaction are at odds': Conference Board report. *Washington Post* <www.washingtonpost.com/wp-dyn/ content/article/2010/01/05/AR2010010503977.html>.

✝ NIOSH (1999). *Stress at Work*. U.S. National Institute for Occupational Safety and Health, DHHS. Publication no. 99-101.

✝ Northwestern National Life Insurance Company (1991). 'Employee burnout: America's newest epidemic'.

Minneapolis, MN: Northwestern National Life Insurance Company.

\ Omega Foundation (25–26 October 2002). 'Stun Weapons and Their Effects'. A draft paper to the International Meeting of Experts on Security Equipment and the Prevention of Torture, London.

\ Princeton Survey Research Associates (1997). 'Labor day survey: State of workers'. Princeton, NJ: Princeton Survey Research Associates.

\ Richtel, Matt (2008). 'Lost in E-Mail, Tech Firms Face Self-Made Beast'. *New York Times* <www. nytimes.com/2008/06/14/technology/14email. html?pagewanted=all>.

\ Roffey Park Management (2003). Survey of 372 managers in the UK <www.roffeypark.com/ SiteCollectionDocuments/Research%20Reports/ manag2003.pdf>.

\ Schmidt, Matthias B. & Schwabe, Lars (September 2011). 'Splintered by stress: The good and bad of psychological pressure'. *Scientific American*.

\ Thompson, Clive (October 2003). 'There's a Sucker Born in Every Medial Prefrontal Cortex'. *New York Times* <www.nytimes.com/2003/10/26/magazine/26BRAINS. html?pagewanted=1>.

\ Turner N., Barling J. & Zacharatos, A. (2002). 'Positive psychology at work', in C.R. Snyder & S.J. Lopez (eds), *Handbook of Positive Psychology* (pp. 715–28). New York: Oxford University Press.

\ Wenner, Melinda (28 January 2009). 'The Serious Need for Play'. *Scientific American*.

\ Zatz, D.A. (1995). 'Job Involvement and Interrole Conflict'. Doctoral dissertation, Columbia University.

Electronic resources

\ Alfonso, Veronica (2009). 'Pessimists' and Optimists' Reactions to Interruptions on a Creativity Task' <http:// dspace.sunyconnect.suny.edu/handle/1951/44812>.

⅄ Bronson, Po & Merryman, Ashley (2010). 'The
Creativity Crisis'. *Newsweek* <www.thedailybeast.com/
newsweek/2010/07/10/the-creativity-crisis.html>.

⅄ Brown, Stuart (2008). 'Play is more than fun'. TED talks
<www.ted.com/talks/stuart_brown_says_play_is_more_
than_fun_it_s_vital.html>.

⅄ Bunce, Jane (May 2011). 'Cult of Apple: Why the
must-have brand triggers brain reaction "similar to
religious devotion"'. *Mail Online* <www.dailymail.
co.uk/sciencetech/article-1389256/Apple-brand-
triggers-brain-reaction-similar-religious-devotion.
html#ixzz1bSMIsZG5>.

⅄ Carr, Austin (2010). 'The Most Important Leadership
Quality for CEOs? Creativity'. Fast Company
<www.fastcompany.com/1648943/Creativity-
the-most-important-leadership-quality-for-ceos-
study?partner=homepage_newsletter>.

⅄ Christensen, Clayton M. & Anthony, Scott D. (January
2007). 'How to Be a Disrupter'. *Forbes* <www.forbes.
com/2007/01/22/leadership-disrupter-christensen-lead-
innovation-cx_hc_0122christensen.html>.

⅄ Cowing, Keith (2003). 'NASA Responds to the Columbia
Accident Report: Farewell to Faster — Better — Cheaper'
<www.spaceref.com/news/viewnews.html?id=864>.

⅄ 'Emotions Can Negatively Impact Investment Decisions'
(September 2005). Stanford Graduate School of Business
<www.gsb.stanford.edu/news/research/finance_shiv_
invesmtdecisions.shtml>.

⅄ Fishburn, Tom (9 January 2011). 'Blamestorming' <http://
tomfishburne.com/2011/01/blamestorming.html>.

⅄ Fox, Catherine 'Workers by design' <www.afrboss.
com.au/magarticle.asp?doc_id=22153&rgid=2&listed_
months=0>.

⅄ Frey, Chuck (September 2002). 'Are we too busy to
think creatively?' <www.innovationtools.com/Weblog/
innovationblog-detail.asp?ArticleID=21>.

⟩ Grant, Andrew, Grant, Gaia & Gallate, Jason (2011). 'Who Killed Creativity Survey' <www.whokilledcreativity.com/survey>.

⟩ Hanna, Julie (14 May 2008). 'Getting Down to the Business of Creativity'. Harvard Business School <http://hbswk.hbs.edu/item/5902.html>.

⟩ Hunt, Jamer (2001). 'Among Six Types of Failure, Only a Few Help You Innovate'. Fast Company <www.fastcodesign.com/1664360/lets-be-clear-failure-isnt-always-good>.

⟩ IBM (2010). 'Global CEO Study: IBM Biennial Global CEO Study Series', 4th edn <www-03.ibm.com/press/us/en/pressrelease/31670.wss>.

⟩ ' "Infomania' worse than marijuana' (22 April 2005), BBC News <http://news.bbc.co.uk/2/hi/uk_news/4471607.stm>.

⟩ Kennedy, Jessica (2011). 'Marketing needs to "pull up its socks" to help sales' <www.bandt.com.au/content/articles/marketing-needs-to--pull-up-its-socks--to-help-sal.aspx>.

⟩ Lewis, Michael (2008). 'The End' <www.portfolio.com/news-markets/national-news/portfolio/2008/11/11/The-End-of-Wall-Streets-Boom>.

⟩ Lindstrom, Martin (18 May 2011). 'The Cure for ADD-vertising'. Fast Company <www.fastcompany.com/1753945/the-cure-for-add-vertising?partner=homepage_newsletter>.

⟩ Major Formula One Technical Innovations (1950–1998) <www.motorsportsetc.com/info/f1_innov.htm>.

⟩ Mueller, Jennifer S. (2011). 'Why people desire but reject creative ideas'. University of Pennsylvania <http://digitalcommons.ilr.cornell.edu/cgi/viewcontent.cgi?article=1457&context=articles>.

⟩ Nader, Ralph (September 2007). 'Fighting Back Against the Commercialization of Everything Wrapping the World with Advertising' <http://moderate.wordpress.com/2007/09/03/ralph-nader-wrapping-the-world-with-advertising/>.

\ 'Overcoming Apathy in the Workplace Smart Manager' <www.smartmanager.com.au/web/au/smartmanager/en/pages/125_apathy.html>.

\ Palmetto Security <www.palmettoalarm.com/crime-statistics.html>.

\ Pink, Daniel H. (2003). 'How to Make Your Own Luck'. Fast Company <www.fastcompany.com/magazine/72/realitycheck.html>.

\ Potter, Janet (2011). 'Mad, Mad World: Jon Ronson's The Psychopath Test'.

\ <www.themillions.com/2011/05/mad-mad-world-jon-ronsons-the-psychopath-test.html>.

\ 'Prudential sells Egg to Citigroup' (January 2007) <www.finextra.com/news/fullstory.aspx?newsitemid=16435>.

\ Richards, Laura (2006). 'Jack the Ripper's face "revealed"' <http://news.bbc.co.uk/2/hi/uk_news/6164544.stm>.

\ Richardson, Laura Sergeant (2009). 'Frog Design: The Four Secrets of Playtime That Foster Creative Kids' <www.fastcodesign.com/1662826/frog-design-the-four-secrets-of-playtime-that-foster-creative-kids>.

\ Robinson, Joe (February 2010). 'Tame the E-mail Beast' <www.entrepreneur.com/magazine/entrepreneur/2010/march/204980.html>.

\ Scott, Duncan (2009). 'The Edge of the World: How the Rule of Three Can Save F1' <http://bleacherreport.com/articles/117975-the-edge-of-the-world-how-the-rule-of-three-can-save-f1>.

\ Shaughnessy, Michael F. (2011). 'An Interview with Jonathan Plucker: Creativity, the Creative Person and the Creative Mind' <www.creativity.or.kr/bbs/board.php?bo_table=2011_01&wr_id=3>.

\ Stern, Stefan (March 2006). 'Wake up and smell the coffee on your corporate culture'. Financial Times <www.ft.com/intl/cms/s/1/7ecca3c4-dba7-11db-9233-000b5df10621.html#axzz1badX4FNW>.

❧ Subhani, Ayatullah Ja'far, 'Being Pessimistic about Others' <www.alhassanain.com/english/articles/articles/ethics_and_supplication/ethics_articles/being_pessimistic_about_others/001.html>.

❧ Tuite, Don (2007). 'Better, Faster, Cheaper — Pick Any Two' <http://electronicdesign.com/article/analog-and-mixed-signal/better-faster-cheaper-pick-any-two14997.aspx>.

❧ Tysome, Tony (2007). 'Creativity Campaign to Attack Red Tape', *Times Higher Education* <www.timeshighereducation.co.uk/story.asp?storyCode=207402&sectioncode=26>.

❧ UK crime hotspot map (2010). <www.dailymail.co.uk/news/article-1258197/The-crime-hotspot-map-Britains-hardened-criminals-live.html#ixzz1Y5DKZwsE>.

❧ US House of Delegates (February 2010). ABA Criminal Justice Standards on the Treatment of Prisoners <www.americanbar.org/content/dam/aba/publishing/criminal_justice_section_newsletter/treatment_of_prisoners_commentary_website.authcheckdam.pdf>.

❧ Virtual Team Performance Facilitation <www.grovewell.com/virtual-team-facilitation.html>.

❧ Watson, Richard (4 October 2004). 'A beginner's mind'. Fast Company <www.fastcompany.com/resources/innovation/watson/100404.html>.

❧ West, Dr Geoffrey (2011). 'Why Cities Keep Growing, Corporations and People Always Die, and Life Gets Faster', interviewed by John Brockman <http://edge.org/conversation/geoffrey-west>

❧ Who Killed Creativity <www.whokilledcreativity.com>.

❧ Workplace Bullying Survey (2010). <www.workplacebullying.org/wbiresearch/2010-wbi-national-survey>.

❧ The 2010 MetLife Study of the American Dream (2010). <www.metlife.com/assets/cao/gbms/studies/10062017_AmDrm_web_version.pdf>.

Videos and movies

Ⳇ Grant, Andrew & Gaia (2009). *Hands Up*. Tirian.

- Part 1: 'How Creative are You?' <www.youtube.com/watch?v=MhBIiNl3edk>
- Part 2: 'Creativity secrets from the kids' <www.youtube.com/watch?v=77LYUTLH6hQ>
- Part 3: 'Creativity secrets from the experts (the teachers' response)', <www.youtube.com/watch?v=AX6VgVQ3CMs>.

Ⳇ Riley, Alex (2011). 'Secrets of The Superbrands' <www.psfk.com/2011/05/secrets-of-the-superbrands-how-apple-products-affect-your-brain.htm>.

Ⳇ Schank, Roger (interview with) (2007). 'The Business of Innovation. Innovators & Iconoclasts', CNBC <http://innovation.cnbc.com/en/programmes/innovators_iconoclasts>.

Ⳇ Wujec, Tom (2010). 'The Marshmallow Challenge'. TED talks <http://marshmallowchallenge.com/Welcome.html>.

More ways to get creative

Andrew and Gaia Grant and their team at Tirian have designed *The Creative Connection* suite of programs. These programs aim to develop creative thinking skills and actions in individuals and teams, and are also designed to help develop organisational innovation. *The Creative Connection* programs can be run independently or sequentially and are available in the following formats:

The Creative Connection introduction: Who killed creativity?

Explore why creativity is important. Match your and your team's knowledge against that of the latest brain research and sociological experts to learn about 'who killed creativity?' and find out how we can get it back.

Available as an interactive workshop, board game simulation and whodunit-style comedy experience.

The Creative Connection 1: individual approaches to creative thinking

Discover ways to improve individual creative thinking skills through seven practical strategies.

Available as an interactive workshop, seminar or keynote.

The Creative Connection 2: team approaches to creative problem solving

Learn effective tools that teams can use to integrate talents and skills to come up with creative solutions—culminating in a practical collaborative innovation task.

Available as an interactive workshop or seminar.

The Creative Connection 3: organisational innovation and applications

Examine deeper platforms for building systematic organisational innovation and linking this to customer needs (outside innovation).

Available as an interactive workshop, seminar or keynote.

Creative Connection 4: the chocolate factory

Experience a simulation that looks at innovation and cross-functional process design.

Available as a business simulation and workshop.

As well as keynote talks, seminars, simulations and workshops, *The Creative Connection* is also available as:

\ downloadable facilitation packages (QuickBITEs)
\ consulting programs
\ train-the-trainer programs
\ licensed programs for independent delivery.

More information, resources, articles, podcasts, blogs, books, interviews, seminars and keynotes can be found at <www.whokilledcreativity.com> and <www.tirian.com>.

Index

The Who Killed Creativity? *Game Pack is an action-packed discovery exercise that can be played in teams. The game can be used to explore the specific creativity killers in any organisation and introduce the best strategies for reviving innovation. With a clever CSI approach, the game stimulates intelligent and lively discussion and provides the tools for targeted action. The pack includes a game board, card sets and instructions, and can be played independently or facilitated by a trained Tirian facilitator (including the authors) in a stand-alone workshop or as part of* The Creative Connection *suite of programs. It can also be used as the basis for a fun whodunit-style themed event.*